30/6/94 05733
23.00 Pout

Europe after Maastricht
American and European Perspectives

♦ ♦ ♦ ♦ ♦ ♦

Europe after Maastricht
American and European Perspectives

♦ ♦ ♦ ♦ ♦ ♦

Edited by

Paul Michael Lützeler

Berghahn Books
Providence • Oxford

Published in 1994 by

Berghahn Books
Editorial offices:
165 Taber Avenue, Providence, RI 02906, U.S.A.
Bush House, Merewood Avenue, Oxford OX3 8EF, UK

Library of Congress Cataloging-in-Publication Data
Europe after Maastricht / edited by Paul Michael Lützeler.
    p.   cm.
Includes bibliographical references and index.
ISBN 1-57181-020-X
    1. Europe–Economic integration–Congresses. 2. European
federation–Congresses. I. Lützeler, Paul Michael.
HC241.E7835 1994   94-33658
337.1'4–dc20   CIP

British Library Cataloguing in Publication Data
A CIP catalog record for this book is available from
the British Library.

Printed in the United States.

Contents

◆ ◆ ◆ ◆ ◆ ◆

Preface

♦ ♦ ♦ ♦ ♦ ♦

As the Director of the European Studies Program at Washington University in St. Louis, I organized the symposium "Europe after Maastricht. American and European Perspectives" during the weekend of 1 to 3 October 1993. As is always the case with endeavors of this nature, it was the result of team effort. I would like to thank all the members of the Administrative Committee of the European Studies Program for their ideas and their help. William Danforth, Chancellor of Washington University, and Martin Israel, Dean of the Faculty of Arts and Sciences, secured partial funding for the symposium. Other sources of financial support were the Andrew W. Mellon Foundation, the North American Office of the German Academic Exchange Service (DAAD), the American Branch of the Friedrich Ebert Foundation, the Delegation of the Commission of the European Communities in Washington, DC, and the German Research Association (DFG). Special thanks go to the DAAD for subsidizing this volume. Henry Schvey, Chair of Performing Arts, and Philip Boehm staged the play *Mad Forest* by the British author Caryl Churchill. This production was a great success and was well suited to the theme of the symposium, since it dealt with the rise and fall of the 1989 revolt in Romania. Shirley Baker, Dean of University Libraries, together with Holly Hall, William Olbrich, and Kenneth Nabors organized an exhibit of the books in the EC's Documentation Center at Washington University's Olin Library. She also gave a reception in honor of the participants, in the course of which she mentioned how proud the library is to have housed the Documentation Center for thirty years.

Furthermore, I would like to express my gratitude to the following colleagues from Washington University who served as session chairs or discussants: Milica Banjanin, Solon Beinfeld, Lee Benham, Nicholas C. Burckel, James W. Davis, Frances Foster, William C. Jones, Charles L. Leven, Wilhelm Neuefeind, John V. C. Nye, Roger Petersen, Christine Ruane, Michel Rybalka, Richard J. Scaldini, and Richard J. Walter, as well as John Gillingham from the University of Missouri, St. Louis.

Last but not least I would like to give special thanks to Ellen Feinstein, the Administrative Assistant in the European Studies Program. She helped with the practical side of making the symposium arrangements, she was always available during the event whenever assistance was needed, and she helped in preparing and copyediting this volume.

Paul Michael Lützeler   St. Louis, January 1994

Introduction

Paul Michael Lützeler

The autumn of 1993 was a good time to discuss European matters. Two years previously, on 1 December 1991, the heads of
government of the twelve member states had met in the old
Dutch city of Maastricht to discuss the future of the European
Community once the goal of a single market had been attained by
31 December 1992. The governments of the EC opted to proceed
in the direction of further integration, an integration that encompassed more than the economic parameter. They envisioned a
European union on the monetary, the strategic, and the political
levels. The meeting place was well-chosen, since in earlier centuries Maastricht was the capital of the Duchy of Limburg, a
region that is now divided into a Dutch, a German, and a Belgian
part. It served to remind those participating in the Maastricht
Conference of the historical relativity of political borders in
Europe, of the common cultural heritage of the old European
regions, and of their significant role in a more unified continent of
the future. On 1 November 1993, the Treaty on the European
Union, the so-called Maastricht Treaty, went into effect. Its adoption followed two years of controversial debates on the various
levels of the political strata and in the media of all the member
countries of the European Community, years of turbulent referenda for and against the treaty as well as of court decisions as to
whether the treaty was in accord with the constitutions of the
individual member states. The ratification of the Maastricht
Treaty brought about a European Union, which is currently
something less than a political union but more than the European
Community, whose focus was primarily economic.

One month before the Maastricht Treaty finally went into effect, a group of American and European scholars, publishers, and politicians met at Washington University in St. Louis to discuss Europe after Maastricht as seen from European and American perspectives. The conference was organized by Washington University's European Studies Program. It was both an interdisciplinary and an international conference with scholars from fields such as law, economics, political science, history, art history, literature, and cultural studies, who came from countries such as the United States, England, Germany, Switzerland, Poland, and Russia. In order to make themselves understood in this community of scholars from very different areas, all were careful to avoid the use of disciplinary jargon. Following the conference, the papers were revised and prepared for publication in this volume. In putting together the symposium, we made sure that a number of pertinent questions regarding new developments in Europe would be addressed, i.e., the anticipated effects of the Maastricht Treaty on: European-American cooperation; the relation of the individual member states to the European Community; questions of international trade, law, and security; the connection between the West and the East European countries; environmental policies within the EC; the situation of European women; and cultural developments in Europe. This volume documents the output of the symposium and presents its lectures as a contribution to the ongoing discussion on Europe's present and future.

The papers of Theo Sommer, Caroline Jackson, Murray Weidenbaum, and James Little deal with aspects of present and future U.S.-EU relations. According to Sommer, the collapse of communism and the breakup of the Soviet Empire have undermined the old commonality that existed between Western Europe and the U.S. during the postwar decades. Sommer points to the shift from the political-military-territorial world of old to the new economic-financial-commercial world of the twenty-first century. In this world the U.S. (or rather North America) will be on equal footing with the European Union and with Japan (together with other East Asian countries). Since all three main players are preoccupied with economic matters, there exists an enormous potential for rivalry and friction among them. Yet unity and cooperation are imperative for the survival of individual nations as well as all mankind. Sommer concludes that only by building a partnership of equals among America, Europe, and Japan can we achieve a peaceful and thriving future during the new century.

Like Sommer, Jackson makes the point that the European Community — with its single market and its intent of further unification — has become a global power during this decade. Her major concern is European competitiveness. She observes that, due to the recession in Europe, the EC's international competitive position is diminishing, particularly in the field of world exports in manufacturing. Jackson raises additional pertinent questions, such as whether EC interventions and the implementation of EC laws are helping the economic recovery or contributing to the recession. She advocates that the Community should participate in international environmental accords and consumer protection policies, regardless of the EC's problems with recession.

To Weidenbaum, the rise of the European Community presents both threats and opportunities for American business. On the positive side, the integration of the commercial, financial, and cross-border markets facilitates a vast potential market. The negative aspect is the imposition of trade restrictions against non-members and tougher competition from the stronger EC businesses in their domestic markets. The winners are likely to be the stronger European companies with highly skilled labor and high-tech production capabilities, as well as many large U.S. firms with an established presence in Western Europe. The different policies of NAFTA and the European Union notwithstanding, Weidenbaum foresees that in the coming century the business firms and consumers of both North America and Western Europe will become increasingly interlinked.

Like Jackson and Weidenbaum, Little addresses the question of European competitiveness. If competition intensifies within the EC as a result of the single market, European companies will become stronger global competitors. Little is interested in the consequences of the two major forces in European business today, i.e., globalization and the new single market situation. He has studied two relatively recent business activities: mergers and joint ventures. There has been a surge in both activities in Europe (and worldwide, for that matter), and the question arises whether this is a result of adjustment to the single market. Little concludes that general strategies for globalization rather than the single market account for merger and joint venture activities in Europe. A "fortress Europe" attitude, i.e., a European fear of globalization, could lead to backlash. Little reminds us that for many of the largest European firms the competitive arena is not the Community but the world.

Alberta Sbragia and Hartmut Kaelble explain the factors underlying the knitting together of the EC and the nation-states of which it is composed. Sbragia looks at the roles played in this process by elites, structural policies, and the mass electorate, while Kaelble cites historical reasons for the possibility of a continuous integration process in the future. Sbragia shows that the socialization process of elites is a central component of the Community-member state relationship. Becoming comfortable with the Community represents a long, slow process for national political and administrative elites. The expansion of the Community's policy scope above and beyond the economic arena has helped force the EC's institutions and those of the member states into closer engagement, with the European Court of Justice being a case in point. While the elites and the policy of European institutions have contributed to an improvement in relations between the EC and its member states, the politicization of the electorate brought about by the Maastricht debate has complicated this relationship, signaling that the engagement between the two is both contested and serious.

In Kaelble's view, an examination of European social history, especially since 1950, can give us some insights into the lasting favorable preconditions for European integration. In comparing the social peculiarities of late twentieth-century Europe with those of non-European industrialized societies, he shows that the family, class and employment structures, the urbanization process, social milieus, elites, and welfare state policies have become similar in nearly all the EC member states. The period of relative economic prosperity and peace between the 1950s and the 1970s has brought about a marked reduction of dissimilarities in many aspects of European life. Exchanges and connections among European societies have led to a turning away from purely regional or national outlooks toward a more European horizon. Like other contributors to this volume, Kaelble acknowledges the fact that during recent years basic contradictions between the EC and national interests have surfaced, but he is confident that they are mitigated by the continuous diminution of differences among European societies.

Peter Rogge and Elke Thiel address the question of monetary union within the member states of the European Community. Both favor this union and point out that vast amounts of unproductive costs could be eliminated if this union were instituted. The old European Monetary System (EMS) is no longer functioning. As Rogge points out, this setback is indeed serious, indicating that Europe's quest for a common currency is untenable economically (stable exchange rates cannot be maintained in recessionary economies) as well as politically (monetary union implies too much loss of sovereignty). Rogge hopes that the newly created European Monetary Institute in Frankfurt/Main will become a clearinghouse for the close cooperation of a nucleus of independent EC central banks, which could rebuild the EMS to a stable system.

For Thiel, the European Monetary Union (EMU) is a key element in the Community's evolution from market integration to political union. Looking closely at those paragraphs in the Maastricht Treaty that deal with the EMU, she finds that according to this treaty, the new European monetary authority will be independent so that it can maintain price stability, and the member states will be obliged to avoid excessive public deficits, among other provisions. In order to qualify for the EMU, member states must meet stringent fiscal criteria; thus, the EMU will start up with only a few qualified members, while those who do not qualify immediately may join at a later time. As Thiel reminds us, the U.S. has always supported European unification in the belief that a united Europe would be a better partner for sharing global responsibilities.

George Bermann and Leila Wexler deal with important legal aspects of the European Union. Bermann evaluates the principle of subsidiarity as described in the Maastricht Treaty; this principle states that action to accomplish a legitimate government objective should be taken at the lowest level of government capable of effectively addressing the problem, i.e., the EU institutions (like the Council of Ministers, the European Parliament, or the Commission) should exercise the power constitutionally vested in them only to the extent that member states are unable to achieve the same objectives satisfactorily. However, there are limits to the uses of subsidiarity, as Bermann points out. For example, it cannot measure values like market uniformity. Another limitation is that the doctrines of subsidiarity and proportionality may operate at cross purposes in the same case. Nevertheless, Bermann asserts, subsidiarity is an important instrument in conveying to the institutions a set of messages that may help them avoid legislating on occasions when member states could do an effective job of attaining the Community's policy goals.

As Wexler points out, defining Europe's goals in a positive manner is important, both to retain political support for the EU and to provide guiding principles upon which the institutions of the Community may base their decisions. The task of the European Court of Justice is to ensure that in the interpretation and application of the EC treaties, the law is observed. However, the Court does have a number of limitations. As things stand now, European citizens may raise issues of EU law before their national courts and receive rulings thereon from the European Court of Justice, but they do not have a right of direct access to the Court. Furthermore, the current Court seems to be backlogged, thus impairing its availability to Europeans and thereby decreasing respect for the Court and its pronouncements on European Union law.

Dieter Dettke, Andrzej Stępniak, and Yuri Fedotov deal with aspects of the new situation in Europe subsequent to the end of the cold war, following the political division of the continent. Dettke describes the peculiar situation in Eastern Europe. Nearly all the East European states have minority problems within or outside their borders, thus creating a strong potential for a conflict situation. These ethnic problems are complicated by the fact that the necessary economic reforms in all of Eastern Europe will entail massive unemployment, at least temporarily. Not only has the Yugoslavian crisis illustrated the explosive force of nationalism and the political use of ethnic parameters as a source of military conflict in Europe, but it has also shown the weakness of the EC with regard to the prevention of wars and the resolution of conflicts. According to Dettke, NATO as well as the European Union must formulate a new vision for a dynamic European multilateralism: NATO should adjust its former regional multilateralism to the new global political conditions, and the European Union should not reject the wish of the Eastern European countries for admission.

The admission of Poland to the European Union is the topic of Stępniak's paper. In December of 1991, Poland became an associate member of the EC. A framework for Poland's gradual integration into the Community was established, a framework to strengthen the political dialog between Poland and the EC; to plan the creation of a free trade area; to enable the harmonization of laws; to improve economic, financial, and cultural cooperation; and to prepare the establishment of common institutions. While these are noble aims, Stępniak does not overlook the problems involved. The liberalization of imports of agricultural goods would be detrimental to Polish agriculture. Poland's dilemma is described by Stępniak as follows: Poland cannot equal the level of economic development of the EC countries until it has gained access to the resources of the Community, but its admission to the EC is dependent on its achievement of the preconditions of membership, i.e., curbing inflation, lowering the unemployment level, and reducing the budget deficit.

As Fedotov shows, cooperation between postcommunist Russia and the EU is even more complicated. The goals of reform have not been attained; in fact, the opposite has occurred: inflation in Russia has risen sharply while industrial and agrarian output — as well as investments — have dropped dramatically. The basics necessary to a market economy are absent from Russia's economy, and this fact — coupled with rampant corruption — has further complicated economic cooperation between Russia and the West. These barriers notwithstanding, Russia's wealth of natural and human resources exerts a long-term attraction for potential business partners. The shortage of consumer goods makes the country attractive to Western manufacturers. As one of the world's richest areas in natural resources, Russia stands a good chance of obtaining investments from the West.

Michael Strübel and Joyce Mushaben address the important issues of European environmental policy and the European Union's attitude toward the emancipation of women. The Single European Act of 1985 introduced the rule that the EC's environmental policy is to be incorporated into all areas of the Community. But according to Strübel, this integration has not been realized. Too often ecological priorities are supplanted by national and economic interests. Member states have used ecological issues as bargaining points; for example, Greece has agreed to accept air emission standards only if the EC rejects the membership of Turkey and meets certain other conditions. While the Green faction accounts for less than six percent of the membership of the European Parliament, the main function of the Greens has been to raise environmental awareness on the part of the general populace.

To date, little research has been done on the EC's attitude toward the advancement of women's rights. Mushaben compares the national legislatures with the European Parliament and finds that women's share of seats there is higher than it is in the parliaments of most member countries. The EC's record on women's issues has been good throughout its history. As far back as 1957, the Treaty of Rome mandated "equal pay for equal work." The European Parliament has emerged as the primary mobilizer around women's causes, issuing a number of directives advocating positive action against discrimination. The changes foretokened by the Single European Act and the Maastricht Treaty — particularly the creation of a transnational core of social rights — can provide an antidote to the immobilism of national governments with regard to gender equality policies. The strongest champion of women's rights, Mushaben points out, has been the European Parliament itself.

Robert Picht's, Udo Kultermann's, and Paul Michael Lützeler's articles shed new light on European culture in its present postmodern situation. Picht reminds us that the problems of mutual understanding among the European countries go far beyond linguistics; traditions as well as industrial constraints and interactions give rise to ways of thinking and acting that may be appropriate in a single European country but may be incompatible with those of neighboring states. But European cultural integration is not impossible; it is spurred by pure necessity. Post-Maastricht Europe is a highly contradictory but dynamic postmodern structure, and the new challenges engender new elements of shared meaning. Educational exchanges among European countries have been encouraged, producing a new generation of Europeans who can understand and overcome cultural differences through mutual respect for diversity. Social and cultural change in Europe is accelerated by the fact that traditional identities are being disrupted by numerous forces, e.g., unemployment, violence, migration. In view of these crises, Picht believes that the reorientation of European societies must occur on a cultural level before new steps toward unification can be taken.

Kultermann analyzes European architecture in its postmodern phase as a unique marker of contemporary transformation, as a signpost for developments before and after 1989. Both the International Style of Modernism, which dominated large segments of architecture in the Western world, and the International Style of Social Realism, which dominated the communist world, are being transcended by regional independent manifestations that no longer adhere to the old political ideologies. European architects have searched for their regional roots and, in many instances, have been able to establish new criteria for buildings in harmony with the history of the site, uniting tradition and new requirements. European identity has emerged from a multiplicity of sources. What is important, Kultermann claims, is a balanced and free diversity of regional manifestations which, nevertheless, remain united in their sharing of mutual values.

Literary essays on Europe — on its political structure and its cultural identity — are the topic of Lützeler's paper. During the past two hundred years most of Europe's leading authors have written on European cultural and/or political unity. Political arguments for continental cooperation have been supported by references to shared history, religion, and art. In these essays it is generally assumed that in Europe idealism, individualism, and unity are embroiled in a constant struggle with materialism, collectivism, and diversity. Endless discussions have been devoted to the specific form of the alliance among the individual nations; the authors questioned whether a united Europe or a federation of states or a Europe of fatherlands would be the best arrangement. As far as their cultural goal was concerned, most authors of the essays on Europe tried to contribute to the elimination of national prejudice, hatred, and warmongery. It is to the lasting credit of the European writers, Lützeler notes, that they committed themselves to the European dimension of their identities during the nineteenth and twentieth centuries, a time when nationalistic movements insisted on the unity and totality of a specific nation's identity and proceeded to enforce these demands, often with catastrophic consequences.

European integration and unification is a highly complex and complicated process. In this collection of articles on the topic of Europe after Maastricht, scholars from different fields have analyzed the political, social, strategic, economic, and cultural aspects of the current situation, in which the transformation of the European Community into the European Union is taking place. The problems addressed are viewed from both American and European perspectives, which should help readers in the U.S. and on the old continent gain a better understanding of recent changes and developments along with their implications for the future.

1
The U.S. and the EC
Cooperation and Competition

◆ ◆ ◆ ◆ ◆ ◆

Theo Sommer

One and a half centuries ago Alexis de Tocqueville made the prediction that America and Russia — alike in outlook, ambition and energy — would come to dominate the world, each establishing its lordship over one-half of the globe. After World War II this prophecy came true. The world designed at Yalta was one-half American, one-half Russian. Now the condominium of the two superpowers has suddenly broken up. Europe — the Old World — is once again taking its destiny into its own hands. A new world is coming into being in the Pacific Region. The Cold War, in 1993, is but a nightmarish memory.

In a way this is exactly what two postwar generations in the West have been wishing for, praying for, and working for ever since 1945. But now that our prayers have been answered, many feel extremely uncomfortable. During the Cold War the risks were familiar, our certitudes unshaken, the need to huddle together obvious for all. The risks of the new dispensation are unfamiliar in the extreme; the old certainties are gone; the imperative of partnership is no longer self-evident.

A shrewd observer, Stanley Hoffmann, had premonitions about this as long ago as 1984. In the summer of that year he wrote (in *Daedalus*): "One external force could strain the [Atlantic] Alliance to the breaking point: the Soviet Union, should it revolutionize its foreign policy and suddenly offer to let its East European protectorates be 'finlandized,' in exchange for a West European reduction of dependency on Nato and the United

States. But, until now, Soviet stolidity, brutality, fear of sacrificing well-established gains for uncertain possibilities, and unwilling-ness to run the risk of German reunification have carried the day." Hoffmann had little doubt that this state of affairs was going to last for some time to come. Giving expression to what was, at the time, almost a truism, he concluded: "There is no reason for anguish."

Barely five years later the unexpected happened. History wrought cataclysmic change in an exceedingly short span of time, upsetting seemingly immutable patterns with the force of an erupting volcano. Within six months in 1989, six East European countries shed the shackles of Communist dictatorship and Soviet tutelage. On 3 October 1990, Germany was reunited after forty-five years of partition. The Warsaw Pact and Comecon ceased to exist shortly afterward. By Christmas 1991, the Soviet Union itself came unstuck; in the process, the imperial legacy of both the tsars and the commissars went up in smoke. All of a sud-den, the Cold War was over.

It was a famous victory for the West. But like the Romans after their victory over Carthage, many Westerners find themselves wondering what is to become of them without the enemy of yes-teryear. Communism is dead, but in the West, too, the foundations are shaking. Organizations such as Nato, the European Commu-nity, and GATT are afflicted by self-doubt, a sense of drift, and a lack of purpose. The economic downturn adds to the general bewilderment, to the areas of friction, and to a rising tide of beg-gar-thy-neighbor attitudes. All around the temptation to go it alone has been weakening the cooperative arrangements that served the Western world so well during the past half century. "With no common enemy," argues Mark Nelson in a recent issue of *Foreign Policy*, "Europe and America are coming unglued."

Human beings tend to be alarmist about the present and nos-talgic about the past. For this reason, I propose to take a brief look at the postwar history of transatlantic relations. It will teach us that our relationship was never trouble-free. But it will also inform us that this relationship was never beyond hope and repair.

II

Twenty-seven years ago, in the summer of 1966, I flew down to Texas to interview President Johnson on his ranch near Houston. He was worried about the cohesion of the Western alliance — about the French pulling out of Nato's military organization; about the Germans balking at paying higher offset payments for the upkeep of the U.S. garrison in the Federal Republic; and about rising opposition to America's Vietnam War.

To illustrate the dangers inherent in the situation, Johnson recounted the anecdote of the young Texan who applied for a job as a railway switchman. He was hauled before an examination board. The chairman told him: "Imagine, young man: you are working on this single-track railroad. You look to the right and see an express train approaching at 100 miles per hour. You look to the left and you see another express train approaching at the same speed. What would you do?" — "I would run and fetch my brother!" — "Why that?" — "Well, he ain't never seen a train wreck. . . ."

Johnson's implication was obvious: he feared that Europe and America were on a collision course. For all we know, they may have been; but as a matter of fact, the collision never occurred. The alliance rode out that storm as it has weathered many others since.

Often its quarrels and struggles had to do with issues of nuclear strategy for defense and deterrence. As recently as ten years ago, Nato's doubletrack decision — basically a decision to arm in order to disarm — rocked Germany, and with it the alliance, to its very foundations. Protesters giving battle to the police outside the gates of the Pershing base in Mutlangen became almost daily fare on the TV evening news. And only four years ago, with the East European revolution already looming on the horizon, American plans to update the "Lance," a tactical nuclear weapon that for want of range could hardly hit anybody besides Germans, caused a deep rift between Bonn and Washington. In the same vein, most Europeans disagreed with the White House when the incumbents belittled arms control and disarmament. In our view, merely building up military strength was not sufficient to obtain security.

Frequently European-American quarrels originated in crisis flashpoints outside the Nato treaty area: Suez, Algeria, Vietnam, the Arab-Israeli conflict, Iran, Afghanistan. More recently the Persian Gulf and the former Yugoslavia fall into this category. Moreover, there was never a total congruence of views about how to deal with the Soviet Union. Europeans agreed that the West must be prepared to *resist* the Soviets whenever resistance was of the essence, but they also argued that the West must be ready to *assist* them whenever and wherever such assistance promised to further our goals. For most Europeans — especially for most Germans — detente was a pragmatic method of bringing about what George F. Kennan had called "the mellowing or the break-up of the Soviet Union." The Germans never shared the Americans' ideological qualms, their reticence vis-à-vis Gorbachev, their reluctance to invest in perestroika.

Finally, economic policy has been a bone of contention between the United States and Europe for at least a quarter of a century. The recent squabbles over oilseeds and steel exports were long ago preceded by "chicken wars" and tariff battles over soybeans. And decades before Mickey Kantor started ruffling the feathers of E.C. negotiators there was Johnson financing the Vietnam War through an inflation that quickly poisoned the other Western economies; Richard Nixon letting the Bretton-Woods System fall by the wayside; Jimmy Carter badgering Japan and Germany to act as "locomotives" for the ailing world economy; and Ronald Reagan with his malign neglect of the dollar exchange rate.

Peoples' memories are notoriously short. It is a matter of historical record, however, that European-American relations have never been entirely free of tension. We have always had our difficulties with each other. We have always overcome them. And for almost half a century, we could confidently add: "We shall always overcome them."

III

The question is: Will we manage once again to resolve our differences? The agenda has not changed basically, although priorities have. We have to make up our minds with respect to the future purpose, doctrine, and structure of Nato. We have to establish a consensus about what to do with out-of-area cases of aggression, with regimes torturing and killing their own citizens, and with "failing states" suffering a total breakdown of law and order. We have to devise a common strategy vis-à-vis the newly liberated countries of Central Eastern Europe and the successor republics of the Soviet Union. And we have to address the economic problems in a spirit of collaboration rather than in a beastly mood of Western infighting. This, I am afraid, will be the toughest part.

While the Cold War lasted, self-preservation provided an overriding rationale for settling differences, accommodating conflicting interests or, if necessary, sweeping disputes under the carpet. The instinct for self-preservation engendered self- discipline. Now that the totalitarian challenge has failed and the Communist model collapsed, the need for discipline, for closing ranks and pulling together may not be felt as keenly as it was felt when Europe and the United States lived under the threat of nuclear annihilation. This is especially true in the field of economics — which is certain to gain enormously in importance as the military arena fades into insignificance, with threats evaporating, armies dissolving, and overseas garrisons being reduced or shut down for good.

The real question today is whether the old cooperative structures will be able to adapt in order to survive in the new post-Cold War age — the Atlantic Community primarily, but also the wider trilateral association — encompassing North America, Europe and Japan — which has evolved over the past twenty years into a most useful, most profitable, and most promising piece of international architecture.

IV

When communism collapsed, the Warsaw Pact dissolved, and the Soviet Union fragmented, the efforts, sacrifices, and sufferings of two generations finally paid off. A new age seemed to be dawning. George Bush spoke of a New World Order; Francis Fukuyama published a book reconfirming his thesis about the end of history.

But history has not ended; rather, it returned — and with a vengeance. In the few years that have passed since the collapse of communism and the breakup of the Soviet Empire, the sigh of relief that greeted the great upheaval has turned into a gasp of horror. As the risk of nuclear annihilation, the iron unity of the Socialist camp, and the worldwide rigidities of the Cold War vanished, national ambitions, ethnic hatreds, tribal zeal, and religious enmities erupted all over the globe. CIA boss James Woolsey put it very well: "The West has slain the large dragon, but we live now in a jungle filled with a bewildering variety of poisonous snakes."

Freed from the restraining hand of the superpowers or the compliance imposed by ruthless communist regimes, suppressed nations, different ethnic groups, and various communities of faith go about settling old scores. Bloody conflicts rage in many far-flung places: Somalia and Sudan; Zaire and Togo and Liberia; Iraq and Haiti; Cambodia and Afghanistan; Tadjikistan and Georgia and Nagorny Karabakh. And — closer to home for Italians, Germans, French, and British — barbarism has returned to the former Yugoslavia. It is a telling and deeply troubling coincidence that Sarajevo, the symbol of Europe's darkest hour at the beginning of the twentieth century, has now become the horrible hallmark of its last decade as well.

The Balkan imbroglio destroyed the hope for a post-Cold War reign of peace around the European heartland. It revealed, to everyone's discomfort, that the veneer of civilization is very thin indeed. Ancient passions eroded it in no time; ideological terror was replaced by ethnic and religious horror. And it exposed the helplessness of the European institutions, of the United Nations and equally of the United States, to end the nightmare.

Grudgingly, the present practitioners of statecraft have been forced to realize that in a world of a thousand points of darkness, there are situations beyond their capacity to handle. To be sure, the jury is still out on the United Nations' effectiveness in Iraq, Cambodia, Angola, and Somalia. But any realist will readily concede that there is too much disorder in the present world for the Western powers to put right. They cannot be everywhere and do

everything. The term "New World Order" promised more than
they can live up to. They will have to say "no" more often than
"yes" as the demands for international action keep increasing.
Douglas Hurd said so a few months ago. It is interesting that, after
a lot of soul-searching and equivocation, President Clinton now
preaches the same message from the pulpit of the United Nations.

Inevitably, global anarchy is a phenomenon that will intrude
more and more on our peace of mind. But it is beyond our capacity to react vigorously to every CNN newsreel. It is, moreover,
almost inevitable that Europe and the United States will not see
eye to eye in every instance. As Pierre Hassner eloquently put it:
"To find legitimacy, military intervention must be based on universal principles, but its implementation depends on a particular
constellation of power and interest." There will always be some
tension between universal rules and particular cases. And it is
national interests rather than moral principles that will guide
Western action. We did not start a nuclear war to put an end to the
Gulag. We cannot possibly start a host of smaller wars to correct
misrule all over the globe.

Any realistic policy is bound to follow the same guidelines that
served us extremely well during the Cold War: let's hold our own;
let's contain the threat; let's not go beyond our borders in search
of monsters to slay; let's wait patiently until the forces of evil have
spent themselves; and let's always keep our hand outstretched to
those who would grasp it.

V

We must not close our eyes to those monsters in the immediate
vicinity or in far-away countries. But after having won the Cold
War, the West has every right to give priority to its internal preoc-
cupations. It is high time to shore up our various domestic foundations — and in doing so we need not feel any compunctions.

This goes, first of all, for the United States of America. It paid
a high price for its triumph over communism and Soviet imperi-
alism — almost as high a price as Moscow paid for its defeat. Trying to outgun and outspend its Eastern rival, it neglected its social

fabric, its public infrastructure, its industrial base, its fiscal sanity. Its economy is still the world's largest, but three-quarters of all Americans worry about its future and, more particularly, about their own futures. The termination of the Cold War coincided with the beginning of a severe recession. The Golden Eighties have been superseded by the Nasty Nineties. The old dream is fading that each generation will be better off than the preceding one. The persistent budget deficit will not go away; the welfare system is still rudimentary by European standards; the health care setup is the most expensive and the most inefficient in the Western world, leaving fifteen percent of the population without any coverage whatsoever. America's domestic agenda can no longer be ignored by any president. In the last analysis Bill Clinton made it into the White House because he promised to devote his efforts to this new agenda.

This turning-inward of the United States does not spell another retreat into isolationism. America won't turn its back on the world — it has become too much part and parcel of it. But it will have to tailor its commitments to its shrunken capacities. The United States has emerged from the Cold War as the only truly global power. Now, however, it is acting in an international setting much less susceptible to big-power manipulation, let alone big-power intimidation. Furthermore, the U.S. no longer has the will or the wallet to play Atlas to the rest of the world. America still aspires to leadership, but given its reduced circumstances and the changed world environment, *hegemonic leadership* is not an option anymore. Even *catalytic leadership* — building coalitions for joint operations or stirring others into action — has obvious limits. And *multilateralism*, the new catchword, is still a slogan without much concrete meaning; it suggests abandonment of U.S. leadership rather than changing the mechanisms of leadership.

It seems to be Washington's bad luck that it reached the pinnacle at exactly the time when the old currency of power — men under arms, nuclear bombs, and ballistic missiles — went out of usage. Geo-strategy is going out of fashion; geo-economy is now the name of the game. But as we move from the political-military-territorial world of old to the new economic-financial-commercial world of the twenty-first century, industrial prowess, technological innovation, and fiscal solvency will become the crucial yardsticks. By this measure, being the sole superpower does not signify a great deal. More than ever before in its history, America is an equal among equals.

Europe, too, feels the excruciating pains of transition. For the first time since 1917, the Old World is whole and free again. It suffers, however, from various degrees of political and economic malaise in the West; and in the East, as Adam Michnik has aptly said, "freedom is grayer than the dream of it used to be."

When the Iron Curtain fell, the European Community was on its way to the Single Market. Its leaders immediately decided to push ahead toward full monetary and political union — that was the whole purport of the Maastricht Treaty. But then, as though the new nationalism rampant in post-Communist Eastern Europe was catching, they stumbled and fumbled, stalled and stuttered, balked and bartered.

I am not a pessimist, but I cannot help noticing that our statesmen tried to rush things beyond prudence. Now they face the task of convincing their skeptical peoples to go along on the next leg of the European journey.

The Single Market entered into force at the beginning of this year, but monetary union and political union are distant as they were three years ago. I would not consider these projects canceled, but they will take longer to materialize than we had thought; different members will get there at different times, moving at different speeds, and not everybody may ultimately participate in all Community endeavors. The Europe of the future will accommodate differences. Yet the Community is bound to widen: first, to include the five EFTA countries; second, to bring in the Central Europeans already pounding on its doors — Poland, the Czech Republic and Slovakia, Hungary and Slovenia; third, to associate the countries further east. If I were to make a wager, I would say by the year 2000 the European Community is likely to have nineteen or twenty members, and it is not unimaginable that the EC will count thirty members by the year 2010.

All the reasons that more than forty years ago impelled the process of West European integration are still present — save one: the communist threat. The Community has an example to offer: that ancient enmities can be overcome; that there are more constructive methods of advancing everybody's welfare and security than pandering to the spirits of the past; and that the victory of freedom need not spell the end of peace and the beginning of fragmentation. European integration is the most potent antidote to ruinous nationalism.

Only a Community evolving into a full-fledged union can spare us a lethal return to history. Only such a Community can provide a *structure d'accueil* to the newly liberated East. And only such an indissoluble Community will be able to handle the turbulent "Third Europe": the Balkan and the Baltic states, Ukraine, Belarus and Moldova, and lastly Russia itself. When I say "handle," I mean both warding off the dangers emanating from those turbulent peoples as well as helping them overcome the present turmoil.

Building the structures of the future, deepening and widening the Community, taming the nationalist spirit rather than enflaming it — these tasks will tax the Europeans' capacities to the utmost, particularly so as they have to tackle them at a moment when they find themselves in the throes of the most cruel recession since 1945. But in a world increasingly characterized by large regional groupings — hopefully, not inimical blocs — Europe is bound to become more than the sum of its nation-states. It will become an actor on the world scene in its own right. It must be a partner for the American Region as well as for the Japanese-Pacific Region, an entity capable of collaborating with the other two but also, if necessary, of holding its own in any sustained rivalry with them.

VI

My topic is U.S./EC relations. Fifteen or even ten years ago, it would have been perfectly permissible to leave Japan out of any discussion of our mutual relationship. In 1993, this is neither permissible nor possible. At this point we cannot create a new order without Japan. It is the world's first and only developing nation that made it to the top of the heap, as its regular presence at the G-7 summits underlines. In 1953, a hundred years after Perry's Black Ships anchored in Tokyo Bay, it still smarted from the bitter defeat it had suffered at the hands of the Americans in 1945. But amid the smoldering ashes of Tokyo and Kyoto, amid the radioactive rubble of Hiroshima and Nagasaki, imaginative men set their sights on new targets. "An army in uniform is not the only sort of army," wrote one of them, Saburo Okita, later to become foreign minister. "Scientific technology and fighting spirit under a business suit will be our future army."

The Japanese Samurai donned gray flannel and single-mindedly went to work, developing their precision engineering, expanding their production, conquering foreign markets rather than foreign countries. They met with remarkable success. In 1950, Japan's GNP was one-third that of Britain, one-twentieth that of the United States. Today it is three times bigger than Britain's and has reached two-thirds of the American GNP. Japan is now the world's number two national economy and the world's second largest exporter. The army in business suits has gained the country global financial-economic preeminence.

But today Japan is also in deep trouble. As one Japanese politician put it: "Our country has a first-rate economy, a second-rate standard of living, and a third-rate political system."

The first-rate economy has recently run into considerable difficulties. Asset inflation was followed by a severe stock crash. Immediately after that crash the global recession forced the Japanese to throttle their industrial production. And now the enormous trade surpluses they have built up in their commercial relations with the United States ($50 billion) and the European Community ($20 billion) are unleashing the forces of protectionism everywhere. The stronger the position of the Japanese on the world market becomes, the more furious a backlash they are likely to trigger.

At the same time, pressure is building within Japan to let the people enjoy a greater share of the fruits of their labor. Today the triumph of Japanese capitalism is expressed in total productivity, not in the advantages accruing to the individual. In a number of respects Japan is a backward country. Its social security system is deficient; its infrastructure, e.g., roads and sewage systems, is deplorable. The Japanese work long hours, take only short vacations, and live in tiny homes ("rabbit hutches"). Clamor is rising to change this, to increase domestic consumption and to improve the overall quality of life.

In addition, Japan has now been engulfed by a dramatic political crisis. After forty years the dominance of the Liberal Democrats has ended. The curious Japanese phenomenon of a one-party democracy kept going by corruption, sleaze, and favoritism has been replaced by a new alignment. But the forces of the future are taking shape slowly, and for some time to come, uncertain leadership is likely to remain the fate of Japan.

VII

This cursory glance at the three main players on the world scene — the U.S., Europe, and Japan — reveals an enormous potential for rivalry and friction between them. Perhaps this is the inevitable consequence of the fact that economic matters preoccupy everyone far more than geopolitical concerns; as the Germans say, "In Geldsachen hört die Gemütlichkeit auf." As long as there existed a clear and present danger, the task was military containment of enemy states; now all too frequently it is seen to be economic containment of partner nations.

We are all tempted to yield to the siren songs of protectionism, but in the end no one would be better off; we would all be worse off. Common sense enjoins us to continue to hang together — lest we all hang separately.

Let me give you just a few reasons for hanging together:

1. The huge dragon we have slain may not be quite dead, or new dragons may grow up in far-away jungles. Global anarchy will promote worldwide instability. Islamic fundamentalism, other millennial demagogues, or ambitious zealots might pose new threats. Mass migrations, the proliferation of modern weapons of mass destruction, violent

explosions of wrath among the have-nots in the Southern half of the globe against the happy few in the North will confront us with highly menacing situations.

2. The industrial democracies will no doubt once again work their way out of the present recession. But behind the conjunctural weakness a daunting problem is becoming visible: the possibility that we might run out of work and that large-scale structural unemployment may be the curse of the future. Technological innovation will soon reach a point at which only one-sixth of the workforce will be engaged in the production of goods. Will the others find jobs in the service sector and in the knowledge industries? Or will progress make human labor superfluous as the tractor made the horse superfluous?

3. All the industrial democracies are in the grip of a grave internal crisis. This crisis made itself felt at the very moment external tension abated — a crisis of governance affecting Socialists and Conservatives alike. Already some people conjure up the "death of party democracy." This is at least premature, but fundamental reform of our various democratic systems is clearly an urgent task everywhere.

4. We need — all of us — a revival of public spirit. During the decade preceding the implosion of the communist world, the nations of the West indulged in an explosion of egotism that all but destroyed the community spirit that is indispensable to the success of any democratic society. What is needed is a redressed balance between citizens' rights and choices on the one hand, citizens' duties and responsibilities on the other, and a renewed dedication to social connectedness, civic virtue and political probity. We must learn to produce values again, not only goods.

All this adds up to a formidable agenda. We are bound to fail if we try to tackle it severally and separately. Our only chance lies in continued cooperation, in deepened and widened collaboration, in one considered and determined joint effort. The rationale for the

American-European alliance, and indeed for the close association with modern Japan, may be different today from what it was in the heyday of the East-West confrontation, but it is just as compelling.

Together we won the Cold War — but we have yet to earn the glory that goes with victory. The Eastern system collapsed. Now the Western system is discovering that it, too, has to mend its ways, drastically and rapidly. Merely enduring will not be enough to survive.

As one historian suggested, there are three sorts of statesmen: those who *make* events happen; those who *watch* events happen; and those who wonder *ex post facto* what has happened. In the years ahead, I submit, we should not simply let the future befall us; rather we should try to give shape to it — shape and meaning.

VIII
The New Agenda

What I said about European integration, i.e.., that all the old reasons for it are still compelling, minus one — the Communist threat — goes for the transatlantic relationship as well. We must hang on to it, for all imaginable alternatives would be far worse. The degree of practical cooperation we have reached during the past half century is a historic achievement that we should not lightly put at risk.

There is battle fatigue in the United States and in Europe. There is a tendency, after our joint triumph in the Cold War, to indulge in spitballing and mutual recrimination. And there is a disquieting trend to consider our proven partnership expendable.

I think we must resist those temptations. Rather, we should work out, jointly and with great determination, a Grand Strategy for the new era. Ours is a world in transit, and it is hard to discern toward which goals it is moving. That is all the more reason to clasp hands across the Atlantic as we address a twofold agenda. One part is the agenda of classical statecraft. It has to do with traditional concerns: how to deal with relations between nations after the end of the Cold War. It is about strategy, international politics, and international economics, about alliances and contractual arrangements, about threats and challenges and responses. This is, as it were, the "hard" agenda of world politics.

But there is another; the "soft" agenda. It relates not so much to the survival and the prosperity of individual nations, or groups of nations; it relates to the survival of mankind. It deals with the problems of ecology (global warming, biodiversity, etc.), of population growth, the alleviation of poverty, proliferation and the arms trade, drug trafficking, AIDS, terrorism, and mass migration. This agenda highlights the threats emanating not from other nations' armies but from human selfishness, stolidity and stupidity, irresponsibility and levity. The hard part of this agenda is difficult enough to tackle.

We have to construct a partnership of equals, which will require new methods and mechanisms of collaboration. This updated dispensation must reflect the shifting priorities — shifting from military concerns, which intrinsically make for cohesion, to economic issues, which are inherently divisive. We must resist the temptation of renationalization and protectionism. We should bend all our efforts to preventing the present trilateral arrangement from degenerating into a three-bloc system of political and commercial rivalry to the hilt. The "soft" part of the agenda poses even more difficult problems. In this regard, the record is pitiful. European-American friction over Rio was indicative of wide divergences. We can do better — and we have to. The dilemmas of global disorder are destined to become the defining determinants of the twenty-first century. We should not flinch before them, but rather close ranks and address them together. European-American cooperation (and, indeed, European-American-Japanese cooperation) is the only front of hope.

In all this, we ought to beware of both complacency and euphoria.

We are living between two ages. The outline of the future is but dimly discernible. Only one thing is certain: We will not wake up one magic morning and find a stable New World Order in place. History teaches, if anything, that there is no end to human drudgery and misery, no end to surprise and shock, no end to ever new beginnings. "The moving finger, having writ/moves on." Like it or not, we have to move along.

Let's stick to what we have, and let's build on it. We have a European-American connection of proven worth. We have a working relationship with Japan that holds great promise. And we have a long list of vital tasks to perform.

Jean Monnet once said: "Nothing is possible without men, nothing will last without institutions." I hope the men — and, of course, the women — will arise to take matters in hand. And I hope that they will have the imagination, the courage, and the votes to create the institutions which we will need if the Atlantic Community is to play a meaningful role in the coming century.

The Tocqueville Paradigm has been scuttled by events. The bipolar world is finished, and it will not return. If we are looking for a new paradigm amid a sea of change, a host of unfamiliar changes, a multitude of new risks, I would suggest the Hugo Paradigm. Victor Hugo, the great French novelist, wrote in 1848, thirteen years after his compatriot Tocqueville published his famous book *Democracy in America*: "The time will come when these two immense systems — the United States of America and the United States of Europe — will come face to face with one another, shake hands and trade their products, their arts, their genius . . . thus improving the state of our world."

The time will come, said Victor Hugo. I put it to you: the time is now. It is no longer the dire necessities of the Cold War that force us together. We — America, Europe, Japan — can now build an association of free nations on the foundations of our ideals, our hopes for the future, our joint visions. I trust that we shall rise to the occasion.

2
The U.S./EC Relationship
Friends and Competitors

◆ ◆ ◆ ◆ ◆ ◆

Murray Weidenbaum

The increasing economic integration of Western Europe resulting from the essential completion of the EC 1992 agenda is an appropriate time to consider the problems and potentials of the developing economic relationship between the United States and the European Community.

EC-1992 and Beyond

This paper analyzes the U.S./EC relationship from admittedly an American point of view. Let us begin with the ongoing economic unification of Western Europe. To an economist, the creation of the single market as it unfolds during the 1990s is essentially a positive event, yet one destined to generate winners and losers on both sides of the Atlantic. Because the formation of the United States represented in a very real sense the creation of the original common market, Americans are basically supportive of the Community's efforts. We have been so from the outset, going back to the creation of the original European Coal and Steel Community, the predecessor to the current European Community.

However, the business and economic relationships among our nations are bound to become more intricate as we both compete in what is increasingly a global marketplace involving numerous third — and fourth — parties. It is vital, therefore, that the European Community and the United States each develop a better understanding of how to be friends and competitors simultaneously during the years ahead. In that spirit, we must acknowledge that, from the vantage point of American business firms, the rise of the European Community presents both threats and opportunities.

The fundamental positive economic factor flowing from developments in the EC is, of course, that the twelve member countries have been reducing restrictions on business, trade, and labor. Many of the goals associated with the creation of a single EC market and the integration of commercial, financial, and cross-border markets were met with the implementation of the EC 1992 program, which in large measure went into effect at the beginning of 1993. Despite some gaps in implementation, people as well as goods and investments are now able to move much more readily from one of the common market nations to any other. That is bound to make Western European businesses more efficient as they achieve greater economies of scale and as standardization replaces twelve varieties of many products and services. The participation of the EC as a single entity representing its member states in the multinational GATT tariff negotiations is another important step in the integration process.

However, the big negative — from the viewpoint of other nations as well as the EC's own consumers — is that the trade wall around the EC is not coming down. In the words of the Federal Reserve Bank of Chicago, "Not only did formation of the EC result in a reduction in restrictions on trade between members, it began the process of setting *common trade restrictions against nonmembers*" (emphasis in original).[1] The contrast between these two very different movements is quite striking.

Actually, the EC is toughening its external barriers to commerce. Enlightened economists are not supposed to use pejorative terms such as "Fortress Europa," so let us cite some numbers instead. In 1960, more than 60 percent of the foreign trade of the twelve EC members was outside of the EC. In 1992, 61 percent of their trade remained in the EC.[2] This is a complete reversal.

---

1. Jack L. Hervey, "Europe at the Crossroads," *Chicago Fed Letter*, August 1993, pp. 1-2.
2. Thomas J. Duesterberg, "Global Competitiveness and U.S.-EC Trade Relations," Hudson Briefing Paper, July 1993, p. 4.

The current ratio is bound to rise further for two reasons. The first is the increasing economic integration of the EC-12. The second force moving in the same direction is the six countries in the European Free Trade Association (EFTA) who are joining in a formal trade association with the Community to form a European Economic Area. Those six are Austria, Finland, Iceland, Liechtenstein, Norway, and Sweden. For the time being, Switzerland rejected participation via a national referendum.

Complying with the terms of the European Economic Area will anticipate approximately two-thirds of the adjustments in national laws necessary for full EC membership. The trade linkages are already very strong. Austria, for example, purchases 69 percent of its imports from the EC nations which, in turn, buy 65 percent of Austria's exports.[3]

Our friends in Brussels tell Americans not to worry about these developments, and that the EC's trade restrictions, such as reciprocity and domestic content rules, are aimed at Japan. However, we do not know how good their aim is. The same restrictions that affect Japan can keep out goods produced in the United States, whether by domestically owned firms or by factories in North America that are transplanted from Asia. Moreover, if the products of Asian rim countries are kept out of Europe, the Western Hemisphere is their major alternate market. So, in the interconnected global economy that now exists, Americans have a vital interest in the maintenance of open trading patterns around the world. EC purchasers, whether family consumers or industrial buyers, likely have very similar interests.

The impacts of greater EC economic unification will surely be uneven, as is expected of any dynamic process. The most likely winners will include the stronger European companies with high labor skills and high-tech production capabilities. They will be enjoying the benefits of both economies of scale and growing domestic markets. These firms also bring a special understanding of European needs, capabilities, and cultures. Many of these enterprises should emerge larger and stronger than ever.

---

3. "Austria: First in Line to Join the EC?" *International Economic Review*, August 1993, p. 12.

In contrast, losers from greater EC economic unification may well include high-cost European companies that have been sheltered within their own national markets. Some of these more tradition-bound firms will be hurt by new continent-wide competition. The economically backward areas — the *mezzogiornos* — may fall further behind. Of course, not all barriers will come down. Each member nation continues to possess individual values, needs, cultures, language — and tax systems. No matter what changes the EC makes, the French are not going to make a stampede for German wine. The British will still want cars with steering wheels on the "wrong" side.

Likely winners will also include many strong U.S. firms with an established presence in Western Europe. The implications of that presence, it turns out, are ambivalent. The overwhelming majority of goods sold in the EC by American multinational firms is produced in the EC by European workers. Only a small fraction of the products sold by American multinationals in the EC is made in the United States and then shipped to Europe for sale by their local subsidiaries.[4]

The rationale for American firms favoring direct investment in Europe over exports from the United States was made clear by a representative of Pfizer, the American pharmaceutical firm:

> Pfizer does not have a choice about whether to manufacture in the European Community or not. If we are going to sell in Europe, we have to manufacture there.[5]

Quite a few U.S.-based companies have encountered similar experiences. However, once established in Western Europe, these enterprises have some special advantages. These high-tech, well-capitalized companies are accustomed to competing on a continent-wide basis. They can use one EC country as a base to sell to the other eleven. General Motors and Ford currently have more Europe-wide strength than such European automakers as

---

4. Robert Lipsey, *American Firms Face Europe: 1992* (Cambridge, Mass.: National Bureau of Economic Research, 1990).

5. Cited in "The New Tax Law's Uneven Bite on Corporate America," *New York Times*, August 18, 1993, p. C-16.

Volkswagen, Fiat, Peugeot, and Renault. The same holds true for computer manufacturers such as IBM, Digital Equipment, Unisys, and Hewlett Packard compared to their European counterparts.

On the other side of the ledger, quite a few U.S. firms are likely to be losers as a result of the creation of the single European market. They will find it more difficult to export to Western Europe. Looking beyond the initial adjustment period, U.S. exports to the EC are estimated to be 2-3 percent lower than they would be in the absence of European integration.[6] U.S.-based companies also will face tougher competition from the stronger EC businesses in their domestic markets. The expected losers will include many provincial American companies that have not yet awakened to developments across the Atlantic.

On balance, there is a positive thrust to these changes in the economic relationship between the European Community and the United States. From the viewpoint of the United States, Western Europe now presents a potential market for a wide range of products and services far greater than most Americans appreciate — and the benefits should flow in both directions. The EC is the largest customer of U.S. products and, at least until the most recent period, its imports from the United States exceed its exports to the United States in most recent years. Here are a few examples of the ways in which U.S. and EC companies are developing closer business relationships:

- Ford has agreements with Cosworth in the United Kingdom and Porsche in Germany for the design and development of car engines used in the models it produces in Europe.

- IBM purchased minority equity stakes in more than 100 software and computer service companies in Western Europe between 1990 and 1992.

- Some models of Boeing commercial jet transports use engines made by the United Kingdom's Rolls-Royce, especially for European airlines. For its new 777, Boeing has

---

6. Linda C. Hunter, "Europe 1992: An Overview," *Federal Reserve Bank of Dallas Economic Review*, January 1991, p. 21.

entered into partnerships with Italy's Alenia to produce the outboard wing flaps and with General Electric of Britain for the primary flight computers.

■ Otis' new elevator, the Elevonic 411, uses electronics designed by its Germany subsidiary, door systems made by its French branch, and small-geared components produced by its Spanish division.

■ Unisys is simultaneously a customer of, and a supplier to, Switzerland's BASF, the Netherlands' Philips, and Germany's Siemens — and also competes with each of these Western European electronics giants.

■ Digital Equipment Corporation and Italy's Olivetti & Co. jointly fund and share the results from Olivetti's research laboratory in Cambridge, England.

■ General Electric and Pratt & Whitney are cooperating with Rolls-Royce and France's SNECMA to develop quieter, more economical, and cleaner-burning aircraft engines.

■ McDonnell Douglas is working on the development of a new radar-equipped version of the Harrier II (a vertical take-off and landing aircraft) jointly with Alenia, British Aerospace, and CASA of Spain.

■ Pacific Telesis is a 26-percent participant in a joint venture led by Mannesmann to provide mobile telephone service in Germany. The American company also holds a 23-percent stake in Telecel, an international consortium building a cellular phone system in Portugal.

Not all developments in the EC have been positive, even from a European viewpoint. Considerable concern has been aroused by the failure of the EC-12 to move more rapidly in approving and carrying out the Maastricht agreement. In retrospect, the early rush to monetary union was faster than could be reasonably sustained. Progress surely will be more cautious in the years ahead, but some positive movement may well continue. Individually, many market-oriented economists sympathize with the reluctance of the citizenry to increase the already substantial power of the EC bureaucracy and of central bankers.

The simultaneous failure of Western Europe to take a forceful stand on the contentious Bosnia issue also has contributed to a feeling of unease in assessing future progress in the Community. However, these political setbacks should not deflect from the genuine accomplishments made in integrating the production, trade, and financial markets of Western Europe.

Moreover, the EC is a dynamic and not a static concept. The Community started with six member nations and gradually doubled that number. Twelve will not be the end of the line. Many other European nations are seeking admission, aside from the special case of East Germany, which already has been unified with West Germany. As outsiders, we can only speculate that the applications of Sweden, Finland, and Norway will be approved fairly expeditiously. Denmark's existing membership is a constant reminder to the other Scandinavian nations of the benefits of Community membership.

Austria's entrance into the EC would be especially strategic, since Vienna is a major gateway to Eastern Europe. The Czech Republic, Hungary, and Poland already have each signed preliminary protocols with the EC. It is likely that their relationship, at least initially, will be that of associate members. Slovakia may be a fourth member of that category and perhaps ultimately will be joined by one or more of the newly independent Baltic republics. Surely, if the Eastern European nations can get their political and economic acts together, they could become low-cost suppliers to Western Europe — or competitors — or both.

Now consider the impact of the EC going from twelve members to fifteen or twenty or more. Adding together all those gross domestic products shows that, later in the 1990s, Western (and Central) Europe will become the world's largest consolidated marketplace and, conceivably, the center of gravity once again of the international economy. That, in turn, requires us to analyze, albeit briefly, the key trends in the rest of the international economy.

The Rise of the Other Regional Groupings

The Asian rim economies are growing rapidly and now constitute a very large regional concentration of economic resources. They are also growing together, although not in a formal structure such as EC or EFTA. An examination of the substantial flows of investment from within the Asian rim — especially from Japan, Taiwan, and South Korea — to the newer industrialized nations in the area such as Thailand, Malaysia, and Indonesia is instructive. Most of their investment capital comes, not from Europe or North America, but from Asia itself. Not too surprisingly, the development of a unified trading area is now taking place in that part of the world. In some cases — notably Malaysia and Indonesia — Japan has become their leading trade partner, for exports as well as imports. By 1995, it is likely that Japan will provide the largest market for the exports and perhaps also the imports of most of the Asian rim nations.

The other more advanced economies in the Pacific rim — notably South Korea, Taiwan, and Hong Kong — are also large providers of investment capital and have become key trading partners for the less economically advanced nations in this region. For example, Hong Kong and the neighboring Chinese province of Guangdong have generated a very considerable cross flow of investment; 50,000 managers and professionals commute daily from Hong Kong to Guangdong. Most of the actual manufacturing activity for Hong Kong-based industries is now performed on the mainland. In fact, what some observers call the greater "Hong Kong enclave" enjoys a gross domestic product approximately equal to that of France and it is growing more rapidly.[7]

Economists are not especially enamored of inward-looking regional trading blocs. Thus, American economists can describe the likely extension of the U.S.-Canadian Free Trade Agreement to include Mexico (NAFTA) as essentially an inevitable response on our part to the market consolidations that are proceeding so swiftly both in Western Europe and in East Asia. Surely, it is important to note that, in the case of the EC as well as NAFTA, this process is essentially a positive one, focusing on reducing barriers to commerce.

---

7. See Murray Weidenbaum, "Greater China," *Washington Quarterly*, Autumn 1993, pp. 71-83.

Important questions then arise: will regionalization improve the relationship between the United States and Western Europe or will we go our separate ways? Will regionalization reduce or increase the volume of world trade? The first question is very judgmental. The second involves data that are very difficult to interpret. On balance, the continued rise in regionalization is likely to coincide with the growth in international commerce. However, it will not be a simple cause and effect relationship. It is another development — the globalization of business — that will pace the growth of world trade. Continual technological advance, especially in transportation and communication, will be a far more powerful force than any static governmentally imposed restraints. Let us explore these relationships.

Regionalization Versus Globalization

It is a commonplace that France exports wine and Japan sells automobiles to the United States and that the United States exports jet airliners to both. In truth, though, nations and governments do little more than record, and tax, those cross-border transactions. It is private, profit-seeking enterprises that typically engage in international commerce.

Examining foreign trade from this viewpoint provides new insights. For example, in the case of the larger, more industrialized nations, about one-half of what governments call foreign trade actually involves cross-border transactions between different parts of the same company. That ratio holds true for Western Europe, the United States, and Japan. An increasingly common occurrence is a domestic firm shipping goods to or receiving items from an overseas subsidiary — or a foreign firm engaging in similar transactions with its divisions in other countries.

In a traditional sense, all this is foreign commerce. From an economic viewpoint, however, these international flows of goods and services are internal transfers within the same firm. Perhaps the most telling case was cited by former U.S. Secretary of State George Shultz. He tells of a shipping label on integrated circuits made by an American firm, which read: "Made in one or more of the following countries: Korea, Hong Kong, Malaysia, Singapore, Taiwan, Mauritius, Thailand, Indonesia, Mexico, Philippines. The exact country of origin is unknown."

That is the global enterprise in full swing. This incident also illustrates the degree to which businesses are generating an increasingly more global outlook transcending regional blocs, no matter how powerful or carefully structured. This broader perspective underlies the strategies that transnational enterprises employ to respond effectively not only to increased competition but also to the inhibiting effects of regionalization.

Here is a rather unusual example of cross-border commerce to illustrate the power of technology in shaping the strategies of the global enterprise: the day of the Iraqi invasion, the manager of a Kuwaiti bank faxed the bank's records page by page to his office in Bahrain. He was forced to stop several times because the gunfire seemed to be coming closer. By day's end, however, he had successfully sent by fax all of the bank's key documents. Having moved this vital information, the bank opened for business the next day as a Bahraini institution. Thus it was not subject to the United States freeze on Kuwaiti assets or to Iraqi control. The bank literally was transplanted from one nation to another by technology.

Technological progress — especially in the fields of communication and transportation — makes possible a variety of business innovations that often overcome the obstacles imposed by governments. Cross-border joint ventures and strategic alliances have moved from the classroom to the boardroom. They are increasingly common in high-technology industries where few companies possess the resources, the technical ability, or the willingness to undertake on their own the risk of a costly new venture. Electronics companies in Europe, Asia, and the United States engage in joint ventures to develop new products and co-produce existing products. The same firms serve as sources of supply for each other, are each other's customers — and compete against each other.

There is no set pattern. Partially-owned subsidiaries, associated firms, licensing, franchising, and correspondent relationships are all increasingly popular ways businesses respond to changing threats and opportunities in the global marketplace. Immunex Corp., a small biotechnology firm in Seattle, Washington, licenses five products for production and sales by the giant Swiss firm Hoffman-LaRoche. Jiffy Lube, Hertz, Budget Rent-A-Car, Rainbow International (a carpet dyeing and cleaning company), and Mailboxes Etc. have franchised many European-based firms to provide the type of services they originally designed for American customers.

The insurance services firm Alexander & Alexander maintains correspondent relationships with All Risk of Norway and Aegis Insurance Company of Greece. It also owns large minority stakes in France's Societé Générale de Courtage d' Assurances and in Ganat Alexander of Spain. A major portion of Corning Glass's revenues comes from joint ventures with Germany's Siemens, Switzerland's Ciba-Geigy, and the United Kingdom's Plessey.[8]

Clearly, technology and business innovation are outpacing traditional political thinking about international relations. The standard geopolitical map is out of date compared with the emerging map of business and economics.

An Optimistic Long-Run View

While private enterprise is increasingly global, government policy nevertheless usually remains very parochial. Understandably, voters still care about the jobs in their country, state, province, and locality. And politicians are not reluctant to exploit those concerns. However, when we examine how the public sector deals with economic issues, it is hard to sustain a feeling of awe. Take the highly visible subject of EC agricultural subsidies. This is a subject that has occupied a considerable amount of the time and energy of U.S. and EC trade negotiators. Yet, it is useful to examine the operation of those supposedly awesome obstacles to commerce. Here is an excerpt from the 79-page book of instructions published by the UK Ministry of Agriculture, Fisheries, and Food. This section

---

8. Harvey S. James, Jr., and Murray Weidenbaum, *When Businesses Cross International Borders* (Westport, Conn.) 1993.

of the manual, which is supposed to instruct farmers how to apply for aid under three of the EC's subsidy schemes, has been described as one of the livelier passages of the book:

> If you are claiming only Beef Special Premium and/or Suckler Cow Premium and are exempted from the stocking density rules, you need not submit an area aid application. You are exempt from the stocking density rules if your total number of Livestock Units (LUs) is not more than 15. This total is based on any milk quota you hold on April 1, 1993, sheep on which you have claimed Sheep Annual Premium in 1993, and cattle on which you are claiming Beef Special Premium or Suckler Cow Premium in 1993. Further details of the calculation of stocking density and LUs are set out in paragraphs 44 to 57 of the explanatory booklet "CAP Reform in the Beef Sector." You will, however, need to submit an area aid application if you wish to claim extensification premium (see paragraphs 58 to 61 of "CAP Reform in the Beef Sector").[9]

There is another and ultimately more powerful force that comes into play in international commerce: the consumers who vote every day of the week, in dollars, guilders, marks, yen, pounds, francs, and lira. That is a compelling reason to end on an upbeat note when pondering the future of the international economy in general and of U.S.-EC relationships in particular.

In each of our nations, the same voters — as consumers — buy products and services made anywhere in the world. They may vote protectionist, but their daily buying patterns are oriented to free trade. Consumers in each of our nations give far more weight to price and quality than to the product's country of origin. Without thinking about it, consumers are adapting to the global economy. After all, if consumers were not open to the global marketplace, the pressures on government to restrict international trade would not arise in the first place.

In the years ahead, the combined power of economic incentives and technological change will increasingly compel voters and government officials to wake up to the positive implications

9. Quoted in John O'Sullivan, "O'Sullivan's Second Law," *National Review*, May 24, 1993, p. 6.

of the global economy. In a basic sense, the mobility of enterprises — of their people, capital, and information — is reducing the power of government. Public-sector decision makers increasingly are being forced to understand that they now have to become internationally competitive in the economic policies they devise. Government programs that impose costs without compensating benefits or that reduce wealth substantially in the process of redistributing income undermine the competitive positions of their own domestic enterprises. The result is either the loss of business to firms located in other nations or the movement of the domestic company's resources and activities to more hospitable locations.

Political scientists and economists have long understood and every American school child is taught that people vote with their feet. They leave regions and nations with limited opportunity in favor of those that offer a more attractive future. In this era of computers, telephones, and fax machines, enterprises are far more mobile than that. The fear of losing economic activity to other parts of the world will surely reshape in fundamental ways the domestic political agendas of the coming decade.

Therefore, despite the difficulties being encountered by governments negotiating at GATT, we can be optimistic about future trends of world investment and commerce. Even if many of those public-sector barriers remain, the private sector will increasingly learn how to overcome them or even just to live with them. Of course, there are costs involved when businesses respond to governmental barriers to international business. At times the costs of crossing these borders may be very substantial, especially in the short run. However, in a global economy these barriers become far from absolute.

Conclusion

The tension between business and government is not new, but the required adjustments may actually reduce the frictions between governments by bringing closer together the people and private institutions of each of our nations. The traditional problems of international relations are being exacerbated by the rapid rate of social, economic, and technological change around the globe. But, as a result, the real liberalization of international trade and investment — and the creation of a truly global marketplace in the years ahead — will be achieved, not from changes in government policy, but from the competition among firms in the private sector of the various national and regional economies.

The rapidly changing global marketplace of the 1990s, and likely beyond, will provide both threat and opportunity for business firms, governments, and consumers. Invariably, developments such as the achievement of the single market will generate both winners and losers. The outcomes for specific individuals and organizations will depend in large part on their ability to understand and to respond effectively to ever-changing economic and technological trends.

While governments continue to react to the global marketplace with new regional associations, businesses will keep on trying to overcome or at least to adjust to these barriers and policies in their relentless effort to meet the needs of their customers.

Looking out toward the twenty-first century, we can readily envision the business firms and consumers of both North America and Western Europe becoming tied far more closely together than is the case today. Happily, those alliances and other cooperative relationships will not be forced by governments. Rather, they will be encouraged by economic opportunities and technological possibilities. We will indeed learn how simultaneously to be friends *and* competitors.

3

The European Community and the Challenges of the 1990s

Change and Competitiveness

♦ ♦ ♦ ♦ ♦ ♦

Caroline Jackson

It is some forty years now since the foundations of the European Community were set down by politicians who had survived the Second World War and who were determined that the nations of Europe would never fight each other again. The problems of European recession and resurgent nationalism have led some—in Europe and in America—to say that the experiment may have run its course; that the Europeans will succumb to the temptation to fall back upon protectionism to support their uncompetitive habits; and that Europe—even though it is a major economic power—is simply unable to find a united voice to respond to international political challenges. For Americans in particular there is a temptation simply to write off Europe and its problems—to turn to their new world, the Pacific, as the number one area of expansion.

The European Community clearly is in a state of agitation and change, heightened by the recession. At this time, we are seeing a number of very serious questions converge upon the Community. Europe now has to debate its future. It has gone through the difficult and sometimes painful process of creating a free trade area; there has been a substantial transfer of national sovereignties to the Community level, and the Community has created and is operating many common policies over and beyond those immediately connected with the free trade area.

Now the Community is in the aftermath of the constitutional conference that took place at Maastricht in 1991, and that agreed on further transfers of sovereignty and the creation of further common policies, with more powers of supervision and control being given to the European Parliament and sanctions being made available to the European Court of Justice. All states had to ratify the agreement that contains these changes, the Maastricht "Treaty on European Union," before it would come into effect.

This is all part of the evolution of the Community, which cannot stand still; policies and institutional arrangements that were right for the small Community of the 1950s have to be changed for the global power that the Community has become in the 1990s. The French are having to adjust to this in the GATT negotiations.

Simultaneously, there is the pressure to increase the number of member states of the Community. Austria, Sweden, Norway, Finland, Malta, Cyprus, Switzerland, and Turkey have applied to join, and their membership applications are at various stages of negotiation. At the same time, the Community has to respond to the needs of Eastern Europe.

On top of this the Community has to find its own response to the recession that is afflicting it. And from the recession has come the increasing need to look at the Community's competitiveness and to examine how far EC policies may contribute to it and/or damage it.

This convergence of forces for change means that questions are now being asked in Europe about the appropriate degree of Community intervention, about how much EC law costs to implement, about whether we should in fact now unravel—by repealing it—law that may cost too much to implement and regulate if it does not bring substantial gains. And questions, too, about how far in fact EC law is being universally obeyed and if it is not, what we should do about it.

These questions are vital to Europeans, but they have a particular relevance at this time in the United States because of the NAFTA agreement. NAFTA is a trade arrangement first and foremost, but it obviously raises important questions about how you arrive at the legislation needed to ensure open markets and free competition: how do you agree on product standards, what environmental and consumer safeguards do you need, how do you deal with differing standards of social protection for workers, and—a very big question—what institutional and regulatory framework do you need? The European Community is not in a position to offer precise answers to these questions, but we do at least offer a working model of transnational cooperation and integration on precisely these issues.

The question of competitiveness is being debated urgently in the European Community as never before. If Europe cannot compete, then it cannot afford many of the policies it is presently pursuing; if it can only compete with the help of protection, then, as we have seen, it menaces the future of world trade.

This is a particularly difficult question for Europeans who have been used to high levels of welfare benefits and social protection. At present, we have unemployment standing at seventeen million and likely to rise to twenty million, or 11 percent of the work force of the Community by the end of 1993. Recently we have seen job losses—real reductions, not all covered by early retirement arrangements—announced in major French and German companies, where real job cuts would have been unthinkable a few years ago. As these losses mount, attention is turning to high EC labor costs. In manufacturing industry these rose by 4 percent a year throughout the 1980s, while in the U.S. the increase was 1 percent a year and in Japan no increase took place at all. In 1993 the average hourly labor cost per hour in manufacturing industry was $24.87 in Germany, $21 in Belgium, $19.83 in Holland and $19 in Denmark—but $16.40 in the U.S. and Japan. (The UK figure was $12.37.)

In 1992 average labor costs in manufacturing in the EC were 20 percent higher than in the U.S. and Japan, and non-wage costs are almost twice as high on average in the Community as in the U.S. Where Europe has experienced growth, it has taken place without a net increase in jobs, largely because of increased female participation in the labor force. Thus, for the Community to reduce unemployment from 11 percent to 7 percent requires the creation of ten million jobs before the year 2000.

Against this background the Community's international competitiveness is falling. Its share of world exports in manufacturing has fallen by one fifth since 1980. It has a widening deficit in trade in high technology: a study by the Commission showed that between 1982 and 1990 the volume of EC high-tech exports to the rest of the world grew by only 2 percent a year, while high-tech imports grew by 7.7 percent a year.

The European Commission, the executive arm of the Community, published its response to this situation in a White Paper on Competitiveness, Growth and Employment. The heads of the twelve EC governments had already acted at the end of 1992 to try to switch public expenditure priorities to support growth and encourage investment, to establish a new lending facility for infrastructure through the European Investment Bank, and to finish putting into place the remaining laws needed to create a completely open market among the twelve.

The controversy over our competitiveness is centering first of all on the Community's social policy. This has its origins in the Treaty of Rome and in the Community's commitment to the "continuous improvement of the living and working conditions of the people of Europe." At the end of 1991, in the agreement concluded at Maastricht, eleven member states, excluding the United Kingdom, signed a commitment, known as the social protocol, to go ahead with proposals for EC-wide laws in a number of important areas, including working conditions and the information provided to, and consultation of, workers.

The protocol does recognize that whatever social legislation is proposed must not impose undue administrative, financial, or legal costs on small and medium-sized firms. But it is difficult to see how some of the aims of the protocol could be achieved without this happening. Indeed, during the recession most member states are cutting back on social protection costs: the Dutch plan to freeze social security benefits in 1994; France is raising employees' social security contributions; Germany has proposed cuts in welfare benefits.

When we turn to environment and consumer protection issues, we find the same conflict between those who want to press on with established programs and those who believe that the Community, because of the recession and because of the need to realize that it will soon be legislating for a Community of perhaps twenty states, has reached something of a turning point.

The original treaties setting up the European Community in the 1950s made no specific reference to the environment, but since 1972 there have been five action programs on the environment, giving rise to over two hundred pieces of legislation covering pollution of the atmosphere, water, and soil; waste management; safeguards in relation to chemicals and biotechnology; environmental impact assessment; and protection of nature.

The Maastricht Treaty on European Union takes European environment policy some steps further. It builds into the Community's tasks the promotion of "sustainable and non-inflationary growth respecting the environment" and places environmental protection on an equal footing with economic concerns as one of the Community's objectives. It also includes in the Treaty for the first time the requirement that the Community's environmental policy be based on the precautionary principle. This is in addition to the principles that "preventive action should be taken, that environmental damage should as a priority be rectified at source, and that the polluter should pay." Furthermore, the Treaty states that "environmental protection requirements must be integrated into the definition and implementation of other Community policies." Last but not least the Treaty removes the ability of individual member states to veto environmental proposals; these will now all be subject to qualified majority voting, with much more involvement by the European Parliament.

How is this likely to work out in practice? Will there be a new tide of European law on the environment? Will this be something that those who are working to make Europe deregulate and become more competitive will see as a threat? Obviously we have yet to put the Maastricht agreement into force, but there are some straws in the wind that enable us to make some predictions about the Community's attitude to the environment in the future.

First, it must be said that whatever its internal troubles with recession, the Community will want to contribute to international environmental accords. We see this most recently in the moves to ban CFCs under the Montreal agreement. There are costs attached there; this comes home to me very much as an MEP directly elected to represent a constituency of some 500,000 people. For example, action to ban CFCs means, at the local level, that dry cleaners have to buy new machines. There is no fund to help them do so; they and their customers must pay the bill for the Community's actions.

Second, there will continue to be a general acceptance that, because environmental problems transcend national boundaries, it is more effective to legislate to protective environmental measures at the Community than simply at the national or local level. It is therefore difficult to see how responsibility for environmental legislation will be "returned" to the member states, although questions have been raised about a number of measures adopted in the 1970s, notably regulating drinking water and bathing water. The drinking water directive especially is now leading to horrendous increases in compliance costs in many member states: in Britain the water authorities believe that the annual cost to domestic consumers will rise by $150 in real terms by 1999.

Third, because of the increased awareness of costs, we in Europe will certainly see much greater reluctance to give agreement to some of the more expensive environmental proposals that are currently under discussion.

Two examples of this are the proposal for a tax on carbon emissions and the draft directive on packaging. The carbon tax is an important part of the Community's action to meet its obligations under the Rio Climate Change Convention. It would amount to an initial tax of $3 a barrel on oil, increasing by $1 a year until it reaches the level of $10 a barrel in 2000. It is accompanied by two programs designed to give incentives to energy saving measures. Explicitly, the coming into force of the measure is conditional upon similar action being taken by other OECD countries.

The idea of the tax has split the Community. Some countries—notably Germany and Holland—favour it; indeed, Holland has already introduced its own small carbon tax. The United Kingdom is against it, arguing with the strong backing of business interests that the tax will burden industry with extra costs without necessarily reducing total CO_2 emissions. Politically consent to the tax is simply impossible because the UK government is in the middle of a political storm over its decision, in part a reaction to the demands of the Rio summit, to levy for the first time Value Added Tax at 17.5 percent on supplies of domestic fuel and power.

Then there is the draft directive on packaging and packaging waste. This is an example of the Community needing to act on a problem, packaging waste, when one country, Germany, had already gone ahead. The German law now requires the recycling of high percentages of packaging within short timescales. Incineration, even with energy recovery, is not a permitted option. German industry has had to introduce a system whereby a levy on packaging, paid ultimately by the consumer, is used to finance the collection and separation of packaging from households; consumers may leave surplus packaging at retail outlets; packaging producers are responsible for its collection and recycling. The problem with the German scheme has been that the market for the recovered material could not handle the amount collected. Although strongly against landfills (and pro-recycling) in their own country, the Germans have been exporting waste for landfills as far away as Indonesia: in 1992, 400,000 tons of plastic were recovered, but recycling capacity can handle only half that amount. German waste paper has been available to foreign paper makers at very low cost, making a paper recovery scheme in other EC countries—including Britain—economically unattractive.

Two governments especially, French and British, have been pressing the Commission to act—in effect to regulate this disorder. A directive has now appeared that seems to satisfy nobody in its initial form. It would commit the member states to recover 90 percent by weight of their packaging waste within ten years and to recycle 60 percent of each material collected. If implemented in this form, the cost impact on industry would have been enormous and the overall environmental gains questionable. The latest development here is that the targets are likely to be adjusted downwards, putting more effort into reducing the initial amount of packaging and ensuring that a recycling capability and a market for recycled products exists before legislation is put into effect. In a communication put out at the end of 1992, the Commission has already looked at how environmental policies impact on industrial costs. There are some pluses on the environmental side: the EC market for environmental protection equipment is worth about $50 billion, with Germany accounting for a third of this; environmentally friendly products are an expanding market; there is a growing waste recycling industry in Europe. But there is a clear cost impact, which is proportionately heavier on small business.

Let me here make a connection with the NAFTA debate. Increased environmental costs may be acceptable if their full implications are known in advance and if they impact, broadly speaking, equally on all participating countries. In the EC we have a big problem because we do not as yet have a full compliance cost assessment for all new legislation that impacts on business. Nor indeed do we have universal compliance. Here the difficulty lies with the unequal transposition of EC law into national law, with implementation of that law, and with its local enforcement.

No member state has yet notified the Commission of the action it has taken to implement all 110 directives covering environmental matters. Some have ignored successive judgments against them in the European Court of Justice for failure to incorporate the requirements of EC directives into their national law. Since the environment is a high profile public issue, the question of unequal observance of the law has tended to reinforce popular objections to the EC in those countries, like Britain, that have a relatively good record of obeying the law and suspect that others are flouting it. The EC has now turned its attention to its regulatory system and is acting to strengthen it. It is setting up an Environment Agency that will analyze data from the member states, and report regularly on the state of the European environment, and it is giving its supreme court, the European Court of Justice, the power to fine countries that ignore its judgments. These are the essential underpinnings if the EC's environmental policy is to develop successfully.

To turn now to consumer protection policy: to date the EC has mirrored the US approach in adopting programs of law that try to articulate certain consumers' rights. The Community has always had a problem because pressure for and interest in consumer protection has not been universal; it is mainly a preoccupation of the northern states. Indeed, the annual Community budget contains financial aid for the establishment of consumer groups in some southern states. The Maastricht Treaty, for the first time, has a separate section on consumer protection that states that the Community shall contribute to the attainment of a high level of consumer protection through measures adopted under the heading of the completion of the internal market, and through specific actions to support member states' policies to protect the health, safety, and economic interests of consumers and to provide them with adequate information.

It is true that the creation of a barrier-free single market has given European consumers the prospect of wider choice of goods and services, increased competition, and reduced border formalities, which should cut delays and speed up the transport of goods. Companies will have reduced production costs, since they are now able to sell the same product in all twelve countries without having to make expensive modifications to suit twelve sets of national laws standards, as before.

But the other side of the single internal market is that any product or service that can be legally sold in any one country of the twelve must in general be accepted by the other eleven, and this clearly does raise issues of both quality and safety. Questions of quality have arisen most sharply in the food sector, where national standards on the use of additives differ very greatly. Any agreed common standards therefore involve compromises: the British use more additives than anyone else, and so face the prospect of some foods disappearing from the marketplace in their wellknown form if the common list of additives is heavily reduced; the French (and others) ban additives in certain traditional foods but face the prospect of manufacturers being able to use them if the common list of European additives is altered to accommodate the British. Wide consumer choice may therefore, in some instances, be seen as a threat to quality. Consumer groups warn that as national standards disappear, the tendency may be for competition to drive down standards until all twelve EC countries reach the lowest common denominator.

On the safety front, the EC has now agreed on a directive on general product safety, but it will probably not be implemented everywhere until June 1994 at the earliest. Until then, national rules will apply in dealing with unsafe goods. One example of a safety problem is flammable furniture. The sale of new furniture containing certain types of dangerous foam filling is illegal in the UK. But similar legislation does not exist in other EC countries, so it is now possible for a Belgian manufacturer to try to export this type of furniture into the UK, where there will be no checks on the frontier. The UK rule will continue to apply but will have to be policed at hundreds of retail outlets. In this case, the need for EC-wide legislation is clear and the Community will have to produce some common standards.

This year the Commission has produced a two-year action program. It contains only one directive, dealing with claims used in the sale of food; for the rest, the aim is to consolidate what has been adopted and to see that it is put into practice. The central consumer budget, spent via the Commission, has also been cut to some $7 million for the whole Community. The consumer lobby in Europe has a much fuller agenda, involving the regulation of distance selling, the need to ensure that guarantees offered in one country are honored in another, and the need to improve access to justice and systems of redress to help resolve disputes concerning goods and services bought in another member state.

But this agenda seems unlikely to make much progress over the next few years. Europeans have some tough problems to deal with at the heart of their economic life, and they have tough political decisions to make about the future shape of their Community and about the pace at which it will change. They will be giving these priority in the immediate future, since it is only from their success in dealing with these that the Community will draw the resources and the assurance to continue to develop.

4
Business Restructuring in Response to the Single Market

◆ ◆ ◆ ◆ ◆ ◆

James T. Little

Introduction

The Ceccheni report, in projecting the consequences of the single market project, paid particular attention to the impact of the single market on economies of scale. Roughly speaking, the reasoning was as follows: in a single market unimpeded by border delays and differences in national standards, European manufacturers could produce with longer production runs in fewer plants. In services, product offerings would tend to become standardized across the Community, and the expected reduction in the number of organizations providing these services would produce administrative scale economies. These expected scale economies were the major source of the projected impact of the single market on income within the Community.[1]

Obviously, it would be premature to assess directly whether these expected scale effects have in fact been realized. Many of the single market provisions have been in place for only a short period of time and others, especially on the service side, have yet to come into effect. Moreover, over a short period of time, the

---

1. Cecchini projects gains of 2.1 percent in Community income as a consequence of the scale economies that would be realized as a result of the single market. Total gains from all sources are projected to be between 4.3 percent and 6.4 percent of Community income. See Paulo Cecchini, *The European Challenge 1992*, London, 1988.

impact on Community economic performance will be swamped
by macroeconomic effects.

However, scale effects should also be reflected in the structure
of European producers. In particular, enhanced economies of
scale should be reflected in a smaller number of producers with
larger shares of the Community market. The adjustment process
that leads to the new market structure will involve a restructuring
of firms,with some growing in size and others disappearing as
their markets are taken away by the more efficient producers.
While some of this restructuring would occur as growth of some
firms and the death of others, the more likely outcome is the
absorption of some firms by others and the restructuring of the
combined operations. Thus, one important consequence of the
scale effects of the single market should be an increase in mergers of existing firms. Indeed, the merger boom in Europe during
the second half of the 1980s was widely interpreted within the
Community as a consequence of the single market program. For
example, the *Panorama of EC Industry —1991—,* published by
the Commission, states in its discussion of merger activity that
"the EC's Internal Market program triggered a surge in takeovers
by companies in one member State of companies in another."

However, the European boom was not unique; merger activity
was high worldwide during this period. One explanation of this
high worldwide level of merger activity is globalization of economic activity. Globalization is really a single market effect but on
a larger scale. With improvements in communication and transportation, the general reduction in barriers to trade, and the free
movement of capital — so the argument runs — surviving producers must exploit scale economies and be efficient on a worldwide basis. The adjustment of firms to globalization of markets
would involve many of the same consequences as the adjustment
to the single market. Thus, the question arises as to the independent effect of the single market project: would the impact on the
size and efficiency of firms producing and/or selling in the EEC
have occurred independently of the single market project?

In this paper, I examine two forms of combinations of firms,
mergers and joint ventures, since the initiation of the single mar-

ket project. The purpose of this is twofold: first, to describe the restructuring of European businesses in recent years and, second, to attempt to sort out how much of this restructuring is a consequence of globalization as opposed to the single market project by itself. I then go on to suggest that some recent developments within the EEC, including those associated with the Social Chapter of the Maastricht Treaty, may hinder the ability of European-based producers to compete on a global basis.

Mergers

In the century that the modern industrial enterprise has been the dominant organizational form in the U.S. economy, mergers have been a significant factor in the evolution of the large, multiunit enterprises necessary to realize economies of scale and scope. In fact, it is difficult to find a large corporation in the U.S. — or Europe, for that matter — that has not been built, in part, via merger. A small number of these mergers reflected a strategy of vertical integration where the value created by the merger was realized via cost reductions and productivity increases generated by improved coordination of the production chain. However, most mergers have been horizontal combinations in which the acquiring firm increased its share of a market either by increasing its market share in a given geographic area or by expanding into new areas. Until recently, the conventional wisdom was that the economic motivation for horizontal mergers was the increased profit to be realized through gaining power over prices and quantities by reducing competition.[2] But it is now recognized that another rationale for horizontal combinations is the lower cost and higher productivity that result from the realization of economies of scale and scope.

---

2. Even Alfred Chandler, who is responsible for much of our understanding of how enterprises have evolved as owners and managers attempted to exploit economies of scale and scope, holds his view of horizontal mergers:"The second [horizontal combinations] aimed at maintaining profits by controlling the price and output of each of the operating units." Alfred D. Chandler, Jr.,*The Visible Hand: The Managerial Revolution in American Business*, Cambridge, 1977, p. 315.

Scale and scope economies are especially relevant in interpreting the cross-border combinations that have been an increasing portion of worldwide merger activity over the past fifteen years. However, it would be naive in the extreme to assert that sometime in the 1970s or early 1980s the world changed so that scale and scope economies that had not previously existed suddenly emerged. The multinational corporation, which by 1914 was already an important element of the worldwide economic structure, provides the vehicle by which enterprises can grow beyond the borders of their home markets. So the question that naturally arises is why cross-border acquisitions have become a significant component of companies' international expansion strategies.

Part of the answer to this lies in the liberalization of capital markets that occurred in the late 1970s and early 1980s. France, Japan, and the United Kingdom all largely eliminated capital controls. With these controls still in place, the high volume of cross-border acquisitions that we will see in the data would not have been possible. Many domestic capital markets were also at least partially liberalized, with larger numbers of companies being publicly traded and the ability of incumbent managements to resist takeover bids somewhat weakened. Finally the maturation of the international capital market, the development of sophisticated international financing vehicles, and the emergence of global merchant banking organizations have played an important part.

However, significant differences in the legal and regulatory structures and the "cultural" context in which national capital markets operate remain. The differences in legal rules and practice that apply to ownership structure and capital markets mean that merger activity will be an imperfect indicator of the restructuring that might result from a change in the economic environment such as the setting up of the single market. In the United Kingdom, for example, the rules governing capital markets and ownership structures are such that takeovers by a domestic or foreign buyer are more easily accomplished than in countries where public shareholders rarely represent a controlling interest (Italy, for example) or where ownership structures involving multiple shareholder classes and differentiated voting rights are allowed.[3] Such factors are especially relevant in Germany. Not only are companies in Germany less likely to be traded publicly than in anglo-Saxon countries, but companies whose equities are traded tend to have voting control in the hands of large banks.

There are also significant differences across countries in the requirements for the public reporting of acquisitions. In any case, in no country is there a reporting requirement for companies whose shares are not publicly traded. This means that measured *volumes* of merger activity, which are based—as they must be—on publicly reported transactions, are not strictly comparable across countries. Nonetheless, if the rules governing legal forms companies and reporting of acquisitions remain the same over time, the *patterns* of merger activity can provide insight into the economic and strategic factors that underlie the combinations.

The best data for volumes of merger activity for a Community member are those for the UK, where government statisticians have been tracking activity for some time. Since 1970, there have been two merger booms in the UK, the first running from 1970 through 1973, the second—which has been attributed by many analysts as a response to the single market—from 1987 through 1990. In terms of number of transactions, the merger wave of the 1970s was at least as significant as that of the late 1980s. For example, the early wave of peaked with 1212 acquisitions of UK companies in 1972, compared to a peak for the second wave of 1224 acquisitions in 1988. On the other hand, the total value of acquisitions, adjusted for price level changes, was about 50 percent higher in 1989 than in 1972. The preliminary evidence provided as to the existence of "single market" effect, therefore, is at best mixed.

---

3. Coopers and Lybrand, in a study of takeovers in the EC, found that as of 1990 only eight of over 200 listed Italian companies had issued more than 50 percent of their shares to the public. Not surprisingly, the study found only one successful contested bid for an Italian company.

Table I: **Acquisitions by UK Companies, 1986-1989**

	EC		North America		World	
	Number	Value[a]	Number	Value	Number	Value
1986	62	958	195	12,139	317	13,313
1987	124	2,292	214	13,513	431	17,112
1988	191	2,655	311	21,389	606	26,064
1989	274	4,230	295	27,426	675	33,704
TOTAL	651	10,135	1015	74,467	2029	90,193

[a] in billions of ECU

The volume of cross-border acquisitions by UK companies during the second merger wave, detailed in Table I, is much more revealing. Both the number and the total value of acquisitions by the UK of companies in the EC more than quadrupled from 1986 to 1989. But even with the increase in the number of EC acquisitions, North America continued to dominate Europe as the focus of UK companies' merger activity. Of the worldwide increase of 20 billion ECU in the value of acquisitions between 1986 and 1989, 15 billion of the increase went to North America compared with slightly more than 3 billion ECU into Europe.

Table II: **EC Cross-Border Merger Activity, 1989**

	As Target		As Acquirer		Target—Acquisitions	
	Value[a]	Number	Value	Number	Value	Number
Belgium	1,286	61	1,016	27	269	34
Denmark	544	34	393	12	151	22
France	5,366	191	9,674	167	(4,308)	24
Germany	5,710	215	6,647	128	(937)	87
Greece	263	7	17	1	246	6
Ireland	174	11	305	21	(131)	-10
Italy	4,122	104	1,681	52	2,441	52
Luxembourg	1	2	12	10	(11)	-8
Netherlands	1,883	98	619	47	1,265	51
Portugal	314	20			314	20
Spain	2,689	128	295	18	2,394	110
United Kingdom	20,832	237	5,512	281	15,320	-44
EC Consortia	762	40		4	762	36
EC TOTAL	43,947	1148	26,172	768	17,775	380
EFTA	1,770	145	3,845	265	(2,075)	-120
US			13,803	85		
Japan			1,482	54		

[a.] in millions of ECU

The hypothesis that the single market program has had but a modest impact on the pattern of merger activity is borne out by the data for the EC as a whole. Tables II and III report the patterns of activity for 1989 and for 1990 and 1991 combined.[4] The data reported in Table II include all reported *European* cross-border mergers in 1989. This implies that the numbers reported for acquisitions include acquisitions within the EC and other European countries but do not include acquisitions elsewhere in the world.

Keeping in mind the earlier caveats regarding the cross-country comparability of the data, they do confirm, as might be expected, that the newer arrivals to the Community—Greece, Spain and Portugal—are net targets of combination activity as larger enterprises based elsewhere in the Community and elsewhere in the world expand their EC operations into these countries. The differences among the big four of the Community—France, Germany, Italy, and the United Kingdom—are significant. France, on net, is a significant acquirer while Italy and the United Kingdom are net targets. The UK is particularly interesting in this regard. The UK has long been the favored entry point into Europe for American companies and, more recently, for Japanese companies. But even if all U.S. and Japanese acquisitions reported in Table II were made in the UK, 5 billion ECU of cross-border acquisitions remain. It simply must be the case that the UK was a significant target for European companies as well. Of the ten largest individual European acquisitions of 1989, seven involved UK targets. In four cases, the acquiring firm was German; the remaining three were American acquisitions. Of the thirty largest deals, sixteen involved UK targets. This pattern surely reflects the fact that the regulatory system makes takeovers easier in the UK, but it may also reflect the generally lower level of regulation of business activity found in the UK relative to other EC countries.

If there is one EC country whose acquisitions appear motivated by the single market, it is France. Nine of the thirty largest

---

4. It must be noted that because of the difficulties in measuring merger activity alluded to earlier, the data in Tables I-III are from different basic sources and therefore will not be strictly comparable.

acquisitions were by French companies, and in all cases they appear to be motivated by their desire to expand their EC presence. It would be very dangerous to generalize from these, however, as four involve a single acquiring company, the BSN food group, which has an announced strategy of acquiring strong national brands and expanding them into pan-European brands. Indeed so active was BSN—it was also the seller in one of the largest thirty transactions—that the five transactions in which BSN was involved account for almost half the total transactions in the food and food retailing segment, which was the most active single industry grouping during the year.

The acquisitions by non-EC companies are worth noting. The low level of Japanese acquisitions should not be interpreted as a lack of interest of Japanese companies in the European market but rather as reflecting the preference of Japanese firms for "greenfield" investment as opposed to acquisition of existing enterprises in their expansion into European markets. The pattern of acquisitions by the EFTA countries, with acquisitions by EFTA companies in the EC more than double the acquisitions by all countries of EFTA enterprises, does seem to reflect a response to the single market.

The United States was the largest acquirer of European companies. But the transaction detail suggests that this investment did not reflect the single market so much as it did the companies' general strategies for globalization. Eleven of the thirty largest transactions involve U.S. companies as the acquirer. Two of the acquisitions, which were typical, involved U.S. automakers, with Ford acquiring 85 percent of Jaguar and General Motors acquiring 50 percent of Saab. Both Ford and GM already were major European manufacturers, and both acquisitions were primarily motivated by a desire to fill a product niche rather than to establishing a geographic position. Of the eleven, only AT&T's acquisition of small minority interest in CIR of Italy could be viewed as a direct consequence of the single market program—in this case, telecom deregulation.

The merger activity for 1990-91 reported in Table III includes worldwide cross-border mergers. Thus, is provides a more comprehensive view of merger activity and allow us to see EC activity within a broader context than at reported in Table II for 1989. As in 1989, Greece, Portugal, and Spain were net targets of merger activity. Spain is, in value terms, the largest net target of all EC members and, as a gross target, the value of acquisitions in Spain is of roughly the same magnitude as the value of cross-border takeovers in France and Germany. However, as in the 1989 data, the UK leads the group in both number and value as a target of cross-border takeovers. But, as the analysis of 1986-89 UK merger activity suggested, UK companies are also significant acquirers, so that while the UK is still a net target in value terms, UK companies made more acquisitions abroad than non-UK companies made in the UK.

Table III **Cross-Border Merger Activity, 1990-91**

	As Target		As Acquirer		Target—Aquisitions	
	Value[a]	Number	Value	Number	Value	Number
Belgium	2,586	120	575	73	2,011	47
Denmark	850	78	1,263	73	(413)	5
France	9,806	414	41,284	565	(31,478)	-151
Germany	11,579	443	14,924	315	(3,345)	128
Greece	554	14	0	0	554	14
Ireland	919	27	1,706	69	(787)	-42
Italy	6,501	204	7,096	145	(595)	59
Luxembourg	1,668	6	718	9	950	-3
Netherlands	3,925	179	9,026	228	(5,101)	-49
Portugal	532	50	239	3	293	47
Spain	9,705	207	3,933	47	5,772	160
United Kingdom	41,565	610	37,780	847	3,785	-237
EC Consortia	1,656	15	307	20	1,349	-5
EC TOTAL	91,846	2,367	118,851	2394	(27,005)	-27
REST OF WORLD	147,282	2151	120,277	2124	27,005	27
WORLD TOTAL	239,128	4518	239,128	4518	0	0

[a.] in millions of ECU

Perhaps the most striking finding in the data is the high level of acquisition activity by French and British companies. With a value of 41 billion ECU, acquisitions by French companies represent more than one-third of acquisitions made by all EC companies during the period and almost one-fifth of worldwide acquisitions. UK companies, with total acquisitions valued at 38 billion ECU, are close behind. Data from another survey[5] suggest that cross-border acquisitions of U.S. companies were roughly 93 billion ECU over the two-year period compared and, therefore, given the size of the French and British economies compared with that of the U.S., these volumes of takeover activity are impressive. As a net acquirer, France overwhelms the remainder of the EC, which is, without France, a net target for takeover activity during these two years while the UK in spite of a high level of activity as an acquirer, is on net a target. In both cases, this is consistent with the activity in 1989.

Overall, the pattern that emerges from the data is that while merger and acquisition activity is significantly altering the structure of European enterprises, this does not appear to be specifically a European phenomenon. The bulk of the activity seems to be part of global restructuring of businesses. This does not mean that the single market project has had no effect but rather that it appears to be of secondary importance to more potent global forces. Interestingly, to the extent that there is European as opposed to global strategy underlying acquisitions, it appears that it is French companies who are in the vanguard. This perhaps reflects the very high enthusiasm among the French political and economic establishment for the Community and, given the big proportion of state ownership in France, perhaps even an informal government policy.

Joint Venture Activity

Until the 1980s, joint ventures were primarily a device for entry into countries that either prohibited private ownership or limited foreign ownership. But in the past decade, joint ventures have increasingly been used by companies as a way of organizing cooperative activities with other firms short of merging their operations. Such joint ventures vary widely in their characteristics. Some represent very substantial cooperative efforts involving production and marketing; others are limited to narrow areas of activity such as cooperation on specific R&D projects. Many

---

5. By the accounting firm of KMPG.

different reasons have been given for the emergence of the joint venture as an organizational form. The most compelling have to do with rapid technological change and the potential benefits of the joint venture in promoting technology transfer and allowing mature organizations to adapt change. Globalization is another important factor for a disproportionate number of joint ventures involving cross-border alliances.

Table IV: **Cross-Border Joint Ventures, 1986–87**

	All Cross-Border		EC Cross-Border	
	Number	Percent	Number	Percent
With EC Partner	90	41.3%	10	11.1%
With US Partner	168	77.1%	62	68.9%
With Japanese Partner	83	38.1%	11	12.2%
US/Japan	60	27.5%	1	1.1%
US/EC	62	28.4%	62	68.9%
EC/Japan	11	5.0%	11	12.2%
High Tech	97	44.5%	53	58.9%
Telecom	15	6.9%	12	13.3%
R&D	24	11.0%	13	14.4%
Total Joint Ventures	218	100.0%	90	100.0%

For our purpose of assessing how the structure of EC companies is changing, an important characteristic of the joint venture is that all partners enter into the agreement voluntarily so that the biases in cross-country comparisons of merger and acquisition activity created by differences in the ability of incumbent managements to resist takeover attempts will not be present for joint ventures. Moreover, since announcements of joint venture agreements frequently include discussion of the rationale for the venture, there is often more information as to the strategic objectives of the companies involved in case of mergers and acquisitions.

Here we focus the two-year period 1986-87. The data are incomplete, as they are based on press announcements, so that, as with the merger and acquisition data, it is the pattern as opposed to absolute levels of activity that are revealed by the data. During the two-year period, 218 cross-border joint ventures were announced. Cross-border joint ventures were a high proportion of the total of 354 joint ventures reported. Two of every five joint ventures announced during the period involved at least one partner from an EC country, a slightly higher participation rate than for Japan but well below that for the U.S.[6] As expected, a high proportion of the joint ventures involve high tech activities.

Table V: **Participation in EC Cross-Border Activity**

| | | EC Cross-Border | | |
	Total	No EC Partner	With European Operations	Telecoms
France	12	10	6	3
Germany	22	20	6	3
Italy	17	12	15	1
Spain	7	2	7	4
United Kingdom	28	22	2	4

As is expected given the high proportion of all cross-border joint ventures involving a U.S. partner, more than two of three alliances with EC participation also involved an American company. Alliances between EC and Japanese partners are much less frequent than Japanese participation rates in all cross-border alliances. Joint ventures involving only EC companies are infrequent, occurring at about the same rate as alliances between EC and Japanese partners. A higher proportion of EC alliances than of all cross-border alliances involve high tech activities. Of the fifteen cross-border joint ventures involving telecom equipment or systems, twelve involve EC partners.

The country-by-country rate of EC participation in the reported joint ventures shows a somehow different pattern of activity than that of mergers. Although UK companies are the most active, the activity of French companies is much less prominent than in merger activity and German companies are more active. Spain is the only other country that participated in more than two joint

---

6. Joint ventures were classified as cross-border based on the home country of participating companies. In a very few cases, joint ventures that were classified as domestic (all partners from the same country) anticipated activity outside the home country. In cases in which one of the partners was a subsidiary of another company, the home company of the parent was used to classify.

ventures. By far the largest proportion of the alliances entered into by French, German, and British companies had no other EC partner. Moreover, for this group of three countries, a minority of the joint ventures anticipated operating primarily within Europe. This is very different from the alliances involving Spanish partners, for which all anticipated European operations and all but two had other EC partners. It is striking that four of the seven alliances with spanish partners involved telecoms.

Overall, the joint venture activity seems to point in the same direction as the merger activity. To the extent that there is an EC focus to the activity, it is on the newer, less developed countries such as Spain. The fact that four of the Spanish alliances involve telecoms and telecom deregulation is one of the major initiatives of the single market program that ties these alliances directly to the single market. On the other hand, the activity of companies from the big four countries appears to be very much externally focused and part of the larger move toward globalization.

Conclusions

In retrospect, the conclusion that much of the restructuring of Community enterprises appears to be motivated by a globalization as opposed to a Europeanization strategy should really be no surprise. Much of the impetus for the single market program came from the belief that Europe was lagging behind other parts of the world in international competitiveness. The single market, among other things, was to provide a large home market as a base from which European companies could build. However, global markets provide an even larger base for the realization of economies of scale and scope, so that it should come as no surprise that ambitious companies chose to compete in the larger market rather than focusing on Europe.

Nor does this imply that somehow the single market program has not succeeded in achieving its goals. Without question, there will be gains from the simplification of the transport of goods, from common product standards, and from the elimination of restrictive practices. Moreover, if competition within the Community does intensify, as the Cecchini Report anticipated, European companies will unquestionably be stronger global competitors. Furthermore, globalization and the competition that comes with it should bring European consumers even larger gains than the single program by itself.

But there is a danger here as well. Just as the fear of globalization among some in the United States leads them to propose reversing the trend toward open and free movement of capital and enterprises, there will be elements within the Community that will propose the rising of barriers. Some product standards that have been proposed by Brussels look suspiciously like trade restricting devices.

Even more disquieting, however, is the tendency among some of the Community's leaders to be Eurocentric in their thinking and fail to see the Community in the context of a global economy. Some Community policies appear to be based on the notion that so long as all firms within the Community face the same regulations and tax provisions, then competition will be "fair." With such a perspective, the Social Chapter of Maastricht would be viewed as largely neutral in its impact as it applies to all enterprises other than those in the UK. But this ignores the fact that for many of the largest European firms, the competitive arena is not the Community but the world. It is well to argue that higher productivity can overcome labor cost disadvantages , but international productivity and its margin relative to other Asian economies is shrinking. Thus recent decisions of Daimler-Benz and BMW to begin producing in the U.S. or of Hoover and Black and Decker to concentrate all European production in the UK may be harbingers of things to come.

Note on Data Resources

Information on mergers and joint ventures is gathered primarily from reports appearing in the press. There are studies that have gathered data from private sources, but these studies do not contain anything approaching time series data.

The merger data reported here were taken from several sources the sources for the data in the tables were various editions of *Panorama of EC Industry,* published by the Commission of the European Communities. These are secondary data, with the primary sources being *M&A Europe, Acquisitions Monthly,* IDD Information Services, and the Central Statistical Office of the United Kingdom. Supporting data were taken from various unpublished reports of international accounting firms and *The Merger Yearbook,* various editions, published by Securities Data Co.

The joint venture data were compiled by the author, with individual transactions reported in *The Merger Yearbook* providing the basic source. Reported transactions that showed the termination of a joint venture were not included, and the data were "cleaned" via the elimination of multiple transactions involving the same joint venture, as would occur when both the signing of the letter of intent and the later signing of the formal agreement were reported in listing of transactions.

5
From "Nation-State" to "Member State":
The Evolution of the European Community

♦ ♦ ♦ ♦ ♦ ♦ ♦

Alberta Sbragia

The European Community has many faces. Analysts from the various member states often differ in the faces they see. Some see the pervasive influence of the French administrative culture, whereas the French themselves find the Community's culture non-French.[1] Some see a Community commanded by Germany. Knowledgeable Germans, by contrast, fear that power is now so dispersed within the German political system that, the monetary sector excluded, the German role in the Community resembles that of a confederation.[2] The British see a Community massively influenced by "continental" traditions and systems of governance. Many continentals find British influence excessive and point to the deregulatory thrust of the single market, the increased concern with administrative efficiency and probity, and the crystallization of British notions of policy implementation. The Italians find the Community "northern" and dominated by the other three big powers, and yet the representatives of those three powers will point to the powerful influence of the "Italian network"

---

1. Vivien A. Schmidt, "Upscaling Business and Downsizing Government: France in the New European Community," paper delivered at the 1993 Annual Meeting of the American Political Science Association.

2. Alberta M. Sbragia, "Maastricht, Enlargement, and the Future of Institutional Change," *Ridgway Viewpoints*, Matthew B. Ridgway Center for International Security Studies, University of Pittsburgh, No. 93-3.

which cuts across policy sectors and mobilizes to protect national interest. And so on.

As an American, I probably see a different face from the one noticed by my Spanish, Italian, German, British, Belgian, or French colleagues. I necessarily view the Community from a different perspective, from that of an outsider rather than an insider. And from that vantage point what strikes me is the gradual blurring of the distinction made between the "Community" and the "nation-states" that agreed to form that Community in the first place. That distinction was pervasive in the early literature on the Community as well as in the spoken discourse: the Community was one thing and somehow the national governments were another. The relationship between the two, whether it was adversarial or cooperative, was nonetheless distant. The tone was one of non-engagement. The nation-state and the Community were waltzing together perhaps but in a very correct and formal manner.

The gradual embrace of the two has happened slowly and incrementally. I would emphasize three dimensions — elites, policy, and politics — in the gradual knitting together of the Community and the states that compose it. Although the two are by no means linked as tightly as are subnational units to the center in the traditional state, the Community-state entanglement is such that the Community is very far from being a traditional regional organization.[3] In the area of domestic policy, entanglement rather than distance is the operative code.

The gradual integration of nationally based elites — governmental, business, and judicial — into the Community has laid the foundation for such entanglement. Many of those who make domestic policy within the nation-state, whether in the public or private sector, now deal with policymakers in Brussels in a fairly routine fashion.

The second dimension has to do with the introduction of a redistributive and social regulatory element to a Community that

---

3. Alberta Sbragia, "The European Community: A Balancing Act," *Publius: The Journal of Federalism*, Summer 1993, Vol. 23, no. 3, pp. 23-38.

otherwise focused on agricultural price supports, tariffs, VAT, economic regulation, and exchange rates. As the Community expanded its policy scope, decisions taken at the European level began to affect the economic health of poor member states as well as issues such as environmental protection, occupational health and safety, and gender discrimination in all member states. The Community had originally been conceived as an *economic* community, but it gradually moved into areas that made it a presence in many non-economic areas of life.

The politicization of the Community — brought about by the public debate over the Maastricht Treaty — is the most recent development in the evolution of the Community-state relationship. Whether the citizens of the states that joined the Community like or dislike Brussels, they are now aware of it. The proper relationship between the Community and the state is now at least debated in the electoral arena (although far more so when referenda rather than political parties are involved). The relationship will never be the same as it was when elites and policies represented the main mechanisms through which the Community and states interacted with one another. Both Community and national actors in the future will need to calibrate their decisions so as to be more in tune with mass electorates.

It is noteworthy that while I have mentioned a variety of actors, I have not mentioned labor. Although labor is very important in many member states, it is not an important actor in the relationship of concern here. Whether labor will eventually find its niche in the same way as other groups have is still an open question, but the tenuousness of its engagement has not prevented the embrace of the Community and the member states from occurring.[4]

---

4. For an interesting discussion of why labor has had so much difficulty in establishing an important presence in the Community's policymaking system, see Gary Marks and Doug McAdam, "Social Movements and the Changing Structure of Political Opportunity in the European Community," paper presented at the 1993 Annual Meeting of the American Political Science Association.

Elites

The Community has often been described as formed and driven by elites, as an organization insulated from the influence of mass electorates. Elites — whether nationally or Community-based — have indeed played the central role in the Community's history. Yet the integration of national elites into the Community's policymaking system has been a fairly long and complex affair. The engagement of national political and administrative officials, of businessmen, and of nationally based judges has been an erratic process in which a great deal of learning and adaptation has had to occur.

Nationally based governmental elites have had to be socialized into the Community.[5] Such socialization takes place in a variety of institutional forums, including COREPER and the numerous Commission and Council advisory committees and working parties on which national representatives sit.[6] For their part, business elites (especially from multinational business) have become drawn into the Community's practices at the Community's invitation. Finally, nationally based judges have become linked to the Community's work through their involvement with the work of the European Court of Justice.

---

5. As national officials have become used to participating in Community business, Commission officials have been forced to accept that national officials have an important and legitimate role to play in the formulation of Community policy. That recognition is now firmly institutionalized. As Peter Ludlow points out, the Council of Ministers works closely with the Commission:

A conflictual model of Commission-Council relations is therefore totally misleading. Of course there are conflicts; that is only to be expected. For a great deal of the time, however, member state officials work loyally beside Commission officials . . . in Commission committees, while Commission officials act as thirteenth members of the Council machinery.

Peter Ludlow, "The European Commission," *The New European Community: Decisionmaking and Institutional Change*, Robert O. Keohane and Stanley Hoffmann (eds.), Boulder, CO, 1991, p. 103.

6. Ludlow, "The European Commission," pp. 102- 103.; Neill Nugent, *The Government and Politics of the European Community*, second edition, Durham, N.C., 1991, pp. 106-110; 82-87; 74-77.

Political and Administrative Elites

The socialization of governmental elites has been, and is, central to the construction and maintenance of the complex relationships that exist between the Community's institutions and the nation-states that belong to it. It takes a great deal of time for the political and administrative elites of a newly admitted nation-state to adjust themselves to the complex routines, procedures, and institutional dynamics of the European Community. The Community's policymaking system operates differently from that of any of its member states, and therefore national officials must become used to decision making procedures quite alien to their previous experience.[7]

Often national representatives have not had much experience in negotiating with individuals from different linguistic, cultural, and political traditions. Knowledge of other member states' political institutions and procedures is rather slight for the vast bulk of national elites.[8] For those actors who come into contact with Community institutions, learning enough about other countries to begin to make sense of both their styles of negotiating and the reason why they take the negotiating positions they do is a time-consuming process.

---

7. In 1971, Emile Noel described the Community as follows:

   Being based on dialogue, the Community system bears little resemblance to the concept of government in the traditional sense of the word. The Community does not have a single head or a single leader. Decisions are collective and taken only after much confrontation of view points. The Communities have in fact been transformed into a vast convention. They are a meeting place for experts, ambassadors and ministers at hundreds and even thousands of meetings." E. Noel, "The Permanent Representatives Committee and the Deepening of the Communities," *Government and Opposition*, 1971, p. 424; cited in Ludlow, "The European Commission," p. 102.

8. It *is* true that the Community's member states have much more in common than do the members of international organizations such as the United Nations. As Helen Wallace has pointed out: Compared with the membership of most other international organisations or alliances their [the EC member states'] economies and political systems are both broadly similar and highly interdependent. Consequently, it has been possible to work from some common values and towards some common objectives

Currently the Spanish government is very aware of the need to expose its own civil servants as rapidly as possible to the Community's ways (Spain is a relatively new member, having joined only in 1986). The government is using its COREPER delegation as a mechanism of socialization, and therefore Spain has the largest COREPER delegation in the Community.

The process of socialization takes place in other political systems, the American especially. When a new President is elected, the shock of Washington experienced by the people who accompany him from his state always provides much grist for the columns of Washington-based columnists and pundits. Yet Washington has a permanent core of policymakers in the bureaucracy, especially on Capitol Hill. Given the longevity of American Congress members and Senators and the semi-permanence of Congressional staffs, the impression of turbulence and turnover presented by the arrival of a new administration in town is always an exaggerated one.

The Community's institutions have a different cast to them. Turnover in the European Parliament is exceedingly high, and Commissioners either serve only one term or switch portfolios if they do stay on in Brussels for a second term. The standard joke about Commissioners — "the first year they have to learn what their job is and the fourth year is spent looking for their next job" — has a great deal of truth to it. Even when Commissioners do receive another term, their portfolio is typically shuffled so that they are responsible for different functions and for different DGs.

For their part, the Community's civil servants do give the Community stability, but their numbers are relatively small. Given the importance of "national experts" who work for the Commission for a maximum of three years and the "undocumented workers" — those free-lancers who work for the various

---

against a background of relative mutual familiarity, shared knowledge and similar administrative and legal practice. Helen Wallace, "Implementation Across National Boundaries," *Policies into Practice: National and International Case Studies in Implementation,* David Lewis and Helen Wallace (eds.), London, 1984, p. 136.

DGs but are not allowed to have either a business card or a tele-phone, as well as those who are allowed those perks but are not officially on the Commission payroll as civil servants — the bureaucratic spine of the Community is far less stable than many would guess.

The institutional anchors of the Community are much more fluid than are those of the American system — which are in turn more fluid than those of most European national policymaking systems. Socializing new actors is therefore a central component of the Community-member state relationship.

The process of socialization is not limited to the period subse-quent to a state's admission to the Community. Each time the Community is given new competences either by treaty arrange-ments or by agreement, the states that are already members need to extend the reach of the socialization process. All of the national ministries involved in the newly added policy areas must gradually become used to working with Community institutions and accept the notion that they will now be responding to direc-tives and regulations from Brussels as well as their own national capitals. Given the firmly established national traditions of law-making, such an adjustment can often be painful. Simply trans-posing one directive from Brussels may require the passage of numerous laws within any single national legal framework. From the point of view of national officials, involvement with the Com-munity leads to greater workloads and much more cumbersome procedures within the national policymaking system.

It is not surprising that the process of becoming comfortable with the Community represents a long, slow process for national political and administrative elites. It may be surprising that they ever feel comfortable at all. Yet the socialization process has been successful enough that most national political and administrative elites do now operate with a fair amount of ease in Brussels. It may well be that they feel far more at home in Brussels than do their national constituencies, a point to which we shall return.

Business Elites

But it is not only political and administrative elites who have come to terms with the Community. Other types of elites have engaged with the Community at different speeds. Business elites tended to deal with the Community through their national governments until the 1980s; political and administrative elites acted as the filters for the business-Community relationship.[9] During the 1980s, however, the business community began to develop direct contacts with Commission officials.

Such contacts developed from Commissioner Davignon's direct consultations with key industrialists in the telecommunications and electronics sectors in the early 1980s. In 1984 the European Strategic Program for Information Technology (ESPRIT) was created, a program developed in collaboration with the twelve largest information technology companies.[10]

Furthermore, European multinationals began to mobilize in support of the single market program and subsequently organized themselves so as to participate in Community policymaking.[11] As Maria Green Cowles has recently argued:

> The political mobilization of European multinationals in the 1980s is unprecedented in the history of the EC.... While European multina-

9. See Emil Kirchner and Konrad Schwaiger, *The Role of Interest Groups in the European Community*, Aldershot: Gower, 1981; W. Feld, "National Economic Interest Groups and Policy Formation in the EEC," *Political Science Quarterly*, 81, 1966, pp. 392-411.

10. David R. Cameron, "The 1992 Initiative: Causes and Consequences," *Euro-Politics: Institutions and Policymaking in the "New" European Community*, Alberta M. Sbragia (ed.), Washington D.C.: Brookings, 1992, pp. 49-50. See also Maria Green Cowles, "The Rise of the European Multinational," *International Economic Insights*, Volume IV, Number 4, July/August 1993, p. 16; Wayne Sandholtz, "ESPRIT and the Politics of International Collective Action," *Journal of Common Market Studies*, Volume 30, March 1992, pp. 1-22; J.Peterson, "Technology Policy in Europe," *Journal of Common Market Studies*, 1991, pp. 269-90.

11. Maria L. Green, "The Politics of Big Business in the Single Market Program," paper presented at the 1993 Biennial International Conference of the European Community Studies Association; Maria Green Cowles, *The Politics of Big Business in the European Community: Setting the Agenda for a New Europe?* Ph.D. Dissertation, The American University, 1994.

tionals were a key force behind the Single Market project, the 1992 program itself engendered a new wave of mobilization. In 1988-89, dozens of multinationals set up government affairs offices in Brussels in order to provide greater input in the EC policymaking process.[12]

Firms such as Daimler-Benz (the largest private employer in Europe) began to lobby the Commission directly rather than rely on their governments or their sector associations.[13] French business, traditionally tied to the French state, became more independent and developed a "closer relationship with the EC bureaucracy and its European business counterparts than with the French government."[14] As McLaughlin, Jordan, and Maloney have argued, "The Brussels office appears to play a crucial role in the representation strategy of the large company."[15]

Judicial Elites

It is now widely accepted that the European Court of Justice has played a central role in the construction of the European Community. Martin Shapiro argues that

> The European Court of Justice has played a crucial role in shaping the European Community. . . . In a sense, the Court created the present-day Community; it declared the Treaty of Rome to be not just a treaty, but a constitutional instrument that obliged individual citizens and national government officials to abide by those provi-

---

12. Maria Green Cowles, "The Rise of the European Multinational," *International Economic Insights*, Volume IV, Number 4, July/August 1993, pp. 15 and 17. See also Svein Andersen and Kjell Eliassen, "European Community Lobbying," *European Journal of Political Research*, 20, 1991, pp. 173-87.

13. Pamela Camerra-Rowe, "The Political Responses of Firms to the 1992 Single Market Program: The Case of the German and British Automobile Industries," paper delivered at the 1993 Annual Meeting of the American Political Science Association; Andrew McLaughlin, Grant Jordan, and William A. Maloney, "Corporate Lobbying in the European Community," *Journal of Common Market Studies*, June 1993, pp. 191-212. See also Jeffrey Anderson,"German Industry and the European Community in the 1990s," in Volker Berghahn (ed.) *German Big Business*, (Oxford/Providence, forthcoming), cited in Camerra-Rowe, footnote 47.

14. Schmidt, "Upscaling Business and Downsizing Government," p. 19.

15. McLaughlin, Jordan, and Maloney, "Corporate Lobbying," p. 198.

sions that were enforceable through their normal judicial processes. A treaty among individual sovereign states was transformed through international law into constitutional and legal obligations directly binding on citizens. ... Thus, not simply in the fancy language of modern political theory, but in a very real and concrete sense, the Court of Justice constituted the European Community.[16]

Judges within the member states, for their part, have played a critical role in permitting the ECJ gradually to become the authoritative judicial body on EC-related legal issues. They have increasingly become linked to the workings of the European Court through the use of the so-called "177 preliminary ruling." In so doing, they have played a key role in the transformation of nation-states into member states.

The "177 preliminary ruling" procedure is one in which a judge in a court within a member state refers a case to Luxembourg because it involves some aspect of Community law. The national judge asks the European Court of Justice to provide guidance as to how he should rule. The use of the 177 procedure can be seen as a rough index of how integrated national judges are into the Community's legal framework. In that context, national judges have over time become far more willing to refer to Luxembourg:

> From a maximum of seven cases per year 1952 to 1966 inclusive, the number of references for a preliminary ruling under Article 177 rose steadily over subsequent years with 23 cases being lodged in 1967 ... 40 in 1972, 61 in 1973, ... 119 in 1978, and 99 in 1979.[17]

In the 1960s and 1970s, such requests came primarily from judges sitting on member states' higher courts. In the 1980s, lower-court judges became much more active. The number of 177 cases coming from lower-court judges increased significantly.

---

16. Martin Shapiro, "The European Court of Justice," *Euro-Politics: Institutions and Policymaking in the "New"European Community*, Alberta M. Sbragia (ed.) Washington D.C., 1992, p. 123.

17. Hjalte Rasmussen, "Chapter VII: The Court of Justice," in *Thirty Years of Community Law*, editorial committee chaired by Giancarlo Olmi (Luxembourg: Office for Official Publications of the European communities, 1983), p. 172.

Burley and Mattli in fact argue that "the Article 177 procedure has provided a framework for links between the Court and sub-national actors — private litigants, their lawyers, and lower national courts."[18] They go on to state that "much of the Court's success in creating a unified and enforceable Community legal system has rested on convincing lower national courts to leapfrog the national judicial hierarchy and work directly with the ECJ."[19]

The cases referred to the ECJ by lower-court judges have often challenged important policy positions defended by the national government. In fact, the challenge to national policy is sometimes extremely significant — so much so that there have been instances in which national public authorities have managed to have cases withdrawn when very sensitive national issues were involved. A recent example involved the withdrawal from the ECJ's docket of a case (brought under Article 86) that would have challenged the current structure of the French electricity market. It is widely believed that French public authorities went to great lengths to ensure that the case was withdrawn. (Some governments, such as the Italian and German, would find it far more difficult, whether for political or legal reasons, to wield the kind of pressure that the French government is reputed to have used.) When a clerk of the ECJ was asked why lower-court judges would act in contravention of the "national interest" his reply was succinct: "Judges are different."

Whatever the policy impact of such activism on the part of lower-court judges, the result has clearly been the creation of significant relationships between the Court and judiciaries within member states. The creation of EC law has been spurred by both national and lower-court judges in such a way that disentangling the Community from the national role in its creation is nearly impossible.

The existence of a common legal framework has also provided an alternative avenue for the highlighting of issues that do not fit

---

18. Anne-Marie Burley and Walter Mattli, "Europe Before the Court: A Political Theory of Legal Integration," *International Organization*, 1993, p. 23.

19. Ibid., footnote 79.

the traditional political agendas of the states themselves. The Court, for example, has been important in the area of sex discrimination, with special emphasis on the issue of equal pay for equal work, including equal pensions (the only section of the Treaty of Rome creating rights between individuals that the Court has ruled to be self-enforcing is that dealing with equal pay for equal work). In that sense, the nation-states have found themselves grappling with issues (such as gender relations) that have not come from either their own agenda setting and policy formulation process or from the Commission-Council legislative procedure.[20]

While a state's lower national courts can cause problems for national policy, the ECJ can also force issues onto a state's policy agenda. The entanglement of the Community and national judicial systems have clearly made life far more difficult for national political leaders than it would have been if the Community's decisionmaking process were monopolized by the Commission and the Council of Ministers.

Policy

Public policies also helped transform the relationship between the Community and its members. The Community was named the "economic community" or, more colloquially, the "common market." Its focus on economic matters was therefore to be expected. In that light, the Community was primarily of interest "to the lawyer, trader, consumer, or farmer."[21] The Community is no longer confined to that policy space, and the expansion of the Community's policy scope helped force the Community's institutions and those of the member states into closer engagement.

The story is too complex to be told in full here, but a sketch will suffice to make the point. "Social policy has been called a

---

20. *Thirty Years of Community Law*, Luxembourg: Office for Official Publications of the European Communities, 1987.

21. Carole Webb, "Theoretical Perspectives and Problems," in *Policy-Making in the European Community*, Helen Wallace, William Wallace and Carole Webb (eds.), second edition, Chichester, 1983, p.1.

'stepchild' of European integration,"[22] and the fact that the welfare state does not exist at the EC level can lead observers to assume that the Community still focuses exclusively on economic matters. Yet the interventionism of the Community in the areas of regional development policy (structural policy in Eurospeak) and social regulation give the Community important policy dimensions that have substantially increased both its visibility with the mass public and its entanglement with national and subnational officials. The use of qualified majority voting in selected areas outside the strictly economic was an important indication of how far the Community-member state relationship had come.

Structural Policy

Structural policy in the Community is concerned with reducing the regional disparities within the Community. It represents a redistributive element within the Community; rather than redistributing wealth among social classes it focuses on territorial units — poor regions within member states. Those units that have benefited from such redistribution include the Italian Mezzogiorno, the former GDR, Spain, Ireland, Portugal, Greece, and declining industrial regions.

Disparities within the Community are significant, far more so than in the United States, and concentrated in a few countries. As Gary Marks points out,

> Of the thirty-two regions with the greatest economic problems . . . all but eight are found in Portugal (counted as one region), Spain, or Greece. . . . At the extremes, the per capita gross domestic product of the poorest regions, including Thrakis in Greece, and southern Portugal, is just one-sixth that of Groningen or Hamburg.[23]

---

22. Stephan Leibfried and Paul Pierson, "Prospects for Social Europe," *Politics and Society*, Vol. 20, No.3, September 1992, p. 335. See also Stephan Leibfried, "Towards a European Welfare State? On Integrating Poverty Regimes into the European Community," *Social Policy in a Changing Europe*, Zsuzsa Ferge and Jon Eivind Kolberg (eds.), Boulder, CO, 1992, pp. 246-278.

23. Gary Marks, "Structural Policy in the European Community," *Euro-Politics: Institutions and Policymaking in the "New" European Community*, Alberta M. Sbragia (ed). Washington,D.C., 1992, p. 205.

Structural policy as such was born with the enlargement of 1973, during which the United Kingdom, Ireland, and Denmark joined the Community. The Italian Mezzogiorno was no longer the only poverty-stricken part of the Community. The accession of Greece, Portugal, and Spain accentuated intra-EC economic disparities. Whereas the creation of the European Investment Bank under the Treaty of Rome had introduced a redistributive element to the Community (which had primarily benefited Italy),[24] the creation of the European Regional Development Fund (ERDF) in the mid-1970s visibly committed the Community to reducing regional disparities. Grants rather than loans were to be used.

As disparities became wider and more widespread, structural policy became increasingly important. While in 1975 the ERDF's budget represented less than five percent of the EC's budget, that figure had climbed to *nine percent* by 1987.[25] Funds were doubled in 1988, and the post-Maastricht era will again see large increases. The Maastricht Treaty reinforces the position of structural policy by establishing a "cohesion fund" that will finance transportation and environmental projects in Ireland, Greece, Spain and Portugal.

Gary Marks argues that the increases in structural funding have in fact been dramatic:

> At the Edinburgh Summit of December 1992 . . . the member states agreed to increase structural spending from its present Ecu 18.6 billion to Ecu 30 billion (in 1992 Ecu) in 1999, of which Ecu 2.6 billion will be devoted to the cohesion fund. That amounts to an increase of 61.3 percent in structural funding, which in absolute terms is even larger than the previous doubling between 1987 and 1993. The share of structural operations

24. The European Investment Bank (a rough equivalent of the World Bank), established at Italy's insistence, was designated as an institution whose primary mission was to assist poor areas within the Community. The Italian Mezzogiorno was, until recently, the major beneficiary of the Bank's loans. See Alberta Sbragia "Italy/EEC: An Undervalued Partnership," *Relazioni Internazionali*, June 1992, pp. 78-88.

25. Marks, "Structural Policy in the European Community," p. 194.

in the total EC budget will rise from 28 percent in 1992 to more than one third in 1999.[26]

Significantly, the formulation and implementation of structural policy has come to involve subnational representatives. They have a seat at the table, thereby ending the previous monopoly held by national officials in the political dynamics of the Community. Marks argues that "whereas the Commission used to deal exclusively with national governments which articulated their own regional plans, since 1988 the Commission has opened up the process to regional and local tiers of government."[27]

The Community is now a presence in councils and areas distant from national capitals. Its commitment to redistribution within the Community perhaps best symbolizes the fact that the Community is indeed far from being simply a common market.

Social Regulation

Although structural policy involved the actual expenditure of funds, the EC as a whole is far from exercising the kind of macroeconomic weight associated with the nation-state. Its budget as a percentage of gross national product is just barely over one percent.[28] The Community's principal impact comes from the laws it passes (in the form of directives and regulations) rather than the money it spends. In that context, the Community has become particularly active in the area of *social* regulation (while maintaining its traditional role in the arena of economic regulation).

---

26. Marks points out that the cohesion fund targets member states with a per capita GNP of less than 90 percent of the Community average rather than poor regions *within* member states,.the latter being the usual recipients of structural funds. Thus, Spain benefits enormously because the Mezzogiorno and Eastern Germany will not receive cohesion fund monies since they are units within wealthy member states. Gary Marks, "Structural Policy and Multilevel Governance in the European Community," *The State of the European Community*, Alan W. Cafruny and Glenda G. Rosenthal (eds.), forthcoming.

27. Ibid.

28. Giandomenico Majone, "The European Community Between Social Policy and Social Regulation," *Journal of Common Market Studies*, Volume 31, No. 2, June 1993, p. 160.

Although social regulation historically belongs to the social policy arena, several scholars have argued that the former is both analytically distinct from the latter and of more significance within the Community.[29] According to Majone, the rationale for social regulation is quite different from the rationale underlying the social service provision traditionally associated with social policy understood in the context of the national welfare state.

Social regulation in the Community has focused on policies in the areas of occupational health and safety, environmental protection, and consumer protection while the welfare state focuses on health, housing, welfare, and social insurance.[30] To use the language of economics, social regulation is justified by types of market failure having to do with negative externalities and imperfect information. By contrast, the types of services provided by the European welfare state are justified not on the basis of market failure but rather on the desirability of redistribution and the provision of merit goods (such as public housing).[31]

Majone argues that

> . . . each successive revision of the Treaty of Rome has expanded and strengthened the competences of the Community in social regulation. The SEA provided an explicitly legal basis for environmental protection. . . . It also introduced the principle of qualified majority voting for occupational health and safety, and the notion of "working environment" which opens up the possibility of regulatory intervention in areas such as human-factor engineering (ergonomics), traditionally outside health and safety regulation. Finally, Art. 100A(3) of the SEA urges the Commission to take a high level of protection as the basis for its proposals relating to health, safety, environmental protection and consumer protection.

---

29. Ibid., p. 158; see also Renaud Dehousse, "Integration v. Regulation? On the Dynamics of Regulation in the European Community," *Journal of Common Market Studies,* Volume 30, No. 4, December 1992, pp. 383-402.

30. Leibfried and Pierson categorize the policies grouped under the rubric of social regulation as "at the margin of traditional social policy domains." Stephan Leibfried and Paul Pierson, "Prospects for Social Europe," p. 335.

31. Majone, "The European Community Between Social Policy and Social Regulation," p. 157-158.

The Treaty of Maastricht, if ratified, will continue this development by establishing consumer protection as a Community policy,
defining a role for the Community in public health, especially in
research and prevention (Title XV) and introducing qualified
majority voting for most environmental legislation.[32]

It is important to note that the Community's activism has come
in areas where many of the member states have been inactive or
have been less progressive than the Community. Although the
conventional wisdom holds that the Community takes a "lowest-
common denominator" approach to regulation (resulting in social
or ecological dumping), empirical research now suggests that the
Community is at times more stringent and innovative than any of
its member states.[33]

Particularly important from a political standpoint was the
Community's active role in the formulation of environmental policy, for environmental issues became "high profile" in many
member states during the 1980s.[34] The Single European Act
strengthened the legal basis for Community environmental protection policy, and the Community gained the reputation of
proposing environmental directives more progressive than
national laws in most of the member states.

As the Community moved into areas other than those associated with economic regulation, its relationship with its members
changed. The Community now became an actor that national

---

32. Ibid., pp. 163-4; for a more cautionary analysis, see Dehousse, "Integration v.
    Regulation?"

33. See, for example, Volker Eichener, "Social Dumping or Innovative Regulation?
    Processes and Outcomes of European Decision-Making in the Sector of
    Health and Safety at Work Harmonization," *EUI Working Papers in Political
    and Social Sciences*, Paper SPS No. 92/28, European University Institute, Flo-
    rence, January 1993.

34. See David Vogel, "Environmental Protection and the Creation of a Single Euro-
    pean Market," *Business & The Contemporary World*, Volume 5, Number 1, Win-
    ter 1993, pp. 48-66; Alberta Sbragia, "EC Environmental Policy: Atypical
    Ambition and Typical Problems? *The State of the European Community: The
    Maastricht Debates and Beyond*, Alan W. Cafruny and Glenda G. Rosenthal
    (eds.), 1993.

bureaucracies in a whole host of complex policy areas had to address. It was no longer compartmentalized in the box marked "economic issues."

Mass Electorates

Although the Community's role in social regulation may have linked certain groups (such as environmental groups) to the Community, it did not propel the Community onto the political stage. The Community was not on the political agenda of the mass electorate even in those countries — such as Britain, Denmark, and Ireland — where referenda had been held on issues related to the Community. Elections to the European Parliament had not engaged the European electorate in ways comparable to national parliamentary elections.

The Treaty of Maastricht changed the political status of the Community in at least some of the member states. The Danish referendum over Maastricht politicized the Community in countries such as France and Germany and raised awareness of the Community in other countries as well.

The Community became a part of democratic politics. In that sense, it became "normalized." Whether further integration was favored or opposed, it became a feature of political discourse and political debate. In that sense, the mass electorate "joined" the Community.

Although the voter may have joined the Community psychologically, he or she does not feel as comfortable with Brussels as do members of the elites mentioned above. Brussels seems to be a forbidding place, filled with arrogant and power-hungry bureaucrats busily intruding into the smallest details of ordinary life. Women are especially suspicious of the Community, particularly in Denmark, where a majority of men voted in favor of the first referendum and a majority of women voted against it.

Although all the major parties in all the member states favor both the Community and the Maastricht Treaty, it is clear that the politicization of the electorate wrought by the Maastricht debate has changed the contours of political debate about the Community. In the past, national leaders could comfortably use the Community as a "scapegoat" for policies that those same national leaders could not support publicly but did support in the secretive Council of Ministers. That game will now be a more dangerous one, as blaming Brussels may serve to corrode the foundations of popular support for a Community that all political elites support. The short-term gain leaders may obtain by blaming Brussels will need to be offset by calculations about possible long-term damage to the Community itself.

Conclusion

The "sovereign" nation-states that created the Community or joined it after its creation have gradually become transformed into "member states." The transformation is both slow and still ongoing, for it involves the knitting together of many elites, electorates, and administrative actors. Given that the Maastricht Treaty was finally ratified, the process of engagement briefly sketched here will continue and deepen. The Community-state relationship will become more contested and more politicized — precisely what one should expect if the engagement between the two is indeed a serious one.

6

European Integration and Social History since 1950

♦ ♦ ♦ ♦ ♦ ♦

Hartmut Kaelble

Introduction

This study of the social history of European integration will explore five main aspects of European social history: (1) the social peculiarities of Europe in comparison with non-European industrial societies in crucial fields such as family, work, social milieus, social conflicts, urbanization and lifestyles, and state intervention; (2) the development of the social differences and cleavages among European countries which, on the one hand, have always been highly valued by Europeans and, on the other hand, have been a major cause of discouragement in the politics of European integration; (3) the development of social exchanges and connections among European countries, i.e., professional migration, student exchanges, business travel and tourism, international marriages, the exchange of consumer goods and lifestyles; (4) the evolution of geographic horizons of Europeans from an almost exclusively regional or national horizon to a more European one based on direct personal experience of other European countries; and finally, (5) the history of the long-standing debate on the social peculiarities of Europe, stressing the many important changes in what was seen as peculiarly European, how European social peculiarities were evaluated, and how certain European peculiarities were regarded in comparison to the nation or the region. Unlike most studies of European integration, this study does not circumscribe the social history of

European integration in time or space; it looks back to pre-1950 periods and includes — as far as possible — all Western and Central European countries. However, to some extent the Central European countries are not dealt with, partly because of the scarcity of research in this area of Europe and partly because many of the conclusions do not apply to these countries, especially during the period between the late 1940s and 1989. Moreover, space limitations do not permit treating all aspects with the same intensity.[1] It must also be noted that not all conclusions presented here are based on detailed research; some are still hypotheses and speculations.

The concept behind this article does not follow the philosophy that social structures determine institution building and that the rise of a European society — i.e, reduced inter-European differences, extensive social exchanges among countries, and clear social particularities in comparison with non-European societies — automatically led to the establishment of European institutions. Any building of European institutions is not merely influenced by a European society in this sense but is even more an act of political will. In the last analysis, however, the emergence of a European society is still an important precondition for European consciousness and long-term institution building.

----

1. For the social peculiarities of Western Europe and for the development of the social cleavages between European countries up to the 1970s, see: H. Kaelble, *A Social History of Western Europe, 1880-1980*, Dublin, 1990; for more detailed conclusions and hypotheses on the social exchanges between European countries, the changing geographical horizon of Europeans and the reduction of social differences and cleavages between Western European societies up to the 1990s see my article, "A Social History of European Integration," in A. Nicholls/C. Wurm, eds., *The History of European Integration*, forthcoming, 1994. The last remarks on the development of the idea of a European society among Europeans since the late nineteenth century are based on a current research project. Final conclusions can not yet be drawn. For a French summary of these articles see H. Kaelble, "L'histoire sociale de l'intégration européenne et la conscience européenne," in R. Girault, ed., *L'histoire de la conscience et l'identité européenne au XXᵉ siècle (The History of European Consciousness and Identity during the 20th Century)*, Paris, 1994.

Furthermore, it cannot be concluded that national and regional societies in Europe have weakened substantially or disappeared. National identity remains crucial in Europe, and there is no sign that it will be replaced by a European consciousness, European politics, or European symbols. At the same time, the totally independent nation of the nineteenth century and the idea of a mere European concert of nations with its congresses and wars is considered to be a phenomenon of the past. It is the intent of this article to show that the isolated, strictly separated *national society* in the nineteenth-century sense no longer exists. Exploring the emergence of a European society in the second half of the twentieth century entails exploring the emergence of a new national society in Europe.

Social Peculiarities of Twentieth-Century Europe

Books by historians who treat European history usually look at Europe as a whole only for the Middle Ages and for the early modern period. Starting with the nineteenth century, the perspective changes and European history is treated nation by nation. In general, for processes such as industrialization, urbanization, secularization, and alphabetization, the national differences are strongly emphasized. However, studies of special fields in social history — such as the history of the family — show that there is no constraint from historical reality to relinquish entirely the European perspective of nineteenth- and twentieth-century social history. European commonalities, which embraced most European countries and most Europeans, did exist and can be shown. They are often part of a European way, of a distinct development of European society different from non-European societies. Such a European way can be demonstrated in five fields of social history: (1) the family; (2) work; (3) European social milieus; (4) state intervention; and (5) consumption and lifestyles. Of course, there are other fields in which more detailed research might also demonstrate a peculiar European way.[2]

---

2. For some other social peculiarities in urbanization, social conflicts and large enterprises, see Kaelble, *Social History of Western Europe*, passim.

The main characteristic of the European family was the establishment by young adult couples of their own household, *independent* from their families of origin. This made the European family different from Asian, Russian, and certain Eastern European families, where young households were predominantly integrated into the households of the parents and the in-laws, respectively. The founding of independent households by young adults also predominated in the "new societies" such as the U.S., Canada, and Australia. However, the material circumstances and the mentalities of Europeans resulted in at least four distinct consequences: (1) The three-generation family was much more rare in Europe than in Japan or in Russia or in parts of Eastern Europe. (2) The age of first marriage for men as well as for women was distinctly later in Europe than outside and, until recently, than in the U.S. (3) Birth rates were and are still lower in Western Europe than in most non-European countries and, until 1989, in Eastern Europe. (4) The rate of those who never married was higher in Europe than outside, since the founding of an independent household requires a measure of economic independence.[3]

European particularities developed not only in the structure of the family but also in family life. Relations among family members seem to have been more intensive, more emotional, and more intimate in Europe than outside. This family intimacy served to separate families from the neighborhood, from the larger family, and from the community. "If an Englishman builds his house," wrote an Anglo-Irish writer in 1914 in a comparison between Europe and the United States, "he surrounds it first of all with high walls. This is no English particularity. It predominates all over Western Europe. Walls outside the house are like doors

---

3. J. Hajnal, "European Marriage Patterns in Perspective," in D.V. Class and D.E.C. Eversley, eds., *Population in History*, London, 1965; P. Laslett, *Family Life and Illicit Love in Earlier Generations*, Cambridge, 1977, ch. 1; Laslett, "Household and Family as Work Group and Kin Group," in R. Wall et al., eds., *Family Forms in Historic Europe*, Cambridge, 1983; Laslett, "The European Family and Early Industrialisation," in J. Baechler et al., eds., *Europe and the Rise of Capitalism*, Oxford, 1988; Michael Mitterauer, *Sozialgeschichte der Jugend*, Frankfurt, 1986, pp. 28-43; A. Burguière et al., *Histoire de la famille*, vol. 2, Paris, 1986; M. Barbagli, *Sotto lo stesso tetto*, Bologna, 1984.

inside. The European wants both because of his want for privacy which is in his blood."[4] Childhood, which was strictly separate from adulthood, was also different than in non-European societies. Gustav Schmoller, a German economist, compared the American and European child in 1886 and was surprised to observe in the U.S. the total lack of what he saw as the European childhood "with its happy playing, with its distinct world of a child and with its poetic charm."[5] A similar conclusion, though evaluated in a contrasting manner, came from the German writer Hans Goslar in 1922: "The Americans like children. They do it not in the European way in which children are often spoilt and become small, pretty, pampered little apes."[6] Because of the independence of young adults from the family of origin, the crisis of adolescence seems to have been more severe and more marked in Europe than outside. Simone de Beauvoir, in her diary of a visit to America in 1947, wrote that to her surprise, the crisis of adolescence "is not lived through by most American young men."[7] Also, it appears that the strict contrasts of gender roles and the special role of the mother as the emotional reference for the children as well as for the husband was a peculiarity of the European family. This would explain why so many European visitors to the U.S. during the nineteenth and early twentieth centuries were shocked by American women. Schmoller, once again, wrote in 1886: "The women [in the United States] are more beautiful and better educated than in any other country, but they do not have the deep soul, the warm sentiment.... Most marriages are based upon mutual respect, much less upon love."[8]

Here one must present some qualifications: the European family started in the Northwestern and in the German-speaking

4. G. Birmingham, in H.S. Commager, ed., *America in Perspective: The United States Through Foreign Eyes*, New York, 1947, p. 281

5. G. Schmoller, "Nationalökonomische und socialpolitische Rückblicke auf Nordamerika," in *Preußische Jahrbücher*, vol. 17, 1866, p. 129.

6. H. Goslar, *Amerika 1992*, Berlin, 1992, p. 146.

7. S. de Beauvoir, *Amerika Tag und Nacht*, reprint Hamburg, 1988, p. 303.

8. Schmoller, "Nationalökonomische und socialpolitische Rückblicke auf Nordamerika," p. 129f.

part of Europe, and it did not become predominant throughout Europe until the nineteenth and twentieth centuries. Most of its characteristics developed first in the European upper classes and were slowly accepted by other social classes. In addition, the European family has changed fundamentally during recent decades. Family forms, gender roles, relations between family members, the isolation of the intimate family have changed dramatically, and new differences between North and South have emerged in Western Europe. Still, some European peculiarities have endured into the present.[9]

A second European particularity emerged in the history of work and the employment structure. Industrial employment grew much more rapidly in Europe than in non-European societies, and in the industrialized countries a larger portion of the active population was employed in industry in Europe. This predominance of industrial employment lasted in Europe as a whole from the 1950s to the 1970s, in Western Europe as a whole from the 1920s to the 1970s, and much longer in some of the highly industrialized European countries, e.g., Great Britain, Germany, Belgium, Switzerland, Austria, and Sweden. In non-European economies such as the U.S., Japan, Canada, the USSR, and Australia the industrial sector was never the largest employer; the agrarian sector was replaced by the service sector as the largest employer. In this respect Europe seems to have been a unique case in world economic history: a period during which the industrial sector was the largest employment sector can be found only in Europe during the nineteenth and twentieth centuries.[10]

---

9. R. Wall, "Introduction," in R. Wall et al., eds., *Family Forms in Historic Europe*, Cambridge, 1983, p. 46ff.; Kaelble, *A Social History of Western Europe, 1880-1980*, p. 16 (for the age at first marriage); *Eurostat. Bevölkerungsstatistik 1984*, Luxemburg, 1984, p. 75; *Statistical Abstracts of the United States 1988*, 108th edition, 1987, p. 83; *Economically Active Population 1950-2025*, ed. by International Labour Office, 5 vols., vol. 5, 3rd ed., Geneva, 1986, pp. 17ff., 85ff.

10. See also for the following remarks on the working population: H. Kaelble, "Was Prometheus Most Unbound in Europe? The Labour Force in Europe During the Late 19th and 20th Centuries," *Journal of European Economic History*, 18., 1989, pp. 65-104.

This exceptional role of the industrial sector had important consequences for European societies: industrial workers were more numerous than in non-European societies; purely industrial cities — such as Charleroi, Sheffield, St. Etienne, Katowice, and Gelsenkirchen — were more numerous; working-class quarters and milieus exerted a much stronger influence on the societies; industrial work was portrayed more often in European arts and literature; reactions to industrial work have been more forceful; trade unions and the labor movement had a stronger impact on political movements in Europe; anxiety about working-class revolutions was stronger and repressive reactions more forceful and dangerous. Following this period of industrial society in the strict sense, industrial employment started to shrink more rapidly in Europe than elsewhere and, since the 1970s, has been reduced more in Europe than in the U.S. or Japan. The collapse of industrial plants in Eastern Europe during the past years is part of this European particularity, differing only in the rapid and brutal way it occurred. In spite of this shrinkage, the share of industrial employment is still higher in Europe than in the U.S. and Canada and slightly higher than in Japan.

Not all European societies have followed this pattern of industrial employment, and in the Netherlands, Norway, Denmark, Ireland, Greece, and Portugal the industrial sector remained the second largest employment sector. In France, the most notable exception, industry has never been larger than the agrarian and service sectors, respectively. The limited industrial employment sector in Northern Europe is partly due to an international division of labor in which Norway and the Netherlands produced a large part of the service work for other countries, while Denmark and Ireland produced agrarian work for other European countries. The exceptionally low birth rates in France during the nineteenth and twentieth centuries kept down its expansion of the industrial sector. The late industrialization in Southern Europe seems to be following a pattern similar to that of the more advanced Third World countries. On the whole, however, Europe is distinct in the strength of its industrial employment.

This European particularity of industrial strength is reflected in European attitudes toward work and non-work, producing a distinct separation between the two. The reduction of working hours during the week and the extension of non-work on weekends was advanced more in Europe than elsewhere. In the Northern European countries the limitation on shopping hours is far more strict than in non-European societies. Holidays are much longer in Europe than outside, giving rise to a highly developed holiday industry and holiday culture. Europeans enter the labor market later in life and retire at an earlier age. Worker protection regulations were introduced in Europe earlier than in non-European countries and they are more stringent. The creation of child labor laws, limitation of work for juveniles and pregnant women — as well as for women in general for certain types and times of work — and for the elderly is European in origin. Women not gainfully employed outside the home are more numerous in Western Europe than in non-European societies and, until 1989, than in Eastern European countries.

This special attitude of Europeans toward work and non-work has various historical sources and is linked to the Protestant ethic, to aristocratic models, to long-term rules of changing generations in family businesses, and to the independence of young adults. The clear separation of work and non-work is also facilitated by the predominance of industrial work; in agricultural societies work and non-work is season- and climate-dependent, while in the service sector it is client-dependent. Hence, within Europe the separation of work and non-work is more strict in the highly industrialized countries than in those less marked by industrial employment.[11]

A third peculiarity of Europe is the development of related social milieus, of which four have been especially important for twentieth-century European society: (1) the middle-class or the "bourgeoisie" ("Bürgertum"), (2) the proletarian working class, (3) the petit bourgeoisie, and (4) the peasant milieu. The aristo-

---

11. For the work and non-work in a life course, see: *Economically Active Population, 1950-2025*, vol. 4, 3rd ed., p. 160.

cratic milieu, which was still important during the nineteenth century, lost much of its force by the beginning of the twentieth century with the fall or loss of power of the monarchies and courts.[12] Even though the professions that comprise these four milieus are found in all modern societies outside Europe, here they have developed specific values, mentalities, social connections, and social separations not found in industrial societies outside Europe.

The oldest of these specifically European milieus — and most notably in inner Europe — is the middle class, which emerged during the late eighteenth and early nineteenth centuries as a social milieu of various occupational groups: the business elite, the professions, Protestant priests, higher civil servants, university and grammar school teachers, and — to some extent — writers, painters, sculptors, musicians, and composers. Although each of these professions formed special professional identities, careers, and organizations, they were simultaneously bound together in Europe by common values and lifestyles; strong social interconnections by marriage; social origins; education; intensive social contacts in associations and clubs; appreciation of fine arts and sciences; and clear social distinctions that initially leaned more toward the aristocracy but gradually inclined more toward the lower classes, especially the proletarian working class. It is important to note that in Europe none of the professions comprising the middle class was clearly predominant in the manner that "businessman" was in the U.S., and this group imposed its value system on the American middle class. To be sure, tensions and even conflicts developed among these various professions — e.g., between the business world and that of the intellectuals and academics — but in the long

---

12. See J. Blum, *The End of the Old Order in Rural Europe*, Princeton, 1978; A. J. Mayer, *Adelsmacht und Bürgertum. Die Krise der europäischen Gesellschaft 1848-1914*, Munich, 1984 (Eng. version: *The Persistence of the Old Regime*, New York, 1984); W. Mosse, "The Nobility and the Middle Classes in Nineteenth-Century Europe: A Comparative Study", in J. Kocka and A. Mitchell, eds., *Bourgeois Society in 19th-Century Europe*, Oxford/Providence, 1993; H.-U. Wehler, ed., *Europäischer Adel 1750-1950* (*European Aristocracy 1750-1950*), Göttingen, 1990.

run, the delicate balance between special professional values and identity on the one hand and common values of the common middle class on the other was preserved during the nineteenth and the first half of the twentieth centuries. In Eastern Europe the middle class was usually much more split into national, ethnic, and religious groups; nor did a comparable middle class emerge in the U.S. or in Japan.

The end of the Second World War brought a weakening of this social milieu and a blurring of its distinctions from the others. Social prejudices against the proletarian working class and the peasant milieu became much less evident. Moreover, increasing professional activities of women and mothers and changes in sexuality eroded the clear separation of gender roles and the predominance of the housewife in the middle class. The two hallmarks of social distinction of the middle class, i.e., property and higher education, also lost their former strength. For the middle class property had a double sense. On the one hand, it was important as ownership of the means of production, becoming much less important with the rise of the manager who directed an enterprise but did not own it. On the other hand, property was an important means to social security of middle class families, to securing the lives of elderly family members, of female members who never married, and of male members who were not gainfully employed. The middle class advantage of social security was lost following World War II, partly because of the creation of the modern welfare state and partly because the ownership of real estate, life insurance, savings, and other titles extended to the other social classes. Not only did property become less important, but the same is true for higher education, which, since the second World War, has expanded rapidly. No longer the privilege of a small minority, professional training is now available to more than one-fourth of Western Europeans. These changes have caused sharper divergences among the lifestyles and values of the various professions of the middle class and, conversely, less visible commonalities and social connections within the middle class. However, middle- class institutions have prevailed, and social distinctions as well as differentials in standards of living have not disappeared; another upper class has emerged, for which a term does not yet exist.[13]

Another important European social milieu, the proletarian working class, emerged during the end of the nineteenth and early twentieth centuries. It was an important development for three reasons in particular: (1) It was a form of everyday solidarity among workers of the same quarter or in the same enterprise and provided a support network during difficult life stages, e.g., young parenthood, illness, death of a family member, unemployment, and old-age poverty — especially before the rise of the modern welfare state. (2) It was an important factor for self-respect and self-assurance in a society that normally excluded workers from society and in which the middle class as well as the lower middle class erected social barriers against the working class. Specific working-class institutions like libraries, educational institutions, pubs, newspapers, and music halls were established for this purpose, and thus eating, drinking, spending money, and the rhythms of life had a different character in this milieu than in the others, though these differences were often aimed at gaining self-respect rather than at distinguishing themselves from other parts of society. (3) In some European countries — e.g., Germany and Austria — the working-class milieu developed a network of associations that mobilized members of the working class for the labor movement and the trade unions.

---

13. See the introductory article by Jürgen Kocka in *Bourgeois Society in 19th-Century Europe* (see for the innner-European comparison the articles by Marco Meriggi for the Italian and German middle class, by Albert Tanner on the Swiss middle class, by Bo Strath on the Swedish middle class, by György Ránki on the Hungarian middle class, by Waclaw Dlugoborski and Elzbieta Kaczynska on the Polish middle class, and my only article on the French and German middle class). On the differences of the education of children in the middle class in Britain and Germany see G. Budde, "Auf dem Weg ins Bürgerleben. Kindheit und Erziehung in deutschen und englischen Bürgerfamilien von 1840 bis 1914" ("Childhood and Education in German and English Middle Class Families 1840-1914"), PhD dissertation, FU Berlin, 1993; H. Kaelble, "Die oberen Schichten in Frankreich und der Bundesrepublik seit 1945" ("The Upper Class in France and Germany since 1945"), in *Frankreich Jahrbuch*, 1991, p. 46ff.

In this sense, the working class consisted of a labor- movement culture rather than a working-class culture and was split into political camps: social democratic, Catholic, and Communist. In spite of important variations among European countries in the relationship between the working-class culture and the labor movement, the working-class milieu was generally an important base for the European labor movement and the European trade unions, which mobilized distinctly larger numbers of worker and which entered into fiercer social conflicts than most non-European trade unions. Because the working-class milieu was in many ways also a reaction to the social distinctions made by the other social milieus, it did not exist to the same degree in non-European industrial societies.[14]

Following World War II, this working-class milieu was also weakened. In Germany and Austria, as well as in the occupied European countries, the Nazis interdicted the institutions of the working class. In Germany the working-class milieu found it particularly difficult to survive, and the German social democrats decided not to rebuild most of the labor movement associations after 1945. Moreover, the rise of the modern welfare state, with its much more comprehensive idea of social security, rendered the solidarity within the working class less necessary. Social distinctions within European societies became less clear, and many of the social distinctions in everyday life disappeared or changed in significance.

---

14. See E.H. Hobsbawm, *The Age of Empire, 1875-1914*, London, 1989; V. Lidtke, "Recent Literature on Worker's Culture in Germany and England," in K. Tenfelde, ed., *Arbeiter und Arbeiterbewegung im Vergleich*, Munich, 1986; K. Tenfelde, "Vom Ende und Erbe der Arbeiterkultur," in S. Miller and M. Ristau, eds., *Gesellschaftlicher Wandel, soziale Demokratie. 125 Jahre SPD. Historische Erfahrungen, Gegenwartsfragen, Zukunstskonzepte*, Berlin, 1988; W. Kaschuba, *Die Kultur der Unterschichten im 19. und 20. Jahrhundert*, Munich, 1990; J. Moser, *Arbeiterleben in Deutschland 1900-1970*, Frankfurt, 1984; H. Mendras, *La seconde révolution française 1965-1984*, Paris, 1988; R. McKibbin, *The Ideologies of Class: Social Relations in Britain 1880-1950*, Oxford, 1990; J.D. Young, *Socialism and the English Working Class: A History of English Labour 1883-1930*, New York, 1990; H. Kaelble, "Europäische Sozialgeschichte des Streiks?" in J. Kocka and K. Tenfelde, eds., *Festschrift fKr Gerhard A. Ritter*, to be published in 1994.

A social milieu to which the attention of the historians was drawn less frequently is the petty bourgeoisie, which was probably also a peculiarly European milieu. It was characterized by a strong appreciation of economic independence, which was often precarious and difficult to maintain. Another of its characteristics was an astonishing upward and downward class mobility. Moreover, it was marked by unusually strong family ties and obligations, values that were needed for keeping up family businesses in a competitive society. This lower middle class also developed a specific culture consisting of choral societies as well as athletic, rifle, and professional clubs. In politics, strong contrasts existed between the more liberal values of the British, the conservative tendencies of the German, and the populist tendencies of the French lower middle classes. But the field of social history recognizes a European lower middle class, which emerged in the second half of the nineteenth century and became weakened during past decades.[15]

The peasant milieu was also an important milieu of European societies as late as the twentieth century. Unlike the American farmer, European peasants were generally not profit- or market-oriented, wishing only to make a living off their property and to preserve it for the family; thus European peasant agriculture was largely a subsistence economy. Beyond a basic education, often inferior to urban elementary education, peasants had no professional training or specialization. Peasants also produced and/or repaired their own farm implements and frequently built their own houses and stables. Peasant agriculture was a family venture, with all members of the family having strict obligations for the work. Geographic and class mobility was very limited; even as late as the 1970s most sons of French peasants became peasants in turn and married peasant girls. Since the distinction between urban and rural life was seen as one of the most important lines of social demarcation in European society (much more

---

15. See "Introduction," G. Crossick and H.-G. Haupt, eds., *Shopkeepers and Master Artisans in 19th Century Europe*, London, 1984; G. Crossick, "The European Lower Middle Class," in H. Kaelble, ed., *The European Way*, forthcoming 1995.

important than in America), the lifestyle of the peasant milieu differed greatly from all the other major milieus — which were mostly urban — in their dining, drinking, clothing, and housing. During recent decades this peasant milieu weakened, the subsistence economy disappeared, and the modern European profit-oriented farmer emerged, well-trained in his field and usually specialized. The family economy disintegrated, enabling mobility into other occupations, social milieus, and geographic locations. The standard of living in farming houses rose to that of urban families. Nevertheless, many of the peasant homes, the villages, and the cultural traditions of everyday rural life have persevered, distinguishing European societies from non-European ones.[16]

Without doubt, some of the characteristics of these four social milieus can also be found in non-European societies, but nowhere else could one find all four milieus, sustained by their contrasts and, simultaneously, their commonalities. Although this European peculiarity has been greatly attenuated, many of the institutions, the architecture, and the lifestyles of the milieus still exist and retain their influence in European society.

A fourth important social peculiarity of Europe is more recent in origin, dating back to the end of World War II and existing to this day: the modern welfare state, which differs from non-European welfare states in several respects. Even today the welfare state in Europe is more advanced, providing social security for a larger part of the population and expending more money. The models for all welfare states came from Europe — the German model as early as the 1880s and the British and Swedish models since the Second World War. Critical decisions regarding welfare

---

16. See R. Huebscher, "Déstruction de la paysannerie?" in Y. Lequin, ed., *Histoire des français, XIXe et XXe siècles* (*The History of the French during the 19th and 20th Centuries*), vol. 2: *La société*, Paris, 1983; H. Mendras, *La fin des paysans* (*The End of the Peasants*), Paris, 1984; A. Ilien and O. Jeggle, *Leben auf dem Dorf. Zur Sozialgeschichte des Dorfes und zur Psychologie seiner Bewohner* (*Life in the Village: On the Social History of the Village and the Psychology of Its Inhabitants*), Opladen, 1978; D. Brüggemeier and R. Riehle, *Das Dorf* (*The Village*), Frankfurt, 1986; W. Rösener, *Die Bauern in der europäischen Geschichte* (*Peasants in European History*), Munich, 1993.

were made in European countries prior to 1914, to be followed decades later in non-European industrial societies. Unlike in the U.S. and Japan, where the alternative to the welfare crisis was found in the family or the market economy, in Europe it was — to a much greater degree — the corporate solution.[17]

A fifth recent social peculiarity of Europe is the development of European patterns of consumption. To be sure, patterns of consumption in food, drink, clothing, and housing are not fully homogeneous throughout Europe, differing among countries and among regions. However, since the second World War the obvious differences in consumption patterns among European countries have been reduced, and today goods found in supermarkets, furniture shops, department stores, restaurants, and travel agencies have a more international — while at the same time overwhelmingly European — character than even in the postwar era. During the immediate postwar era Europe was split into highly industrialized and urbanized countries — mainly in inner Europe — and primarily agrarian and rural societies in the Northern, Southern, and Eastern periphery; this split resulted in contrasting lifestyles and patterns of consumption. During recent decades industrialization and urbanization have reached the European periphery, making consumption patterns more similar all over Europe and reducing the differentials in national levels of

17. See P. Flora, ed., *Growth to Limits: The Western European Welfare States Since World War II*, 5 vols., Berlin, New York, 1986; P. Baldwin, *The Politics of Social Solidarity and the Bourgeois Basis of the European Welfare State, 1875-1975*, Cambridge, 1990; G.A. Ritter, *Der Sozialstaat. Entstehung und Entwicklung im internationalen Vergleich (The Social State: Beginnings and Development in an International Comparison)*, Munich, 1989; J. Alber, *Vom Armenhaus zum Wohlfahrtsstaat (From the Poorhouse to the Welfare State)*, Frankfurt, 1982; B. Schulte, "Die Entwicklung der europäischen Sozialpolitik, in H.A. Winkler and H. Kaelble, eds., *Nationalismus - Nationalitäten - Supranationlität (Nationalism - Nationalities - Supranationality)*, Stuttgart, 1993; S. Leibfried, "Sozialstaat Europa? Integrationsperspektiven europäischen Armutsregimes ("Europe as a Social State? Perspectives on the Integration of the European Reign of Poverty"), in *Nachrichtendienst des Deutschen Vereins für öffentliche und private Fürsorge*, 70., 1990, pp. 296-305; Liebfried, "Wohlfahrtsstaatliche Entwicklungspotentiale. Die EG nach Maastricht," in ibid., 71., 1992; OECD, *Social Expenditure 1960-1990*, Paris, 1985.

consumption expenditures. In addition, the geographic horizon
of Europeans has widened substantially since the war so that
most Europeans learned to appreciate foreign foods and goods,
becoming more international in their consumer behavior. The
period from the 1950s to the 1970s was marked by common economic prosperity, bringing about a dramatic modernization in the
European way of life with the introduction of the automobile,
standardized consumer goods, new methods of food preservation and preparation, and new forms of marketing. The American
model in this modernization was important, since the U.S. took
the lead in developing new lifestyles during the period when the
European way of life was marked by the impoverishment of two
world wars. In spite of a substantial resistance among Europeans
during the immediate postwar period against the "Americaniza-
tion" of life, the majority of Europeans accepted the revolution in
everyday lifestyle because most of its elements were invented
and developed in Europe as well as in America. Another factor in
the Europeans' peculiar consumption is the emergence of a European consumer market, which was made possible by the policy of
the European Community and was realized by the strategy of
European enterprises, which wanted to sell the same products in
as many European countries as possible.

Less Distinct Differences
among European Countries

Another aspect of the social history of European integration[18] is
rapprochement, i.e., the reduction of social cleavages among
European societies. Two factors were especially important for
this *rapprochement*: the industrialization of all of Europe and the
interventionist state. It is incorrect to consider the industrialization of Europe as a nineteenth-century phenomenon because as
late as 1950 the agrarian sector was still the largest employer in
all of Europe (except the Soviet Union). Industrialization was a
long process that evolved from its beginning in late eighteenth-
century Britain until the industrialization of the European

---

18. For more details see H. Kaelble, "A Social History of European Integration"
    (see note 1).

periphery during the 1950s and 1960s. Economic convergence during the final stages of industrialization ushered in three types of convergence in social history.

Around 1950 the contrasts between countries with predominantly agrarian employment (especially in the Southeast of Europe) and those with predominantly industrial employment were still strong. These contrasts became mitigated so that in the 1980s no European country — with the exception of Albania — was primarily agrarian. Service employment, which became predominant in the 1970s and 1980s, did not vary significantly in the different European countries. Similarly, around 1950 strong contrasts still existed in Europe between the highly urbanized countries and predominantly rural ones. During recent decades urbanization spread rapidly to the European periphery and, except for isolated regional societies, urban life — with its concomitant urban values and lifestyles — became predominant throughout Europe. Finally, there was convergence in patterns of consumption expenditure. In the 1950s, huge differences existed between industrialized inner-Europe and the poor periphery.[19] During the three decades between 1960 and 1990, a substantial reduction of these material cleavages took place in Western Europe, and one can only hope that a similar reduction of new cleavages will occur between Eastern and Western Europe.[20]

The interventionist state, which arose following the second World War, is also a factor in the mitigation of differences among Western European societies. Especially during the 1950s and 1960s, public revenues and public expenditures boomed at rates of growth unthinkable before and since. The activity of the public authority became more and more service-oriented. It was extremely important for the differences among European soci-

19. This reduction of differentials was calculated from statistics in *Historical Statistics 1960-1990*, Paris, OECD, 1992, pp. 14ff., 18ff. (private final consumption expenditure per capita U.S.$).

20. Variation coefficients for cars, telephones and television sets per capita of population between European countries fell drastically between 1950 and 1980. Calculated from B. R. Mitchell, *International Historical Statistics. Europe 1750 to 1988*, 3rd ed., Basingstoke, 1992, pp. 3ff., 714ff., 750ff.

eties that this growth of public intervention took place during a
period in which the same political and economic system existed,
at least in Western Europe. Hence, there were liberal exchanges
among Western societies about models and methods of public
intervention so that at this time, in contrast to the nineteenth and
early twentieth centuries, the increase in state intervention did
not lead to distinctly different paths of development.

These convergences may have taken place in other areas of
public activity (e.g., housing and city planning, health and environmental policy), but they are most apparent in the fields of
social security and public education. There is no homogeneity in
institutions of public insurance even in Western Europe, and differences are especially pronounced between the rich European
countries and the poorer ones; Europe as a whole now faces
strong differences in social security between Eastern and Western
Europe. At the same time, four main branches of public insurance
— against illness, invalidism, old-age poverty, and unemployment
— became predominant all over Western Europe. The share of
the population that benefited from social security became less
dissimilar, as did social security expenditures. The impetus for
these convergences was the common experience of the world
economic crisis and of World War II, as well as the broad political
consensus in most European countries and across most political
parties regarding the necessity for public social security. The crisis of the welfare state in the 1980s was also common to the countries of Europe; it did not lead to drastic cuts or dramatic new
divergences of expenditures in relation to the GNP. These tendencies toward convergence with respect to the welfare state are
a European particularity[21] that is not shared by non-European

---

21. Besides the titles in footnote 17: H.G. Hockerts, "Die Entwicklung vom
    Zweiten Weltkrieg bis zur Gegenwart" ("Development from the Second World
    War to the Present"), in P.A. Köhler/ and H.F. Zacher, eds., *Beiträge zur
    Geschichte und zur aktuellen Situation der Sozialversicherung* (*Essays on the
    History and the Present Situation of Social Security*), Berlin, 1983; J. Alber, *Vom
    Armenhaus zum Wohlfahrtstaat* (*From the Poorhouse to the Welfare State*),
    Frankfurt, 1982; P. Flora and A.J. Heidenheimer, eds., *The Development of the
    Welfare States in Europe and America*, New Brunswick, 1981; H. Heclo, *Mod-
    ern Social Politics in Britain and Sweden*, New Haven, 1974; F.X. Kaufmann,

welfare states. In public education, too, one can see huge differences between institutions like the French *grandes écoles*, the colleges of Oxford and Cambridge, and German universities. Nevertheless, the end product of public education in Western Europe has become more similar. It is not well-known that following the second World War, great differences in alphabetization existed, which were clearly mitigated during the past decades. It is more widely known that student rates — i.e., the percentage of students in respective age cohorts — has become more similar in recent decades. This is not a global tendency, and rate differences between Europe and the U.S., Japan, and the former Communist countries in Eastern Europe are great, making the tendency toward convergence in public education a European particularity.[22]

Exchanges and Connections among European Societies

Five major factors have led to a clear intensification of exchanges and connections among European societies since World War II;

"Nationale Traditionen der Sozialpolitik und europäische Integration" ("National Traditions of Social Policy and European Integration"), in L. Albertin, ed., *Probleme und Perspektiven europäischer Einigung* (*Problems and Perspectives of European Unification*), Cologne, 1986; M.G. Schmidt, *Wohlfartsstaatliche Politik unter bürgerlichen und sozialdemokratischen Regierungen. Ein Internationaler Vergleich* (*Welfare State Policy under Liberal and Social Democratic Governments: An International Comparison*), Frankfurt, 1982; G. Esping-Andersen, *The Three Worlds of Welfare Capitalism*, Cambridge, 1990.

22. P. Flora, *Growth to Limits*; F.K. Ringer, *Education and Society in Modern Europe*, Bloomington, 1979; P. Windolf, *Die Expansion der Universitäten 1870-1985* (*The Expansion of Universities 1870-1985*), Stuttgart, 1990; P. Gruson, *L'enseignement supérieur et son efficacité: France, Etats Unis, URSS, Pologne* (*Higher Education and Its Efficacy: France, The United States, The USSR, Poland*), Paris, 1983; A.J. Heidenheimer, "Education and Social Security in Entitlements in Europe and America," in P. Flora and A.J. Heidenheimer, eds., *The Development of the Welfare States in Europe and America*, New Brunswick, 1989; R. Schneider, "Die Bildungsentwicklung in den westeuropäischen Staaten 1870-1979" ("The Development of Education in Western European States 1870-1979"), in *Zeitschrift für Soziologie*, 10., 1982; H. Kaelble, *Social Mobility in the 19th and 20th Centuries: Europe and America in Comparative Perspective*, Leamington Spa, 1985, pp. 31-93.

the barriers to Eastern Europe have been reduced since 1989.[23]
(1) International economic connections through foreign trade,
international investments, and multinational enterprises have
resulted in more social interconnections among European societies. The effects of these connections were not purely quantitative: openness toward the business methods and lifestyles of
other countries has also increased. (2) In addition, the rise in living standards, especially since the 1950s, decreased relative
household expenditures for basics and opened up the possibility
for spending on other items such as education and tourism,
which has led to more knowledge and better understanding of
foreign societies. (3) Another factor is the reversal of educational
levels. Whereas Europeans who had only an elementary education were still the overwhelming majority in the postwar era,
those leaving after elementary school have become a small
minority during recent decades. Higher learning has become
accessible to a substantial part of the population. More educated
people have a greater interest in traveling to other countries and
are more open to foreign lifestyles. More students went abroad to
study, and these educational exchanges have also led to more
interconnections among European countries. (4) The transport
and information revolution has resulted in a reduction of dis-
tances in Europe and has made it a smaller space. (5) The policies of the European Community have also contributed to
increased exchanges and interconnections by establishing a
European market not only for goods but also for labor; by developing exchange programs for students in higher education during the 1980s; and by facilitating travel and tourism across
national borders. While these factors can be found in all modern
industrial societies, their effects were peculiar in Europe, where
by far the most travel, migration, educational exchanges, and
international marriages among Europeans took place.

All this brought about an opening of the geographic horizon of
the common European. Prior to the middle of the twentieth cen-

---

23. Research on this aspect of the social integration of European societies is
scarce. For more details see once again H. Kaelble, "The Social History of
European Integration."

tury only a small minority of upper-class Europeans or Europeans in special occupational activities had any direct personal knowledge of other European countries; the vast majority based their impressions not on direct personal experience but on information from the media and from hearsay. A certain number of Europeans experienced other European countries under circumstances that were often traumatic, i.e., as soldiers, deportees or prisoners of war, or migrant laborers who ended up in ghettos for migrants. Non-traumatic encounters with other countries were often experienced outside Europe, in the European colonies or in the Americas, the main continent of European out-migration. Since World War II, experience by Europeans of other European countries has increased dramatically. Europeans traveled to other European countries with much greater frequency and, with the decline of colonial empires, they settled far less frequently in countries outside Europe. At the same time, this experience was different in nature: it did not occur during extreme situations such as war or enforced migration but rather under favorable circumstances such as holidays, business, marriage, or education in foreign countries. The new experiences took place under more normal everyday situations, could be repeated, and were frequently undertaken in a spirit of European cooperation, which was rarely seen before the 1950s. Thus the geographic horizons of common Europeans became broader, and more Europeans ventured beyond the borders of their own regions or countries.

Awareness of a European Society

The awareness of all these tendencies among Europeans has not yet been explored. A long-term study parallel to the study by P.M. Lützeler of European manifestos by European writers remains to be written.[24] There is no doubt that such a study will produce interesting results, since an intensive debate about European society was being conducted during the nineteenth and twentieth centuries in which such well known European writers as Alexis de Tocqueville, James Bryce, Werner Sombart, Max Weber, and

---

24. P.M. Lützeler, *Die Schriftsteller und Europa. Von der Romantik bis zur Gegenwart*, Munich, 1992.

Simone de Beauvoir participated. I would like to offer a few brief conclusions from my own study: (1) The idea of a European society has changed fundamentally. Prior to 1914, Europeans unconsciously had a Euro-centered perspective, believing Europe to be the leader of modern civilization and world progress, and therefore they viewed non-European societies as exotic and strange. The catastrophes of the two World Wars caused Europeans to become more self-conscious and to realize that Europe is only a part of a much wider modern world. As they began to reflect on the real meaning of civilization and progress, Europeans gained more insight into other societies, and their attitudes began to change. (2) The debate about the peculiarities of European society has been controversial since the nineteenth century when it was part of the more general debate on modernization, and became even more so during the two postwar eras when Europe was in deep crisis. European social peculiarities in comparison with the U.S. were either fiercely defended by opponents of social modernization or vigorously attacked by its supporters. Although the controversy has lessened since the 1950s and 1960s, European social peculiarities have evolved only slowly into a core of European identity, with national societies as objects of identity remaining much more important than European society. (3) Before European institutions started to emerge in the 1950s, the idea of a European civilization with common European roots in previous historical periods was often used as a compensation for the lack of such supranational European institutions. Once these institutions were established and took on increasing power, the idea of a European society became less needed in this comparative way; society and culture even sometimes came to be regarded by a rising number of intellectuals as a refuge against an economic overstandardization and a political overconcentration of power in Brussels.

Conclusion

On the whole, fundamental changes have taken place in the integration of European societies since 1945. Differences between European societies have become less distinct due to the industrialization of all of Europe and the advent of the welfare state. Exchanges among European societies have intensified, widening the geographic horizon of Europeans. The perceptions of European society have changed and have become more consensual, based on direct personal experience.

No doubt one should not overestimate the political consequences of this emerging European society. It was the result of many favorable factors and conditions rather than the product of a purposeful European strategy. Hence, one cannot conclude that a European society can be created in the same way that European supranational institutions were built. The emerging European society did not automatically lead to greater political integration of Europe, nor has it become an object of European identity. Nevertheless, the emerging European society has made a difference in the political integration of Europe. Basic contradictions of national interests have been mitigated by the reduction of differences among European societies and by more inter-European exchanges, thus facilitating compromises in the European Community. More exchanges lead to an increased interchange of information as well as to a better understanding of the mentalities and interests of European neighbors. These increased personal experiences of other European countries and the reduction of differences among European countries, as well as the rise of new European social peculiarities, might one day lead to a rational European identity, a consciousness of the strengths and the weaknesses of European society.

7

Monetary Union in Europe
End of a Dream
or Beginning of a Nightmare?

♦ ♦ ♦ ♦ ♦ ♦

Peter G. Rogge*

The stability of the much vaunted European Monetary System (EMS) with its Exchange Rate Mechanism designed to attain some measure of exchange rate stability in Europe has now finally collapsed under the onslaught of massive capital flows. At the beginning of August 1993, the EMS widened its intervention limits to plus/minus 15 percent around central parities. For all practical purposes, this meant that it had moved to free floating. This appears to mark the end of a drama that seems to have fatally shattered a noble—some would say an unrealistic—dream about one Europe with one currency.

It may therefore seem an anachronism to talk about Monetary Union today, when stable European exchange rates appear further away than ever before. Yet there are strong reasons not to forget the issue. First, the Community's efforts to establish monetary integration have in the past again and again been subject to setbacks as big as the present one, but it has never yet backed away from its persistent effort to tie Europe's currencies more closely together. Second, in spite of all economic and political adversities, the ratification of the Maastricht Treaty on Political and Monetary Union in Europe has gone ahead. The next stage

* With important contributions by Dr. John Noorlander, SBC Economics Department

of the EMU process is therefore just about to begin, and it may very well bring further significant progress on a road that temporarily seemed to be closed altogether.

Still, there is no denying that EMS plans have recently suffered a very painful reappraisal (and seen a downgrading of the common currency denominator, the ECU). The beginning of the downfall should probably be set in December 1991, when the EC heads of state signed what then appeared to be one of the boldest blueprints yet drawn up for the New Europe: the Maastricht Treaty on Political and Monetary Union. What was meant to set the stage for the final step to the full integration of European currencies appears now to have ended in complete monetary disintegration instead. In the ruins of the shattered EMS the future of the envisaged Economic and Monetary Union (EMU) indeed seems doomed to many observers—for several reasons.

First of all, the yielding of sovereign rights as envisaged in the Treaty has provoked a degree of political resistance that the EC heads of state had totally underestimated when they convened in Maastricht in December 1991. This has amply been demonstrated in the meantime; the project to widen the EC into monetary as well as political union has split public opinion all over Europe right down the center on just how far the nation-states of yesterday are ready to part with sovereign rights in favor of a yet undecided supranational grouping of tomorrow. And these are really no minor sovereign rights if running one's own money has been a central prerogative of states (and fiefdoms) at least since medieval times. Accordingly, the proposition to have this core substance directed by a supranational body seems more than problematic to many people, not to mention the abandoning of the highly respected German mark, or the highly accepted British pound, or—for that matter—the highly revered French franc, in favor of something highly "artificial," something out of central bankers' cookbooks (or worse, of economists' textbooks).

Next on my list of reasons for doubt about a common currency in Europe is the disappearance of EMS stability itself. When the Treaty was signed, the EMS had already experienced five years without realignment. Formal monetary union seemed to call merely for further progress in areas where convergence had not yet been complete and for some new institutional arrangements to pave the rest of a straight path toward the common currency. Instead, stable exchange rates have now been blown away, and it seems hard to imagine how European currencies can ever be completely tied together.

What is more (and this is my third point), Europe has fallen prey in the meantime to a very unsettling recession; and with the many plans this recession has shattered, it has also acted as a brake for the European integration process in general (as has always been the case in the past when the economic going got rough). The critical turning (breaking?) point for the drive toward a common currency came in September 1992, when the EMS stability came apart under the attack of huge international capital flows in their search for safer haven or a quick buck. The United Kingdom, Italy, and Finland stepped out of the ERM (Exchange Rate Mechanism) system by reverting to freely floating exchange rates, a step taken a little later by Sweden and Norway as well; and others—Spain, Portugal, and Ireland— devalued their currencies by officially lowering the central parity (sticking, however, to fluctuation margins 2.25 percent above and below this newly established parity). Obviously, Europe's blueprints for monetary union had proved to be as yet unfit for real life. The reality was that macroeconomic conditions in Europe had, after the heady boom years of the late eighties, become bery divergent again, with Germany deviating from the rest based upon its unification bubble and raising both short-term interest rates to contain inflationary pressures and effective real exchange rates to reflect Germany's increased demand on global savings.

Unfortunately, this was by no means all. Many of the countries whose currencies came under pressure had seen their international competitiveness shrink appreciably over the years, and this erosion was compounded for some of the countries by precarious fiscal positions and a high degree of financial fragility. And, just to remind Euro-centered Europeans that they are not alone in this world, the divergence of monetary conditions between Germany on the one hand and the U.S. and Japan on the other acted as a further impulse to drive the German mark up—and thus make it even more difficult for other European currencies to stay on board, i.e., defend their parities at what had come to be assumed to be stable rates. This called for a turn toward a highly restrictive monetary policy, driving short-term interest rates up and thus making their currencies scarce and dear as well; this was, however, increasingly inconsistent with these countries' domestic policy needs in view of deepening recessions and mounting unemployment figures. This mixture proved to be explosive for the Eurocrats' most ambitious brainchild. Sticking to the adopted monetary regime meant—for some countries at least—that they had to push their interest rates up much too high for comfort for their recessionary economies, with an eye to defending an exchange rate that had clearly become questionable. Breaking away from this regime was taken by many as the freedom to act in what was perceived as their own country's best interests.

Still, Europe's monetary engineers, decided as they were in their quest for a common currency, surveyed the damage and concluded that the system did not have to be scrapped (or reinvented); it could be mended. In essence, with the central parities left in place and intervention margins left untouched, more frequent, earlier realignments whenever the need should arise were deemed to be the adequate answer for problems that were obviously not yet definitely overcome. And that is where matters were left until July 29 of 1993.

This was the day when the Bundesbank's surprise decision not to lower the key discount rate touched off another huge wave of selling of currencies deemed by market participants to be artificially propped up by interest rates that clearly had become a burden. The objects of the massive attack this time were the currencies of Denmark, Spain, Portugal, and—most important—of France and Belgium, the latter two definitely belonging to the essential core of the system. Hardest hit was the Banque de France, which spent approximately $ 35 billion in a futile effort to stem the tide; the Bundesbank joined in with another $ 34 billion worth of purchases of French francs. This process could not go on for a prolonged period of time, it had to be stopped, if only because of the inflationary effects these useless efforts might have in Germany due to the sudden oversupply of German marks. Significantly, EC finance ministers and central bankers quickly discarded two of three possible solutions to the crisis as terminal blows to European monetary integration: let all currencies float freely, i.e., abandon any central parity as a common goal; and/or reintroduce capital and exchange controls, i.e., scuttle one of the EC's cherished four liberties. Instead, it was decided to allow EMS currencies as of 2 August 1993 to fluctuate 15 percent above or below their prescribed central rates, as against the previous range of plus or minus 2.25 percent—a system coming pretty close indeed to a virtual free float—and in essence abandoning, at least for the time being, the notion of fixed (if adjustable) exchange rates.

This sad progress report would seem to lead to the conclusion that Europe's quest for a common currency was built on shifting sands. It seems unsustainable economically—stable exchange rates appear to be a fair-weather phenomenon—as well as politically—monetary union implies too much loss of sovereignty. Thus the financial markets acted as the executor of an economic and political judgment and seemed to have dealt the right answer (and blow) to the schemes dreamed up by the Eurocrats. Will the EMS, the EMR, the ECU (and all the rest of those E-words) be struck definitely into a tombstone for the United States of Europe, soon to be overgrown by the ivy of time? And should there not be rejoicing in front of this tombstone, instead of mourning? The answer to these questions seems to be all too obvious; and yet, another look at some of the underlying trends and causes would seem to unveil some hidden truths (and misconceptions as well) and, in the process, generate quite a different answer. Let us concentrate on only a few outstanding points.

First, is the venture of a common European currency really worth it? One answer is offered by statistics: tens of billions of ECU's unproductive costs could be done away with if Europe's internal trade were conducted on a common currency basis.

Another answer is less obvious, less quantifiable, but even more important: low inflation combined with the elimination of currency risks within Europe could significantly lower interest rate levels all over the Continent, since interest rates are at least in part risk premiums demanded by the investors as a hedge against the vagaries of exchange and inflation rates. Thus a large number of potential fixed investments all over Europe would turn from unprofitable propositions into viable, feasible projects, meaning that levels of (industrial, public, housing) investment could be realized in Europe that would otherwise be clearly unattainable. And this does not pertain only to future investment, *all* investments made in the past would be freed from a measure of risk and uncertainty arising out of the volatility of exchange rates between the currencies of neighboring countries! Last and by no means least, a common European currency does appear to be a most worthwhile prospect with regard to its beneficial effect upon the stability of moneys. As long as such a union is built upon sound criteria with respect to money and fiscal policies for eligible union members, it should help ensure enhanced discipline over excessive fiscal deficits as well as appreciably lower inflation.

Having said this, we now come to the key critical question: even if the quest for a common European currency is in fact worthwhile, must it still not be deemed utterly unrealistic, at least under the circumstances prevailing at present and in the foreseeable future? One is reminded of the fact that the experience gained with monetary cooperation in Europe during the eighties has amounted, by all accounts, to a remarkable success story: the working of the European Exchange Rate Mechanism. This system was built upon an agreement between central banks to keep exchange rates stable within very narrow limits around a central parity vis-à-vis the German mark as a common denominator; this was to be accomplished by unconditionally buying or selling other system currencies threatened by devaluation due to short-term oversupply or by appreciation due to short-lived waves of excessive demand. Aided by friendly business conditions in all the EC countries and by fiscal policies following similar lines (with minor exceptions) Europe's central banks—by also coordinating their acts—had achieved a high degree of convergence in monetary policies and, in so doing, had been able—over a span of almost a decade—to get national inflation rates much more in line than they used to be and, most important, on a lower level on balance.

This served, in turn, as a necessary condition for stabilizing interest rates on a significantly lower level as well, due to the consequential reduction in the premium demanded against inflation risks.

All of this resulted in (and the word "result" is important in this context) a notable increase in the stability of exchange rates of the currencies involved: less frequent and wide-ranging deviations from a middle-of-the road trend that was adhered to by the European currencies until September 1992, or even July 1993.

The implicit message of this experience is as forceful as it is important: in order to arrive at a convergence of exchange rates, money policies must be coordinated as closely as possible; having attained this end, one operates, in principle, *as if* there were one currency.

Is that really sufficient to do the trick? Unfortunately not, as Europe has come to learn, because the value of money rests not only on the amount of money supplied by central banks; it also depends on the amount of deficits run by governments and financed out of peoples' savings or out of newly created money, with interest rate reactions inevitable in both instances. Thus, a central truth has now been exposed: a common currency (or even just stable exchange rates) cannot be introduced by government decree; rather, it must be the result of national government policies generally in line with each other, i.e., of an effective coordination of national monetary *and* fiscal policies of the countries involved. This has to be achieved prior to any formal step to Union, as proof that the countries concerned are prepared to live with the full economic consequences of sound and coordinated policies. This is the basis of the famous Convergence Criteria in the Maastricht Treaty.

Low inflation, low public deficits, and *therefore* low interest rates, and *thus*, a high degree of exchange rate stability as the necessary *prerequisites* for a country to join the EMU and for a transition to a stable and, ultimately, a common currency—these are the necessary ingredients of European Monetary Union-in fact , of any monetary union built on the principles of monetary and fiscal prudence.

Are these criteria overly ambitious in view of the fact that at present almost none of the EC countries, including Germany, comply with them? Maybe—but they do make sense economically, even if they call for a long and tough road ahead! But here we are thrown back from noble goals to more mundane realities: today's recessionary climate clearly does make for swift achievement of these criteria. True, inflation has abated throughout the Community as a consequence of EMS discipline, with many members already fulfilling the inflation criterion set out in the Treaty. Much more difficult to achieve in today's recessionary climate are the convergence criteria relating to public sector deficits and debt; at present, hardly any of the EC members stand up to these exacting benchmarks.

And let us be realistic: that governments will successfully be able to balance budget at short notice by raising taxes or even by cutting expenditures can hardly be expected in the current environment of recession and rising unemployment.

So what to make of this state of affairs? Are we still asked to forget any dreams about European currency in exchange for what may indeed develop into most unfortunate nightmares of wildly fluctuating currencies, competitive interest rate cuts and devaluations, and renewed national protectionism in Europe? Or has it not been the unrealistic attempt to tie unequals together that has constituted the real nightmare, and are we not about to enjoy once more the dream of free markets deciding upon the true value of currencies?

As always when economics become complicated and confusing (and they usually do!), it pays to be as elementary and clear as possible. Yes, it is unrealistic to defend stable exchange rates against huge capital flows unleashed by widely diverging policies (and policy prospects) of the countries involved. No, the return to completely uncoordinated policies and completely uncontrolled exchange rates certainly does not hold out the promise of a dream world for Europe. So where is Europe headed in this respect? This question brings us finally to the prospects for the future.

These prospects are certainly not very promising if countries continue along the lines that led to the monetary turmoils of the recent past, i.e., if they continue to put national economic goals above Europe's. However, there is hope: what has happened over the past two years has been the result of (first) entirely abnormal conditions, with the deviation of the German economy from what has come to be a general European business cycle entirely due to the historically singular event of unification, (second) of an almost complete lack of important institutional prerequisites such as step one—uniformity of central banks in regard to their political independence and their policy goals, as well as step two—a common monetary authority in Europe to coordinate effectively monetary policies and to influence the fiscal policies of the countries involved.

As to the first point, business conditions in Europe are set to return to much more normal conditions, i.e., a situation where inflationary pressures in Germany brought on by the unification bubble will abate and where the Bundesbank will markedly trim down German interest rates. At the same time, fiscal policies all over Europe will simultaneously aim at a reduction of deficits. Moreover, a modest recovery is expected to take the European economies back onto more parallel routes. This is a set of conditions needed to gradually rebuild stability in the EMS; this will probably come about through a successive narrowing of the gaping intervention limits of today toward narrower margins built around central parities that have been maintained during the recent turmoils. However, this is not sufficient to reinstall stability dependably. This takes us to the second point.

The lack of full central bank cooperation in Europe along the lines followed by the U.S. Federal Reserve System must be regarded as the most important institutional "fault line" of the

EMS. This is hard to overcome completely as long as national central banks remain accountable to their national jurisdictions alone; short of a European Central Bank, however, institutional changes may create a platform for much closer, much more effective central bank cooperation. These are further steps toward monetary integration laid down in the Maastricht Treaty to be taken by January of 1994 when "Stage 2" of the EMU process is set to begin.

Most important is the setting up of the European Monetary Institute (EMI), which is to lay the foundation for monetary union and for the operation of the future European Central Bank (ECB). Additionally, in "Stage 2" member central banks wishing to participate in EMU are required to become independent.

The significance of this institutional move is that the European Monetary Institute is entrusted with an essential preparatory task: its duty will be to supervise and coordinate all the measures required from member countries to ensure full economic convergence on the eve of monetary union. In the domain of monetary policy, its powers will be limited to making recommendations to member central banks, but these could be very forceful recommendations indeed, if only for their potential impact on capital markets and the public at large. All the more, the EMI could very well provide a roof for the close cooperation of a nucleus of independent EC central banks, which could rebuild the EMS to a stable system with a core of coherent currencies. The European Monetary Institute should thus be watched closely: it could turn out to be the first step to eliminating the most important institutional "fault line" of the current EMS.

✗ Building one currency for all of Europe is still going to require an immeasurable quantity of foresight, courage, and action on the part of all parties concerned. Still, Europe may be more advanced toward a single currency than many observers believe. If countries can achieve the low inflation criterion (an expectation that would seem to be justified for the foreseeable future), we shall soon see a general relaxation of monetary policies all over Western Europe and a convergence of interest rates on a lower level. At the same time, the tightening of fiscal policies, required for many countries to comply with the joint criteria of Maastricht, will become mandatory *and* possible as cyclical deficits of decline. This could turn out to be the environment in which a more stringent, institutionalized cooperation can take hold. While political problems have been the reason for past and present troubles on the European currency markets (a collective retreat from the exigencies of monetary union in Europe), the political commitment to sound (and identical) monetary and fiscal goals has essentially remained intact; and as these goals come back into reach, it becomes much less problematic to coordinate effectively national policies via supranational institutions. The name of the game will continue to be convergence and, as it happens, the rebasing of fixed parities and the restoration of stable exchange rates, which are prerequisite for a common currency, will become technically possible and politically feasible again. When will this happen? Effective dates are immaterial, only conditions count. And as these conditions are not at all beyond the horizon, it may still happen sooner than later ...

One often says, "the darkest hour is just before dawn." With regard to the European Monetary Union, one cannot base confidence on aphorisms of this sort alone. But experience tells us that politicians respond to crises (and sometimes only to crises), and the EC should thus be expected to react with new initiatives to the recent shake-up of the EMS. European integration, including monetary integration, has entailed a history of successes and setbacks. The process of integration has often stalled, but it has never been reversed. So let us by no means forget all about those E-words; let us not, as Europeans, abandon the quest for a common currency as the adequate means of payment in a common market; let us not, as Europeans as well as Non-Europeans, be misled by Europe's troubles on its way to closer integration (the absence of which would have been the real wonder!) to discount the European Community as an obsolete blueprint! Instead, what is called for when one assesses Europe's monetary future is insights and patience on the part of observers, and perseverance on the part of participants: insights into the true benefits of running (part of) the old continent on a single currency; patience with regard to watching the progress of this justified but ambitious effort; and perseverance in making it happen.

8

The European Economic and Monetary Union
Economics and Politics

♦ ♦ ♦ ♦ ♦ ♦

Elke Thiel

The Significance of the EMU in the Overall Process of European Unification

A Retrospect

"Europe se fera par la monnaie ou se ne fera pas!"
"Europe will be united through money or it will not be united!"

Jacques Rueff, a monetary expert and adviser to the French government, made this statement in 1950. It was the year in which Robert Schuman, then French foreign minister, delivered his proposal for the creation of the European Community for Coal and Steel, the first of the three communities that shaped the EC. The preeminent objective was to reconcile Germany and France after a long history of rivalries and wars. Four other European neighbors joined the coal and steel project: the Benelux countries and Italy. These were the countries that later assumed a pivotal role in the evolution of West European integration.

European unification was a distant vision in the early fifties and the next step was a failure initially. The European Defense Community, which was to be complemented by a European Political Union, did not receive approval in the French parliament in 1954. The lesson was that approaching European unification directly via federal institutions and high-level politics—such as defense—was not yet feasible.

In 1957, therefore, the fathers of the Treaty of Rome adopted a more indirect approach. The basic idea was that Europe should be built up gradually from the bottom by market integration. The European Economic Community (EEC) was launched on 1 January 1958 with the objective of creating the Common Market with free movement for persons, goods, services, and capital.

Community aims, however, have never been confined to market integration alone. The EEC was not founded to become a free trade area like EFTA or NAFTA. Instead, the overall objective was to promote political unification by integrating the European economies. Accordingly, the legal and institutional framework of the Community contains supranational elements, distinguishing it from all other international organizations.

The Treaty of Rome also includes a clause for evolution should common activities be extended to areas not covered by the initial treaty. Based on Article 236, the Community so far has seen two fundamental revisions of the founding treaties. The first treaty amendment, the European Single Act, came into force on 1 July 1987. The Treaty of Maastricht, officially called Treaty on European Union, is the second substantial amendment.

X   The European Economic and Monetary Union (EMU) is a key element on the Community's path from market integration toward political unification. Although the EMU was not an explicit goal of the Treaty of Rome, the issue already came into focus during the European Summit at The Hague in December 1969. The Custom Union, i.e., the elimination of all tariffs within the EC, was completed at this time, one-and-a-half years ahead of schedule. In line with the strategy of the founding fathers to advance political unification via economic integration, approaching the EMU was considered a subsequent step.

In the Hague, EC heads of state and government agreed to implement the EMU in 1980 and to transform their countries' overall relationships into a European Union by that year. This sounds familiar: the evolution of the European Union is the overall objective of the Treaty of Maastricht and the Economic and Monetary Union is a significant step in this endeavor.

The Community still consisted of six members in 1969, but its first enlargement was in sight. The Hague summit gave a green light for entrance negotiations and Great Britain, Denmark, and Ireland joined the EC on 1 January 1973. On the eve of the enlargement, however, the Community of Six had reconfirmed its willingness that West European unification should go beyond the markets.

Great Britain has traditionally favored a less committing approach toward European integration, more in line with free trade arrangements. Divergences between the British and other members' views regarding the political destination of the EC did not matter so much in the seventies, when the Community moved very slowly. However, since the Community has tackled the single currency issue, it has become obvious that these differences still exist.

✗ One Market—One Currency

As is well-known, the first approach toward the EMU failed because member states pursued rather divergent economic policies that were unsuitable for pegging currencies together. The internal market, a central ingredient of the EMU, remained incomplete as well. Circumstances became more encouraging during the second half of the eighties, however.

The European Monetary System, a system of fixed—though adjustable—exchange rates, founded in 1979 by a German-French initiative, had been very successful. It had advanced convergence in economic performance and policies among its members. The Community had launched the internal market program, to be completed on 1 January 1993, and had introduced reforms that rendered the project feasible.

Bearing in mind that market unification had always been viewed as an intermediate goal in the overall evolution of the Community, particularly by its founding members, it was not much of a surprise that the objective of a single European currency surfaced once again. Although delicate, the EMU seemed to be achievable and would further the momentum of the internal market.

In June 1988, the European Council, meeting in Hanover, established the so-called Delors Committee, with the mandate to investigate and recommend steps for implementing the European Economic and Monetary Union.[1] The initiative came from the then German foreign minister Hans Dietrich Genscher, and French-German cooperation helped to advance the project.

Implementing the Economic and Monetary Union is high politics. A single European currency certainly offers numerous advantages.[2] It will enhance the benefits of the internal market by eliminating transaction costs among national currencies. It will save money for European businesses and tourists and, of course, for American businesses in Europe as well.

A common currency will make European economies less vulnerable than they used to be to disturbances emanating from the global monetary system. It will improve the Community's ability to pursue its intrinsic economic priorities and goals more autonomously. In this regard, the Community will become more similar to the United States when it achieves the EMU.

In the final stage of the EMU, however, member states will have to transfer sovereignty in monetary policy to a common institution, the European Central Bank. The economic prosperity, welfare and social peace of a country depend to a large extent on the conduct of its monetary policy. Adopting a single currency will link the fates of member states closely together. Such a far-reaching and irreversible step cannot be justified by economic gains alone; it must be based on broader political considerations and goals. Therefore, it is very important to understand that the political rationality of the Economic and Monetary Union derives from the overall objective of proceeding further with European unification.

1. Committee for the Study of Economic and Monetary Union, Report on Economic and Monetary Union in the European Community, April 12, 1989.

2. See also Commission of the European Communities, Directorate-General for Economics and Financial Affairs, "One Market, One Money: An Evaluation of the Potential Benefits and Costs of Forming an Economic and Monetary Union." *European Economy*, October 1990, no. 44.

The Political Union

The Treaty of Maastricht results from two intergovernmental conferences, one that negotiated the EMU and the other that was to negotiate the Political Union. While the treaty is very elaborate on the EMU, it remains rather preliminary on the Political Union. This is partly due to the functional approach toward European unification, assumed with the Treaty of Rome, i.e., the strategy to advance the Community gradually, starting with the markets and the economies.

Moreover, the EMU conference had a clearly defined mandate and was well-prepared. The conference on the Political Union had to find out how much progress was possible in a "residuum" of various matters covering institutional reforms as well as new fields of common activities. Regarding its far-reaching implications, the treaty had to be comprehensive and solid with respect to the EMU. While EMU negotiations could benefit from common experiences in the European Monetary System, the conference on the Political Union had to move into rather new territories, such as a Common Foreign and Security Policy and Cooperation on Justice and Home Affairs.

In these realms, integration is far less advanced than in the economic and monetary field. Although European Political Cooperation (EPC) started as early as 1970, it is still pursued on a strictly intergovernmental basis. Cooperation on Justice and Home Affairs is a prerequisite for eliminating border controls within the EC in line with the internal market. Focusing on visa, asylum, and immigration policies as well as on combating crime, cooperative endeavors have already been initiated on several intergovernmental levels. With the Treaty of Maastricht, these activities have been introduced into the framework of the European Union, but for the present, cooperation remains intergovernmental.

The Treaty of Maastricht entered into force on 1 November 1993, following its ratification by all EC member states. Accordingly, European Union has become the proper name for the European Community. This may be puzzling for many observers, since the treaty does not provide for a clear definition of what the

European Union really is. It is less than a "political union"—if this term is associated with something like a federal state—but it aims to be more than the former EC, which was primarily an economic community. Nevertheless, the "acquis communautaire" achieved by the EC is still the main support of the Union, while its two supplementary pillars, the Common Foreign and Security Policy and the Cooperation on Justice and Home Affairs, remain to be built up.

Notably, the Treaty of Maastricht is not "of" but "on" the European Union which underlines the evolutionary mode of European unification. The treaty shall mark "a new stage in the process of creating an ever closer union among the people of Europe" (Art. A). Like the Treaty of Rome, it is intended to be a starting point, not a point of arrival. Negotiations for additional treaty revisions are already scheduled for 1996.

The agenda for 1996 is manifold. It includes specific issues such as advancement from the present intergovernmental cooperation toward more efficient forms of common decisionmaking on the part of the second and third pillars of the Union, as well as an overall strengthening of the Union's institutions. The latter is of particular importance since the Union faces a new round of enlargement. Without fundamental institutional reforms, a European Union of sixteen or more members would lose the capability to act.

All the issues are very delicate, and much effort will be required in order to achieve progress. If the Union proceeds, "Europe 1996" could become a new catchword for forthcoming academic conferences. In any case, "Europe 1996" can be viewed as a test for the evolutionary potential of the European Union.

Challenges

Since Maastricht was signed in February 1992, the Community has run into several difficulties. The Danish voted against the treaty in the first referendum in June 1992, though by a small margin. This problem was solved by some concession to the

Danish[3] and a pro-Maastricht vote in the second referendum. Yet, although the treaty was finally approved by all the member states, the Maastricht debate revealed discomfort among the population. Individual states and regions suspect that Brussels will assume too much power and that they may lose their national identity in the Union.

Subsidiarity has become the key word for distributing responsibility within the European Union, with the view that the Union shall only act on matters that cannot be properly dealt with on the regional or nation-state level.[4] How this principle will be applied in practical terms, however, could easily become a source of conflicts between the Union and its members as well as within the member states themselves.

On the German part, for instance, the Bundestag and the Bundesrat have used the ratification of the Maastricht Treaty in order to strengthen their right to participate in formulating German politics with respect to the European Union. The Bundesverfassungsgericht, the German constitutional court, has rejected complaints against the Treaty of Maastricht. Yet it has emphasized that the principle of subsidiarity has to be strictly obeyed and that the court will pay close attention to it. Moreover, according to the sentence of the German constitutional court, the European Union is still a Staatenverbund (confederation) wherein the nation-states are the main source of power and legitimacy. With this clarification, the court refused the complaint that Germany would cease to be an individual state when it joins the Union, a step not covered by constitutional law. Of course, this judgment does not rule out the Union's evolution into a federation in a longer-term perspective. However, like any previous institutional changes, this would require a new treaty that would have to be ratified by the member states. And more than one treaty amendment will probably have to occur before the Union reaches its final stage.

---

3. At the European summit in Edinburgh in December 1992, Denmark ensured an opting-out clause for the final EMU and for its participation in the evolution of a common defense policy.

4. See also George Bermann's paper on subsidiarity in this volume.

Uneasiness with the European Union is being spurred by an economic recession in all the member states. Advantages of economic growth, promised by the internal market project, are not immediately apparent. The European Monetary System, which used to be considered a success, has run into several currency crises, starting in September 1992. There is no reason to assume that the national economies would have performed better without the internal market and the EMS—the problems would likely have been even more severe. It also holds that economic and monetary policy is still the responsibility of the member states. Nevertheless, failures tend to be blamed on the Community or the European Union, respectively, primarily because rising expectations have not been fulfilled.

Regaining people's support can thus be viewed as the main challenge facing the Union. This applies to its economic performance as well as to its ability to achieve further reforms. Regarding their experiences with Maastricht, governments will have to be very cautious to ensure that the next treaty amendment will be more appealing to their constituencies. In this respect, establishing a proper balance of power between the Union, the nation-states, and the regions in line with subsidiarity should be one aspect. Yet subsidiarity should not be applied one-sidedly. If member states could, for instance, agree on a common foreign policy, a major topic for the 1996 negotiations, then this would enable them to act more forcefully than they could unilaterally.

The central question is whether the Union can keep alive the momentum that has promoted European integration since the middle of the eighties. The Economic and Monetary Union is a crucial issue in this regard.

The Framework of the EMU

The stability-oriented approach

In order to gain public approval, the single European currency has to become a strong currency in terms of price stability. This holds true for the German population, anxious not to give up the mark for a less stable currency. But it applies to other member states as well, since they have successfully combated inflation in recent years down to levels below the current German performance.

Maastricht creates the legal and institutional framework that should ensure price stability within the EMU. The basic provisions as follows.

First, the priority of monetary policy is to maintain price stability (Art. 105). In order to pursue this goal without any interference by national governments or EC institutions, the new European monetary authority will be politically independent. The treaty strictly prohibits any attempt by political authorities to influence the members of the decisionmaking body of the European Central Bank or of the national central banks (Art. 107). Decisions on the exchange rate with respect to third currencies have to be taken by the Council in close consultation with the Central Bank in "an endeavor to reach consensus consistent with the objective of price stability" (Art. 109).

Second, member states are obliged to conduct fiscal policy so as not to undermine monetary stability. They shall avoid excessive public deficits and debts. A procedure for multilateral surveillance, including sanctions, is aimed at enforcing the rule (Art. 104 c). Financing public debts by the European or the national central banks is strictly prohibited (Art. 104). This treaty provision can also be seen as a denial of Keynesian-style policies, applied by some EC member states in the seventies, when the first attempt to create the EMU failed.

Finally, member states have to qualify for the final EMU through a set of criteria specified in the treaty (Art. 109j). They will have to prove that they have achieved price stability and fiscal stability sufficient for the final EMU.

The qualification criteria for the final EMU are:

- The country's inflation rate shall not "exceed by more than 1.5 percentage points that of, at most, the three best performing member states in terms of price stability."

- The member state shall not be the subject of a Council decision in accordance with multilateral surveillance that an excessive public deficit exists.

- The member state shall have participated in the EMS exchange rate mechanism with its normal margin for at least two years without devaluation.

- The durability of convergence achieved shall be reflected in the long-term interest rate level, which shall not "exceed by more than two percentage points that of, at most, the three best performing members in terms of price stability" (Art. 109j).

Adherence to the entry conditions is highly important. It should prevent the final EMU from starting with large economic imbalances among its members, which would be detrimental to the pursuit of the Union's stability goals. In fact, suspicions that the EMU may not perform properly derive largely from the view that the EMU is going to be implemented simultaneously with all EC members. However, if the treaty provisions are strictly applied, the final EMU most likely will begin with some core members.

The dynamic approach

The Union's approach toward a single currency can be viewed as a double strategy. It will ensure the stability orientation of the EMU by limiting membership through qualification on the one hand, and it will keep alive the evolutionary momentum in the Union on the other.

Since the preeminent concern is to make the European currency a strong currency, it is indispensable that members conform with the requirements. Yet waiting until all EC member states meet stability conditions simultaneously would delay the project into a far distant future. In the meantime, the Union could lose momentum, and the final goal could easily recede out of sight. However, if some core countries proceed, the project would be kept alive. Member states that do not fulfill entrance conditions immediately may strengthen their efforts in order to qualify at a later date.

Maastricht sets a timetable for implementing the final EMU. No later than 31 December 1996, the European Council will decide by a qualified majority whether a majority of member states conform for the final EMU and, if so, will set the date for its beginning, possibly 1 January 1997. If no date has been set by the end of 1997, the final EMU will start on 1 January 1999 with those members whose eligibility has been confirmed by the European Council. This decision has to be made before 1 July 1998.

For those countries not joining the final EMU in the beginning, a derogation will be applied, but it will be limited to the specific EMU provisions such as the European Central Bank; all other parts of the treaty will apply to them as well. They will participate in the internal market and associated policies, as well as in the evolution of the Common Foreign and Security Policy and Cooperation in Justice and Home Affairs. They will take part in the Union's procedures of multilateral economic policy surveillance. And most importantly for the less prosperous members, they will benefit from the Union's financial funds, which were substantially augmented at the Edinburgh summit in December 1992. Their performance will be tested again, at least every second year, with the view to their eventual admission to the EMU.

Maastricht, in this regard, is not a concept for a Union of various circles. The overall emphasis is on keeping member states together. This also holds for the members with an opting-out clause for the final EMU: Great Britain and Denmark. They can notify the Union at any time that their exceptions should no longer apply.

Prospects

Last year's turmoil in European monetary markets have caused doubts regarding the feasibility of the EMU. What happened?

For many years, the European Monetary System has functioned smoothly. It has provided an anchor of stability for the weaker currencies of the system. Although some experts had, for a long time, recommended a currency realignment, the markets did not expect such a step in view of the forthcoming monetary union. But when the first Danish referendum turned out with a small majority against Maastricht, the markets lost confidence in the EMS, and candidates were singled out for devaluation.

In the course of events, Britain and Italy stepped out of the system in September 1992. Spain, Portugal, and finally Ireland had to devalue their currencies. The inner core of the EMS held together. But the French franc and the Danish crown came under pressure time and again, although economic fundamentals did not justify a currency depreciation. On 2 August 1993, market pressures finally led to the decision to extend the margin for currency fluctuations in the EMS from the normal 2.25 percent to 15 percent.

It should be mentioned at this point that speculation against an EMS currency was not very risky. If it came to a devaluation, profit could be made; if not, not much was lost, since currency fluctuation was limited to a narrow 2.25 percent margin. Yet central banks, obliged to support the currency under pressure, could spend enormous amounts of money in exchange market interventions. The expanded 15 percent margin has thus raised uncertainty with a view to holding down currency speculations.

Of course, a system of pegged exchange rates, permitting currencies to deviate from the central rate by plus or minus 15 percent up and down, may not deserve the name, as many commentators have argued. On the other hand, member states did not really use the extended margin, which is the more significant observation. They did not shift policy toward a less stability-oriented course in order to counter unemployment. This could be considered proof that a precondition for the EMU, namely a basic understanding of economic priorities, is still in force.

Member states are preparing for the final EMU. Stage one already started on 1 July 1990, and stage two is set for 1 January 1994. The main objective of both stages is to improve performance for the final stage. Member states have submitted economic programs that should enhance convergence by reducing inflation and fiscal deficits. Where necessary, measures have been introduced that should render central banks independent from governments, a precondition for participation in the final EMU.

Except for Denmark and Great Britain, no member state wants to dissociate itself when the Union implements the EMU. This also applies to those countries that most likely will not be in the first wave. In other words, members have conceived the EMU as a kind of guideline for their own economic policies. For countries with major convergence problems such as Portugal or Spain, recent currency depreciation may facilitate domestic adjustment as well.

Whether the final EMU will start on 1 January 1997 or on 1 January 1999 is, of course, hard to predict. The early date requires a majority of members to meet convergence conditions, which might not be feasible. The only question for 1999 is who will qualify at that time. For political reasons, the final EMU will probably not come about without France and Germany.

The Atlantic Relationship

When the Union advances with Maastricht and the Economic and Monetary Union, what will be the implications for the Atlantic relationship? There are advantages but also challenges. Americans have come to perceive the European internal market as an opportunity for their own business, and a single European currency will increase these benefits. Yet with a unified financial market the size of the U.S., the European currency will have a larger potential than the D-mark. It will likely become the key currency in Europe and will compete globally with the dollar.

As an economic partner, the European Union will be on a more equal footing with the United States in international economic negotiations and cooperative endeavors as pursued in the current Group of Seven. In macroeconomic policies, for instance, the Union may assume a more independent course from the U.S. in line with the stability goals of the EMU.

The impact of a single European currency for the United States depends very much on the policies pursued. For instance, both sides may follow a domestically oriented course of macroeconomic policies, and tolerate exchange rate fluctuations between the dollar and the European currency. But neither the Union nor the U.S. can neglect its external balance in view of volatile capital markets. They may thus be compelled to induce policies more in line with each other.

Americans have supported the idea of West European unification from the beginning, believing that Europe, speaking with one voice, would be a better partner for sharing burdens and responsibilities. The challenges that need to be addressed by common efforts are tremendous—in Eastern Europe, the former Soviet Union, the Mediterranean, etc.[5] The European Union and its members have already shouldered burdens and responsibilities for Eastern Europe that would otherwise have been relegated to the United States.

There are more tasks ahead. The international economic order is not in good shape, especially GATT. The world economy may not yet be falling apart into trading blocks, but it runs the risk of doing so. The European Union and the United States, along with NAFTA, could prevent such a development by keeping their economic regions open and by striving for open markets elsewhere as well. The fact that the Uruguay negotiations were finally concluded on 15 December 1993 is good news in this regard.

---

5. See also Elke Thiel, "Ein Neuer Atlantizismus in der Wirtschaftskooperation," in Albrecht Zunker (ed.), *Weltordnung oder Chaos?* Baden-Baden, 1993, pp. 262-273 (Internationale Politik und Sicherheit, Stiftung Wissenschaft und Politik, vol. 35).

9
Subsidiarity and the European Community

♦ ♦ ♦ ♦ ♦ ♦

George A. Bermann

The notion of subsidiarity in European federalism labors from all manner of burdens. It seems elusive by nature, commentators claiming that they do not know what subsidiarity means or, if they do, that they do not see in it anything new. At the same, time subsidiarity has been presented at least in some quarters as a panacea for the Community's current malaise. It clearly is not that. Even if subsidiarity has not been oversold, it is almost certainly overexposed, a condition that the present article is unlikely to cure.

My purpose in this article is simply to help make some sense of subsidiarity and even to make a case for it as a Community standard. Thus, after offering a basic definition and rationale for subsidiarity (Part I), I attempt to justify subsidiarity first by reference to the legal and political circumstances that gave rise to it (Part II), and then by reference to the specific functions it may usefully perform in the workings of the Community institutions (Part III). On the other hand, precisely because it does risk being oversold, subsidiarity's chief difficulties need to be explored and understood (Part IV). This is not because these difficulties are necessarily easily overcome, but because their acknowledgment should help lower the expectations that continue to be brought to the subject.

This article was published in *Hastings International and Comparative Law Review.* 17.1 (Fall 1993), pp. 97-112.

The Meaning of Subsidiarity

Subsidiarity stands for the proposition that action to accomplish a legitimate government objective should in principle be taken at the lowest level of government capable of effectively addressing the problem. Though originally an ecclesiastical precept,[1] subsidiarity has been seized upon as a principle of contemporary power-sharing between the institutions of the European Community and those of the constituent member states. More specifically, it posits that the Council of Ministers and, to the extent that they also enjoy decisional authority, the European Parliament and the Commission as well should exercise the power constitutionally vested in them by the Community Treaties and by Community legislation only to the extent that the member states are unable, acting separately or in concert, to achieve satisfactorily the same objectives.

Subsidiarity's affinity to federalism is clear. Like federalism, subsidiarity seeks to ensure that when political entities unite in order to serve better their common ends (be they military, economic, or any other), they nevertheless retain sufficient decisional authority on the relevant subjects so that their subcommunities and populations enjoy in substantial measure the benefits of localism. Not surprisingly, then, proponents of subsidiarity tend to evoke an assortment of virtues similar to the ones that the architects of federalism in the U.S. and elsewhere have promoted. These virtues include self-determination (the right of local communities to select the rules that they deem best for governing their own affairs and their relations with others within the community), flexibility (the opportunity to tailor rules to fit the special characteristics of the community and the facility to modify those rules as local conditions and circumstances happen to change), preservation of local identities (a virtue difficult to define but to all appearances readily appreciated) and diversity (increasingly considered a good in itself, but also traditionally favored as creating opportunities for experimentation and progress). The impulse to safeguard these values

---

1. Quadragesimo anno, § 79 (Pius XI, 1931).

drives the rhetoric of subsidiarity much as it has elsewhere driven the decisions to establish federal structures of government and to devise for those systems specific mechanisms for maintaining a decent equilibrium in the exercise of power between the center and the states.

This is not necessarily to equate subsidiarity with federalism. The practical meaning of subsidiarity depends very much on the content that one gives to the notion of achieving objectives "adequately," "satisfactorily," or "effectively" at the state as compared to the Community level. I explore in Part IV of this article some of the ambiguities lurking behind the subsidiarity formula and I suggest what their resolution may mean, practically speaking, for subsidiarity as an analytic device. The task of situating subsidiarity in the theory of federalism is, however, one that I take up fully in another article.[2]

The Legal and Political Rationale for Subsidiarity

In its brief thirty-five year history, the European Community has experienced a wide variety of political moods, and it has experienced change in accordance with quite different rhythms. These moods and rhythms are of course the subject of a rich political science literature. It is fair to say, however, that by the mid-to-late 1980's, the Europeans had an overwhelming sense of momentum in the Community's legal and political integration; many believed it to be irreversible. This momentum can most visibly be traced to the Commission's 1985 White Paper,[3] which established an ambitious legislative program for completing the internal market ("the 1992 Program") on a scale that the population could appreciate as never before. The White Paper was followed shortly thereafter by adoption of the Single European Act,[4] which, apart from its other contributions, introduced important procedural

---

2. George A. Bermann, Taking Subsidiarity Seriously: Federalism in the European Community and the United States, 94 COL. L. REV. 331 (1994)

3. Commission of the European Communities, The White Paper on Completing the Internal Market, COM (85) 310 (June 1985).

4. 30 O.J. EUR. COMM. (NO. L. 169) 1 (1987) reprinted in 25 I.L.M. 506 (1986).

changes that would facilitate adoption of the 1992 Program. Prominent among these was the substitution in many areas of qualified majority voting for unanimous voting in the Council of Ministers. The change clearly strengthened the Community's capacity to act over the objections of a minority of states, and it permitted the institutions to harmonize, on an unprecedented scale, fields of law long thought to be reserved exclusively to the states. The theory was that divergences in member-state rules, even on subjects within member state jurisdiction and even as applied to strictly local transactions, might represent barriers to interstate commerce and thus to the internal market, and that their reduction or elimination by law was a legitimate Community enterprise.

The Single European Act also amended the Community Treaties to bring new, essentially noneconomic matters into the Community's legislative sphere, including environmental protection[5] and worker health and safety.[6] In so doing, it also raised the prospects of yet further jurisdictional expansions, such as the Maastricht Treaty would later introduce. The Act also formalized the member states' program of coordination of foreign policies.[7] The institutions in turn gave every sign of legislating vigorously within the new fields of authority conferred upon them.

There is fairly clear evidence that subsidiarity is a response to such widening in the Community's sphere of competence. Subsidiarity's first mention in the Community's Treaties in fact came with the Single European Act.There the inclusion of a new jurisdictional chapter on environmental protection was accompanied by a statement that the Community was only to take action relating to the environment if "the objectives can be attained better at [the] Community level than at the level of the Member States."[8] Later, the 1989 Delors Report,[9] which foreshadowed the creation of an eco-

---

5. Single European Act, adding Articles 130R-T to the EEC Treaty.

6. Single European Act, adding Articles 118A and B to the EEC Treaty.

7. Single European Act, tit. III ("Provisions on European cooperation in the sphere of foreign policy").

8. EEC Treaty, art. 130r(4).

9. Bull. EC 1989-4, at 8 (Apr. 17, 1989).

nomic and monetary union, called by name for application of the subsidiarity principle. Economic and monetary union (including an eventual central bank and single currency) was of course among the Maastricht Treaty's most adventurous substantive chapters.

Rather than tag only its most controversial chapters with the subsidiarity label (as the Single European Act had done), the Maastricht Treaty makes subsidiarity a general principle of Community law, one might even say of Community constitutional law. Thus, the new Article 3b, which the Maastricht Treaty specifically adds to the Treaty Establishing the European Economic Community, provides that in areas of concurrent competence "the Community shall take action only if and in so far as the objectives of the proposed action cannot be sufficiently achieved by the Member States and can therefore be better achieved by the Community."[10]

It should not be forgotten that, by this time, the Court of Justice also had established through its case law a number of far-reaching constitutional principles designed to secure the primacy and effectiveness of Community law in the national legal orders, and that the highest member state judiciaries had largely accepted them. These include notably the principles of supremacy, direct applicability, and direct effect. As a consequence of these principles, each and every new Community initiative, whether in the internal market arena or in one of the Community's newer competences, stood to enjoy immediate recognition as supreme and, where possible, also directly effective law throughout Community territory.

Besides constructing a powerful federal structure based on the supremacy, direct applicability, and direct effect of Community law, the Court of Justice also developed a jurisprudence of interpretation and a jurisprudence of remedies that further strengthened the Community's position vis-à-vis the member states. This jurisprudence may be summed up in terms of several different ideas. One such idea was that the grant of legislative

---

10. Treaty on European Union (signed at Maastricht, the Netherlands, Feb. 7, 1992) (EC Office for Official Publications 1992), reprinted in [1992] 1 CMLR 719.

powers to the Community by the Treaties should not be narrowly construed. This result was achieved in part through expansive readings of the Treaty's jurisdictional language,[11] in part by generous use of the implied powers clause,[12] in part by the Court's relative inattention to the notion of the enumeration of powers,[13] and in part by a judicial doctrine of federal legislative preemption.[14]

A second idea that the Court's jurisprudence conveyed, albeit less directly, was that the political institutions of the Community were free to legislate as fully as they chose within the outer limits of Community competence, provided they observed the procedural conditions set out in the Treaties themselves as well as certain very basic and general unwritten principles—notably equality, proportionality and the protection of legitimate expectations. These general principles have played a vital role in judicial protection of the individual against substantive unfairness on the part of the Community institutions,[15] but they did not seek directly to protect the member states themselves from the Community's unwarranted intrusions on their sovereignty.

Third, Court of Justice case law laid great emphasis on the requirement that the administrative and judicial branches of the Member States make fully adequate remedies available to private parties for vindicating the claims they derived from Community legislation.[16] The States' essentially procedural obligation to enforce private claims based on Community law is of course a reflection of both the supremacy and direct effects ideas because

---

11. *See generally* Joseph Weiler, *The Transformation of Europe*, 100 YALE L.J. 2403 (1991).

12. EEC Treaty, art. 235. *See generally*, George A. Bermann et al., Cases and Materials on European Community Law 31-36 (1993)

13. *See generally* Joseph Weiler, The Transformation of Europe, *supra* note II.

14. *See generally* Michel Waelbroeck, *The Emerging Doctrine of Community Preemption: Consent and Re-delegation*, in 2 Courts and Free Markets (T> SANDALOW & E. STEIN, eds.) 548 (1982).

15. *See generally*, George A. Bermann et al., *Cases and Materials*, pp. 129-49.

16. E.g., Rewe-Zentralfinanz eG v. Landwirtschaftskammer für das Saarland, Case 33/76, [1976] ECR 1989, [1977] 1 CMLR 533, [1976] Common Mkt. Rep. (CCH) ¶ 8382.

it serves to ensure the primacy and efficacy of Community law in the national legal orders. But the Court's jurisprudence of remedies also offered repeated reminders that the member states' transfer of legislative powers to the Community and the exercise of those powers by the Community's legislative institutions is only the beginning of the story. Member state agencies and courts are also bound on a continuing basis to ensure that Community legislation, once made, is given adequate effect. Overall, the combination of Treaty-based enlargements of Community competence and the Court's various doctrinal assertions of federal authority produced an important shift in the equilibrium of power between the states and the Community.

Finally, the transition I have described was, as I have already suggested, accompanied by a steady retreat from unanimous voting by States in the Council of Ministers in favor of qualified majority voting. Departure from the rule of unanimity in the legislative process of course helped the Community to accomplish its legislative goals of the mid to late eighties, notably the 1992 internal market program. But from a dissident member state's point of view, the loss of power to block or weaken legislative proposals by the Commission represented a significant political change. States might thus find themselves powerless to prevent the Community from adopting legislation to which they were opposed. That legislation, which once enacted stood to be given the fullest possible effect by the Court of Justice, covered ever-widening fields of law, some of them quite controversial. During debate over the Maastricht Treaty, three subject areas acquired particular notoriety from this point of view: expansion of Community competence over social policy,[17] further empowerment of the Community institutions in foreign and security policy[18] and, above all, the ambitious blueprint for economic and monetary union.[19] The rocky process of national ratification of the Maas-

---

17. Protocol on Social Policy, Treaty on European Union.

18. Treaty on European Union, tit. V ("Provisions on a Common Foreign and Security Policy").

19. Treaty on European Union, adding Title VI to the EEC Treaty ("Economic and Monetary Policy"), and related protocols.

tricht Treaty—particularly in Denmark, France, Ireland and the U.K.—is testimony to the misgivings with which this latest and greatest step in European legal and political integration was greeted in some member states.

Subsidiarity, clearly enough, was a doctrinal response to the Community's new critics. Inscribing the principle in the revised EEC Treaty itself seemed a suitably solemn way of affirming that the Community leaders were not about to efface the separate national identities composing the Community population. Although the drafters of Maastricht left in doubt the question of subsidiarity's justiciability, the European Council (consisting of the heads of state and government) took up the matter at its December 1992 Edinburgh Summit. It there opined that, while subsidiarity would not have direct effect (in the sense of entitling private parties to invoke the principle in support of their claims or defenses in national litigation), it would form the basis for direct legal challenge of a Community measure in the Court of Justice in a suit by a party having standing to sue in that forum.[20]

Given the high legal and political stakes of the game into which it was introduced, subsidiarity carried with it quite high, perhaps unrealistic expectations. Proponents hoped, in reliance on subsidiarity, to apply the brakes to the Community engine sufficiently to preserve some necessarily vague sense of localism, yet without compromising the institutions' political capacity and willingness to continue attending to its essential tasks. A particular problem with subsidiarity, however, is that it tends more to describe an abstract goal than a method of achieving it. This perception could only strengthen the hand of those who considered subsidiarity a politically weak and intellectually thin defense against the European Community tide. Designed to help solve a real problem, subsidiarity needed to be conceived of in real, even operational, terms.

Subsidiarity as a Working Instrument

Even though subsidiarity may, as noted, be judicially enforceable in part, it plainly speaks first and foremost to the political institu-

---

20. European Council in Edinburgh, Conclusions of the Presidency, Annex 1 to Part A, at 4.

tions of the Community. It bids them to take action to address a problem of legitimate Community concern only if the member states, acting individually or collectively, are incapable of effectively addressing it on their own. To that extent, subsidiarity expresses a policy of federal legislative self-restraint. The evident assumption is that if the institutions refrain from acting except when they must, member state and local communities will be left with sufficient freedom of decision to capture the values of localism.

As a political injunction, subsidiarity speaks to a wide variety of actors. It addresses the Commission, one of whose principal tasks is to draft and propose new Community legislation for eventual adoption by the Council of Ministers and, under co-decision, also the European Parliament. It addresses the Commission in its other functions as well, namely (1) exercising decisional authority vested in it directly by the Treaty of Rome, (2) exercising law-making authority delegated to it from time to time by the Council, and (3) administering Community law on a routine and daily basis as the Community executive. Subsidiarity likewise admonishes the Council of Ministers, faced with legislative proposals by the Commission, to confine the Community's legislative interventions to cases where its objectives cannot otherwise be met. To say that the Council should act legislatively with due regard for the states' own capacity to act is, of course, to say that the states, which after all themselves compose the Council, should assess their *own* capacity to act before acting in the Community's name.

Although the European Parliament has not figured heavily in discussion about subsidiarity, the principle can readily inform its actions as well. In fact, subsidiarity should have special appeal to a body whose very mission is to express the will of the peoples of Europe. Whether in rendering purely advisory opinions, or participating in the Single European Act's parliamentary cooperation procedure, or actually exercising legislative co-decision as provided for in many areas by the Maastricht Treaty, the Parliament has in subsidiarity a yardstick for gauging the wisdom of what is proposed. Conceivably, every advisory body of the Community—the Economic and Social Committee, for example—should have subsidiarity on its mind.

For all these bodies, subsidiarity implies a particular mode of legislative reasoning and analysis. It assumes an objective falling within the outer limits of the Community's concurrent legislative authority.[21]Before advancing a Community measure to achieve this objective—and, depending on the institution in question, advancing a measure may once again mean proposing, commenting favorably on, assenting to, or actually adopting it—the institution will presumably consider and assess the states' capacity to achieve the objective through the means at their own disposal. If those means are in fact adequate, the measure contemplated by the Community should not be supported or adopted.

While trying to understand subsidiarity's message as clearly as possible, we should also recognize that it typically implies both a difficult factual inquiry and a delicate exercise in judgment. On the factual level, subsidiarity entails all the usual inquiries, such as whether there is a problem in fact to be addressed and whether the Community has the means to address it. It also entails a factual inquiry that may easily escape consideration in the federal legislative process and that it is precisely subsidiarity's mission to call to mind. This inquiry concerns the capacity (legal, political, financial, technical, or otherwise) of state and local government to deal with the problem at hand. This capacity will be difficult enough to establish, even before having to discount the results to reflect the possibility that state and local governments will not in fact use it, or not use it fully and effectively, or that the performance of state and local government may be adequate in one or more member states but less than adequate in others. The speculative element, which is necessarily present in all political analyses, is positively central to subsidiarity. Even after the facts are in, so to speak, subsidiarity presents more than the usual measure of political judgment: judgment about the efficacy of state action, judgment about the tolerability of a situation in which the states

---

21. (If the objective falls within the Community's exclusive legislative authority, the states have no constitutional business acting even if they could do so more effectively than the Community; if the objective falls outside the Community's legislative sphere, it is off limits to the Community altogether, subsidiary notwithstanding.)

are relied upon to act and fail to do so adequately, judgment about the costs to Community objectives of variations in levels of performance from state to state, and so on.

These operational aspects of subsidiarity received conspicuous attention from the European Council when it met at Edinburgh in December 1992.[22] The heads of state and government assembled on that occasion, which happened to fall during the period of national ratification of the Maastricht agreements, were aware that the European public needed reassurance and not just rhetoric about the future of local self-government within the Community. A first operational initiative by the European Council was to develop guidelines by which institutional participants in the Community legislative process might in the future determine whether a proposal before them comported or failed to comport with the principle of subsidiarity and, on that account, deserved or did not deserve their support.[23] I comment on the specific value of these guidelines elsewhere.[24] Second, the European Council advised the Commission to consult with the member states at an early stage in the formulation of legislative proposals, specifically on "the subsidiarity aspects" of those proposals.[25] The dialogue presumably would acquaint the Commission with the States' own views on the necessity for Community intervention and perhaps even with specific steps that the States might be taking or thinking about taking, singly or in concert, to deal with the subject matter before the Commission. It also called on the Commission to include in every legislative proposal that it might eventually submit to the Council a reasoned statement of its conclusions on the subsidiarity issue.[26] What the European Council was here envisaging may be in the nature of

---

22. European Council in Edinburgh, Conclusions of the Presidency, Annex 1 to Part A.

23. Ibid. at 7.

24. George A. Bermann, Taking Subsidiary Seriously: Federalism in the European Community and the United States, *supra* note 2.

25. European Council in Edinburgh, Conclusions of the Presidency, Annex 1 to Part A, at 10.

26. Ibid.

what we would call, in the parlance of U.S. regulatory practice, a "subsidiarity impact analysis."

Third, the European Council encouraged the Commission to take a second look at all pending legislative proposals, and all proposals still in the initial drafting stage, to see whether they pass muster under subsidiarity. It also invited the Commission to take up the more daunting task of reexamining all Community legislation already in place—and presumably adopted without conscious reference to subsidiarity—to see if it comports with that principle.[27] In fact the Commission had already partially conducted such a review, and the European Council was therefore able to announce at Edinburgh the Commission's withdrawal or modification of a certain number of still pending proposals. The exercise doubtless reinforces the idea that subsidiarity means something and that it counts.[28]

Fourth, the European Council directed a number of specific suggestions to the Council of Ministers. Besides the obvious admonitions, it called upon all of the Council of Ministers' working groups, as well as the Committee of Permanent Representatives, to comment specifically on the subsidiarity aspects of any proposal before them for advice.[29] The European Council also recommended that the Council of Ministers make a separate inquiry and take a separate vote on the subsidiarity aspects of any measure up for adoption (that is, separate from the inquiry and vote on the merits of the measure), but that the decision on both aspects be taken on the same occasion.[30]

There remains to be discussed the role the Court of Justice and the Court of First Instance should play in enforcement of the subsidiarity principle. Let us take first the situation in which the Community institutions adopt a measure despite doubts over the

---

27. Ibid. at 4.

28. European Council in Edinburgh, Conclusions of the Presidency, Annex 2 to Part A, at 1-2.

29. European Council in Edinburgh, Conclusions of the Presidency, Annex 1 to Part A, at 12.

30. Ibid. at 11.

measure's compliance with subsidiarity. One possibility in these situations would be for the Court to enforce subsidiarity rigorously as a procedural principle. By this I mean that the Court might readily, in a direct legal challenge to a Community measure, review whether at least the Council of Ministers (and the Parliament where it also has a decisive legislative voice) made a serious inquiry into the measure's conformity with subsidiarity. (An earlier section of this article detailed what such an inquiry might entail.) This would resemble the "hard look" that some have urged U.S. courts to take in reviewing administrative action.[31] On the other hand, it seems highly unlikely that the Council will ever fail utterly to conduct a subsidiarity analysis or that it will conduct and present one in such a way as to cause the Court to consider it a sham.

That would leave the Court of Justice with only the possibility of reviewing substantively the judgment that the challenged Community measure satisfies the requirements of subsidiarity. Given the profoundly discretionary character of this judgment—which once again entails at a minimum measuring the "adequacy" of State action, assessing the likelihood of such action across the states, and comparing its efficacy with that of the proposed Community measure—the Court will almost invariably consider it deserving of an extremely high level of deference.

In the event the Community institutions decline to adopt a measure, out of consideration for subsidiarity, the opportunities for judicial review are even slimmer. Although the Community system provides a judicial remedy for the institutions' failure to act,[32] that remedy presupposes a duty to act, and in the case of legislative measures the element of duty is almost always absent. Even if it were not, the institutions' exercise of discretion to refrain from acting in the belief that the states are perfectly capable of doing so effectively will certainly receive no less deference, and probably more deference, than their exercise of discretion to intervene. On the other hand, while there is thus virtually no

---

31. See generally Stephen G. Breyer & Richard B. Stewart, Administrative Law and Regulatory Policy: Problems, Text, and Cases 363-93 (3d. ed. 1992).

32. EEC Treaty, art. 175.

prospect that the courts will review the institutions' decision not to legislate, the political operation of subsidiarity as I have described it above offers some hope that the institutions will be able to correct on their own the errors they make in this direction. A decent subsidiarity analysis by the political branches should leave a fairly clear record of the elements of fact and judgment upon the basis of which they decided not to act. This record may become the yardstick for determining whether the States in fact eventually acted effectively to address the problem at hand, and it may contain a recipe for federal action on a deferred basis should such action prove to be necessary.

Despite the practical limitations of judicial review, it is highly desirable that subsidiarity be considered a justiciable principle. Justiciability should promote subsidiarity's being taken seriously by the political branches. It will also enable the Court to intervene in the truly exceptional case in which those branches in fact egregiously ignore subsidiarity as a procedural or substantive mandate. Overall, however, judicial review cannot be heavily counted on as the mechanism for making subsidiarity work. We thus return to the hope that the political institutions will in fact genuinely ask the questions that subsidiarity raises and that they will genuinely act in the legislative process upon the conclusions to which their inquiries and analyses lead them.

The Limits of Subsidiarity

Defining, justifying, and operationalizing subsidiarity are all necessary if the principle is to be taken at all seriously by the Community at the present juncture. This will not, however, necessarily suffice to dispel the doubts surrounding the notion. Subsidiarity itself has significant limitations as a principle of legislation for a federal state. Subsidiarity's most severe limitations stem from its neglect of other legitimate factors of legislative judgment. Those factors may be, like subsidiarity itself, peculiar to systems based on power-sharing and may help shape such a overall federalism balance. Other factors may be of the sort that all federal systems, federal and non-federal alike, ought to take seriously. In this section I describe only briefly what seem to me the prime examples of these shortcomings on subsidiarity's part. I develop them much more fully elsewhere.

A. Subsidiarity and the Internal Market

As previous sections have shown, subsidiarity presupposes the existence of a regulatory objective over which both the Community and the member states have a claim to competence. Subsidiarity then guides the institutions in determining whether Community intervention is needed in order to satisfactorily achieve that objective. The newer Community competences—environmental policy, occupational safety and health, consumer protection, economic and monetary policy, to name the more prominent—are ones in which it is relatively easy to imagine the institutions asking subsidiary's questions and acting (to the extent they can tell) as subsidiarity suggests.

Ironically, subsidiarity cannot possibly work this smoothly when the institutions pursue the Community's original and core purpose, which was and probably still is construction of an internal market in which persons, goods, services and capital move freely across member state borders.[33] In legislating aspects of the common market—for example, in harmonizing member state rules on the packaging of goods or the licensing of professions—the Community's central purpose is not so much the adoption of a specific policy as the creation of an orderly and consistent regulatory environment. If the Community were seeking to maximize the orderliness and consistency of the internal market, it would impose uniform standards and rules. More often though, especially under its "new approach to harmonization,"[34] the Community only pursues agreement on the essential regulatory requirements and, instead of demanding uniformity on the part of the states, tends to prefer the mutual recognition of different national standards provided they meet those essentials. The point is that the principal legislative questions to be decided in con-

---

33. EEC Treaty, arts. 2, 3(a)-(c).

34. Council Resolution of May 7, 1985, 85/C 136/01, 28O.Journal of the European Community (NO.C 136) 1 (1985)

structing the internal market—whether the rules on a given subject need to be harmonized, to what extent uniformity in those
rules is desirable, how much national variation to accept and on
what issues, and what the content of the harmonized Community
standards themselves should be—are not ones to which subsidiarity, at least as defined up to now, is very responsive. They
cannot be answered meaningfully in terms of the states' capacity
to deal adequately with a regulatory problem because the regulatory problem is not itself the issue. The issue is whether and to
what extent the Community's unquestioned interest in creating
and improving the common market justifies restricting the states'
otherwise unfettered right to regulate whatever regulatory problem is at hand.

Judgments about the need for and content of internal market
legislation thus turn essentially on whether the gains in the functioning of the common market produced by such legislation are
sufficient to justify the resulting curtailment of the policymaking
freedom of the states to act in areas basically within their jurisdiction. The analysis, not coincidentally, is very much like the
analysis one might expect Congress to make before deciding to
use its Interstate Commerce Clause powers to regulate, in the
interest of unburdening interstate commerce, a subject otherwise within the legislative competence of the states.

It is consequently unrealistic to expect that the Council or
Commission will find subsidiarity to be much help in determining
whether the burdens on interstate commerce flowing from the
states' separate regulation of an issue justify the enactment of legislation on that issue at the Community level. Market uniformity
is simply not a value that subsidiarity is capable of measuring.
Community policymakers will have to approach issues of that
sort with a quite different set of analytic tools, and it is to be
hoped that subsidiarity will not get in the way.

B. Subsidiarity and other Principles of Legislative Judgment

The preceding section shows that, even if we limit our inquiry to
federal systems, the standards for judging the proper scope of
federal legislative action may well differ according to how we

frame the federalism issue. Subsidiarity states a perfectly intelligible principle for allocating responsibilities between the federal government and the states in the regulation of a subject matter within their concurrent competence. It does not, however, aid us significantly in determining when the states' freedom to regulate a subject matter within their competence should be curtailed in the interest of unburdening interstate commerce.

Subsidiarity's limitations become all the more apparent when we consider that the choice between regulating at the federal or the state level may also properly be influenced by considerations that have nothing much to do with federalism at all, but that properly guide legislative judgment in all systems whether federal in structure or not. Legislatures can consult a variety of principles of legislative judgment in determining whether and, if so, in what form to intervene. "Proportionality" is the example of a legislative yardstick that comes most readily to mind because of its prominence both in Court of Justice jurisprudence and in academic literature on the Community generally.

The doctrine of proportionality basically requires that government measures (1) bear a reasonable relation to a legitimate governmental purpose, (2) produce benefits that outweigh the corresponding costs and, most important for our purposes, (3) represent the least burdensome or intrusive alternative among the various governmental means that were available.[35] Necessarily general in formulation, proportionality nevertheless expresses the most widely-accepted set of guidelines in Europe for the exercise of legislative discretion and for the conduct of judicial review of those exercises of legislative discretion that are made. The doctrine seeks in essence to guarantee that government acts rationally in a plurality of ways.

When we hold subsidiarity and proportionality up to the light together, we see how easily pursuit of the one may actually foil attainment of the other. For example, it might be the case that the purposes for which a federal-level measure is contemplated could also adequately be served by a measure taken at the state or local

---

35. See generally, GEORGE A. BERMANN et al., see above note 12, at 129-33.

level. Under these circumstances, the doctrine of subsidiarity would ordinarily point to state or local level, and not to federal - level action. We may safely assume that, in bowing to subsidiarity, federal authorities would also be heeding the first two require- ments of proportionality; unless the state or local measure is rationally related to the purpose to be served, and unless its ben- efits outweigh its costs, the measure can hardly be described as "adequate" within the meaning of the subsidiarity doctrine. But the third requirement of proportionality is more difficult to meet, for the simple reason that the state or local measure may simply not be the least drastic means available for achieving the stated purpose; the federal measure, which subsidiarity normally prefers, may have that particular advantage in its favor.

In other words, the doctrines of subsidiarity and proportion- ality, taken in their ordinary senses, may easily operate at cross– purposes in the same case. It is of course possible to escape the tension by refusing to consider a state measure as "adequate" for subsidiarity's purposes unless it is also the least drastic means available, in accordance with proportionality's final demand. But this would amount to overloading the term "adequate" within the meaning of the subsidiarity principle and, in the process, severely weakening subsidiarity as an instrument of localism.

It is not my goal here to navigate a path between subsidiarity and proportionality that will satisfy them both. That is a topic for another day. But it is my view that, if subsidiarity is allowed to accomplish too fully its relatively narrow purpose of confining Community legislation to matters that the member states cannot themselves adequately treat, it may leave insufficient scope for other principles of allocation of power between the Community and the states that are equally valid and no less important.

Conclusion

Subsidiarity is a rhetorically important instrument of federalism in today's European Community. It also conveys a set of mes- sages to the institutions that may help them avoid legislating on occasions when the member states could do as effective a job of accomplishing the Community's policy goals. It is all the more important that the political branches themselves practice subsidiarity since, although subsidiarity is now widely assumed to be a justiciable principle, the Court of Justice and Court of First Instance will probably seldom find themselves in a position to enforce it.

Subsidiarity's chief weakness is perhaps its own content. As a general matter, it addresses the problem of federalism as if the latter required no more than keeping federal intervention to an absolute minimum. However, even within the Community's own legal tradition, not to mention other federalism traditions, we encounter competing principles that on occasion will dictate different results. I cite in this article the Community's commitment to an integrated internal market and the Court's doctrine of proportionality as criteria that may point in different power-allocating directions than subsidiarity would if it alone were taken into consideration. This suggests that maintaining the proper balance between Community and member state governance for all occasions is a bigger and more important task than any single criterion—including subsidiarity—can itself perform.

10
The Role of the
European Court of Justice
on the Way to European Union

◆ ◆ ◆ ◆ ◆ ◆

Leila Sadat Wexler

Introduction

The troubled adoption of the Treaty on European Union (TEU) has led to much soul-searching about the future of Europe after Maastricht. The seemingly interminable difficulties surrounding the ratification process — the Treaty's initial rejection by Danish voters in 1992, the very narrow French vote and the skirmishing between the various factions of John Major's Tory party in England, the Constitutional challenge in Germany — have left the Treaty on European Union in place, but much the worse for wear. Particularly distressing was the emphasis on the negative that surrounded many of the campaigns favoring ratification: in France, for example, President Mitterand's call to vote *oui* for Maastricht often appeared to rest less on a desire to advance European integration than a desire to battle effectively the American and Japanese economic menace.

It is not the purpose of this paper to comment upon the pros and cons of European Union or what concrete form that Union should take. Yet the secret for a strong and healthy European Community clearly lies in the Community's ability to negotiate successfully the transition from a dynamic of integration that is in effect negative, to one that is, instead, positive.[1] The question that this paper will address is: what role, if any, can or should the European Court of Justice play in such a transformation?

The Role of the European Court of Justice

As originally conceived, the Court of Justice of the European Communities consisted of seven judges, appointed with the "common consent" of the governments of the member states. Each judge served a renewable term of six years, and the judges elected from among their number a President (who could be reelected) with a three-year term. No guarantee of salary or specific qualifications were imposed by the Treaties, although the Euratom and EEC Treaties did require that "the Judges . . . shall be chosen from persons whose independence is beyond doubt and who possess the qualifications required for appointment to the highest judicial offices in their respective countries or who are jurisconsults of recognized competence."[2]

Although the founding Treaties did not specify the nationality of the judges, an informal arrangement of the member states has made it the practice that there shall be one judge from each member state.[3] Thus, the judges depended upon their respective national governments both for their appointment and their reappointment at the end of their six-year term. In practice, their term was usually renewed, and their independence was preserved by the absolute secrecy of their deliberations and the absence of any dissenting or concurring opinions in their judgments.

---

1. For a discussion of "negative" and "positive" integration in a technical sense, see Werner Weidenfeld, "Basic Questions of European Integration," in *The European Community in the 1990s* , Nelson, Roberts and Veit, eds. 1992, pp. 32-33; see also Clarence Mann, *The Function of Judicial Decision in European Economic Integration*, 1972, pp. 37-46.

2. Euratom Treaty, article 139; EEC Treaty, article 167. The Treaty establishing the European Coal and Steel Community did not require that the prospective judges be jurists, but imposed only the requirement that they be persons of recognized independence and competence.

3. See, e.g., Werner Feld, *The Court of the European Communities: New Dimension in International Adjudication,* 1964 p. 17.

The task ordained for the judges by the Treaties was to ensure that in the interpretation and application of the Treaty the law would be observed,[4] and to this end they were granted jurisdiction over a wide variety of cases brought to them as direct actions by member states, Community institutions, or, in limited circumstances, by private parties. They were also granted jurisdiction over a second critical category of cases: preliminary references on questions of European Community law certified to them by the courts of the member states. They would be assisted by two Advocates-General, having the same rank and tenure as the judges, who would not render judgments, but who would issue reasoned and impartial opinions of law on the cases to be decided.

As new member states joined the Community, the number of judges and Advocates-General increased. Their task and jurisdiction remained the same, however, as did their method of appointment. There are now thirteen judges and six Advocates-General. In October 1988, the Council established the Court of First Instance (CFI), pursuant to article 168a of the EEC Treaty, with twelve judges. It was granted jurisdiction over staff and competition cases. On 8 June 1993 the Council adopted a decision, effective 1 August 1993, transferring all direct actions (except anti-dumping cases, whose transfer will be deferred to a date to be later determined by the Council) brought by natural or legal persons to the Court of First Instance.[5] The CFI does not now have any jurisdiction over actions brought by member states or the EC institutions. It also has no jurisdiction over preliminary references. The Court of Justice hears appeals from the CFI on points of law only.

Positive Integration and the European Court of Justice

To evaluate the role of the European Court of Justice in the European Community, one needs to start by looking at the Commu-

---

4. Euratom Treaty, article 136, ESCS Treaty, article 31, and EEC Treaty, article 164.

5. Council Decision 93/350/ECSC, EEC, Euratom, 1993 O. J. L/144 (June 8, 1993). (LEXIS, Intlaw library, ECLAW file).

nity's evolution as a whole. Many of the steps taken in the first phases of the development of the European Community were, in a sense, negative: the removal of barriers to trade, the removal of restrictions on capital, the abolition of discrimination based upon nationality, etc. While I do not mean to imply that these activities did not bring about positive goods, they did not create an environment — either social or political — in which the institutions of the European Community could become active forces for positive social and economic change (to the extent required) in the member states of the European Community.

Much of the current disillusionment with the state of the European Community stems from the problems of psyche and of soma (or structure) generated by this kind of integration. The problem of psyche is essentially Europe's failure to formulate a consensus as to what a United Europe will be like.[6] The structural problems embody a psychological component, yet they are separate: they involve adapting, and reforming if necessary, the current institutional structure in order to carry out the Community's agreed-upon goals. Both of these kinds of problem affect the Court, although often to a lesser extent than is experienced by the other Community institutions.

The Failure to Formulate a Consensus

The role of the European Court of Justice in guiding the EC toward a consensus is obviously confined by the limitations upon it inherent in the judicial function.[7] Nevertheless, defining Europe's goals positively is important, both from the aspect of retaining political support and respect for the European Community, and to provide guiding principles upon which the institutions of the Community, including the Court of Justice, may base their decisions.

---

6. "A sense of community — a consensus on some fundamental values and a willingness to enforce them — is the indisputable prerequisite for a viable legal order." Mann, see above note 1, p. 6.

7. See, e.g., Lord Mackenzie Stuart, *The European Communities and the Rule of Law,* London, 1977, p. 6. As Lord Mackenzie points out, the Court cannot repair legislative inaction or neglect of the Community by the EC institutions or the member states.

The ideas usually cited as representing the original vision of Europe were the desire to secure a lasting peace and prosperity and to fashion Europe into a leader of the post-WWII world. To oversimplify somewhat, these goals would be achieved, according to the vision of founders such as Jean Monnet, through a functional approach whereby economic integration (which would create "real solidarity"[8]) of the various sectors of the Community's member states would be followed by an eventual political integration, one day — maybe — leading to European Union. "Europe" was not presented as a choice but as a necessity; Europe had been devastated by two horrific wars in less than fifty years, providing any doubters with empirical proof as to the correctness of Monnet's views.

While not irrelevant to the present, to some extent these visions are no longer inspiring, as Europeans have come to take for granted their own success.[9] The great advantage of Monnet's vision was its capacity to inspire; but the reality of everyday life in the Community, particularly in times of economic difficulties such as the present, is anything but inspirational, riddled as it is with the minute details of the seemingly infinite numbers of Community regulations, directives and decisions promulgated each year. Moreover, new generations either unborn or too young to have experienced the great wars now take the peace and prosperity that they do enjoy (such as it is) for granted.[10]

The Court has been keenly aware of these problems from its inception and has not remained a bystander. Indeed, most scholars would agree that the European Court has been instrumental

---

8. ECSC Treaty, Preamble.

9. Weidenfeld, *supra* note 1, at 32; Jean Paul Jacqué and Joseph H.H. Weiler, "On the Road to European Union — A New Judicial Architecture: An Agenda for the Intergovernmental Conference", *Common Market Law Review*, 27, 1990, p. 187.

10. Statistics quoted by Clarence Mann show that in the first ten years of the EEC's existence, intra-Community trade increased by 338 percent in comparison with a world trade figure of 89 percent. Moreover, Community trade with the rest of the world nearly doubled, and the GNP of the member states grew on average by 60 percent. See Mann, see above note 1, p. 45.

in bringing European integration as far along as it has.[11] Taking the laconic provisions of article 164 of the Treaty of Rome to heart, the Court has done more with the command that it shall "ensure in the interpretation and application of [the] Treaty the law is observed" than any of the Community's founders might have dreamed:

> Tucked away in the fairyland Duchy of Luxembourg and blessed, until recently, with benign neglect by the powers that be and the mass media, the Court of Justice of the European Communities has fashioned a constitutional framework for a federal-type structure in Europe.[12]

Some have likened the decisions of the European Court of Justice to the judicial activism that came to be characteristic of the United States Supreme Court under Justices Marshall and Warren,[13] which stepped in due to the structural inadequacies that translated into inertia in the other Constitutionally-ordained institutions. The Court has actively furthered the interest of the Community through its articulation of the doctrines of direct effect and the supremacy of Community law, for example, and has thus worked hard to promote positive rather than negative integration,[14] even though this has at times alienated it from one of its most important constituencies, the member states of the European Community.

---

11. See, e.g., Jacqué and Weiler, see above note 9, p. 186; Feld, see above note 3, p. 3; Joseph H.H. Weiler, "The Transformation of Europe", *Yale Law Journal* 100, 1991, 2407.

12. Eric Stein, "Lawyers, Judges and the Making of a Transnational Constitution", *American Journal of International* Law, 75, 1981, p. 1.

13. Hjalte Rasmussen, *On Law and Policy in the European Court of Justice*, p. 61, 1986.

14. van Gend en Loos v. Nederlandse Administratie der Belastingen, Case 26/62, [1963] ECR 1, [1963] C.M.L.R. 105; Costa v. Ente Nazionale Per L'energie Elettrica (ENEL), Case 6/64, [1964] ECR 585, [1964] C.M.L.R. 425. See also Joseph Weiler, Community, Member States and European Integration: Is the Law Relevant? *Journal of Common Market Law*, 21, 1982, pp. 39-56, 42-47.

Problems of Structure

A large part of the Community's current difficulties stems from the inadequacy of its political institutions. In order to win popular support, the Community must eventually wean itself away from its largely intergovernmental structure, in which the Council is the chief decisionmaker, and adopt a more democratic form. European government by benign authoritarianism is simply not acceptable anymore. The TEU recognized this and accorded the European Parliament an increased role, but it did not go nearly far enough (indeed, there have been reiterated calls for reform this fall). In addition, although change was called for, the TEU did not propose any real change in either the role or the structure of the European Court of Justice. Yet, to successfully achieve positive integration, the European Community must probably do both.

Even among those who praise the Court, there is a recognition that there now exist problems that, if left untreated, "will jeopardize the very success story which the Court and the judicial architecture of Europe have been to date."[15] Recently, the institutional affairs committee of the European Parliament presented a report calling for fundamental changes to the operation and the jurisdiction of the European Courts.[16]

The brief summary of the Treaty provisions governing the Court in Part II above suggests that, as originally conceived, the Court was not intended to function as a constitutional court at all, but rather as an administrative court with relatively low prestige and little importance.[17] Although not all felt that the Court's role in the Community would be so limited,[18] this concept of the Court

---

15. Jacqué & Weiler, see above note 9, p. 199.

16. "Parliament Recommends fundamental Changes to Operation, Jurisdiction of European Courts", *Eurowatch* Sept. 20, 1993, p. 1.

17. Rasmussen, see above note 13, pp. 205, 220.

18. According to Maurice Lagrange, one of the Frenchmen involved in drafting the Treaty and an Advocate-General at the ECJ for the first twelve years of its existence, the model used for the Court was the French *Conseil d'Etat*, hardly a body of low prestige. He does agree, however, that the inspiration for the Court was the *contentieux administratif français* and that the Court was to act

would be consistent with the Court's now heavy workload, the relatively short terms served by the judges, and their lack of a guaranteed salary.

Yet, whether or not this was the founders' intent, the Court has, in its forty-odd years of existence, evolved into a court wielding constitutional power, just as the treaties can be said to have been "constitutionalized" by its activities. At present, the Court exhibits characteristics of an international, administrative, and constitutional tribunal wrapped up in one.[19] This requires, at a minimum, that the relatively brief terms and appointment process of the judges be rethought in order to better insure their independence.[20]

This evolution also requires the judicial system of the European Community to be made coherent with the role that the European Community courts do and will play. To do so necessitates examining the Court's relationships with respect to its major constituencies: the public and the "European" legal community, the other Community institutions, and the courts and governments of the member states.

Making the Court more accessible to the citizens of Europe is not a new idea. As the Tindemans Report on European Union, delivered to the European Council on 29 December 1975, stated:

---

as the *juge interne* of the Community. Maurice Lagrange, "La Cour de Justice des Communautés Européennes: du plan Schuman à l'union européenne", *Rev. trim. droit européen*, Janvier-Mars 2-17, 1978, pp. 3,5.

19. Feld, see above note 3, at 37-80.

20. Lord Slynn, one of the United Kingdom's judges at the Court, suggests that this might even lead to a "little freshness in style" and, more radically, the issuance of individual opinions by the judges. Gordon Slynn, *Introducing a European Legal Order* Stevens & Sons/Sweet & Maxwell, 1992) pp. 161-62. The recent report of the European Parliament on September 14, 1993 calls for the joint election of the judges by the Council and the Parliament, to a single nine-year term of office. This would not only act to guarantee their independence, but would, according to German MEP Willi Rothley, provide the Court with "democratic legitimization." *Eurowatch,* see above note 16, pp. 1, 8.

The Construction of Europe is not just a form of collaboration between States. It is a *rapprochement* of peoples who wish to go forward together, adapting their activity to the changing conditions in the world while preserving those values which are their common heritage. In democratic countries the will of governments alone is not sufficient for such an undertaking. The need for it, its advantages and its gradual achievement must be perceived by everyone so that effort and sacrifices are freely accepted. Europe must be close to its citizens.[21]

The Report recognized the need to strengthen the Community's institutions, improving their authority, their legitimacy, and their efficiency.[22] With respect to the Court, the Report suggested, *inter alia*, that individuals should be able to appeal directly to the Court of Justice against an act of one of the Community's institutions infringing upon their basic rights.

This would go to the legitimacy question and, I would argue, should be taken one step further: the citizens of Europe should be able to bring suit before the European Court (or some European court of first degree) to protect not only their fundamental rights but all of their rights under Community law.[23] Article 173 of the Treaty is seriously deficient in this respect, essentially permitting Europeans to bring direct actions against decisions (and not other forms of Community law, for the most part) addressed to them or of direct concern to them.[24] Although it is true that European citizens may raise issues of EC law before their national courts, and through the preliminary reference process receive rulings thereon from the European Court of Justice, that cannot replace a direct right of access:

> the litigant who seeks to invoke Community law, but whose plea for a "compulsory" reference falls on deaf ears in the national court of last instance, has no direct access to the Court of Justice

---

21. Article IV, Leo Tindemans, "Report on European" Union, *Bull. E.C.Supp.* 1/76.

22. Ibid., at article V.

23. Defining the content of these rights is a task I leave for another day.

24. Similar criticisms apply to actions brought by individuals under article 175 or via article 184.

in Luxembourg and finds himself in the unfortunate position of possessing a right without a remedy.[25]

Eventually, too, some thought must be given to the transformation of the European citizen from the passive recipient of EC law to the active formulant of EC law — as the European Parliament grows in power and stature, the ability of the European citizen to use the European Court of Justice to bring about active change in EC law should be considered as well. Of course, transforming the ECJ into a "people's court" could not be undertaken lightly. It would likely overburden the Court (if the Court retained its present form) and would be seen as a major incursion into the powers of the Council and the Commission.[26]

In discussing the Court's availability to Europeans,[27] another problem that must be addressed is that the current Court, even with the addition of the Court of First Instance, is overworked. In 1990, 384 cases were brought to the Court — 141 references for a preliminary ruling, 222 direct actions, 16 appeals, and 5 special proceedings. Three hundred and two cases were actually decided (some from that year and some from prior years) and 583 cases were still pending at the end of the year, up from 501 on 31 December 1989.[28] The average duration of the proceedings increased from 19.9 to 22.6 months overall, and from 16.6 to 17.4 months in waiting time for preliminary references.[29] By 1992, the

25. G. Federico Mancini & David T. Keeling, "From CILFIT to ERT: The Constitutional Challenge Facing the European Court," *Yearbook of European Law*, 1991, p. 1.

26. The addition of the ombudsman position by the TEU is a significant concession by the Council toward improving the citizen's access to the EC, and would remedy this problem somewhat, although it is a much less direct manner of calling the Community's institutions to account before Europe's citizenry.

27. Access is obviously a problem for other litigants before the Court, such as the Community institutions and the member states, as well.

28. *Synopsis of the Work of the Court of Justice and the Court of First Instance of the European Communities in 1990,* p. 101 (Luxembourg 1991). During the same time period, 59 cases were brought in the Court of First Instance, and 79 decided, leaving 145 pending as of 31 December 1990. Ibid., at 130.

29 Ibid., at 102. Interestingly, the creation of the Court of First Instance has not appeared to make a huge dent in the Court's caseload, which, although dipping

average duration had further increased to 25.8 months for direct actions and 18.8 months for preliminary references.[30]

Although comparisons between legal systems are always somewhat hazardous and reliance on statistics to measure "judicial output" somewhat dubious,[31] it is interesting to note that the Supreme Court of the United States, while generally able to dispose of its cases within one year, has complained of a similar trend and has lowered the numbers of opinions issued in recent years from 164 in 1986 to 112 in 1990.[32] Comparing the number of opinions actually issued by the two courts suggests that the judges of the European Court of Justice appear to be at least as overworked as their American brethren, although they are free from the tedium of reviewing literally thousands of petitions *in forma pauperis* and for *certiorari*.

Professors Jacqué and Weiler postulate that the increased workload of the Court has at least three injurious effects. To begin with, it imposes an unfair burden on litigants, who, particularly in a preliminary reference case, must wait an inappropriately long time before a final judgment on the merits is reached. This frustration is bound to be translated into disrespect for the Court and the European Community as a whole. Thijmen

---

slightly in 1991, increased from 284 cases brought in 1988 to 438 in 1992. "Statistical Information", *European Law Review,* 18, June 1993, p. 177.

30. Ibid, p. 177.

31. As Marc van der Woude, a Commission Official, has remarked: "Courts cannot be compared to factories. Their output cannot be predicted, planned, or measured; each case has its own characteristics. This makes it very difficult and hazardous to give a statistical overview of judicial activities." Marc van der Woude, "The Court of First Instance: The First Three Years," *Fordham International Law Journal,* 16, 1992-1993, p. 424.

32. In the Supreme Court's 1989 term, a total of 5,746 cases were on the docket, 2,416 appellate cases (2,032 pending from the prior term and 384 new cases) and 3,316 *in forma pauperis* cases. Of these, 4,705 were denied, dismissed or withdrawn, 79 were summarily decided, and review was granted in 122 cases. The Supreme Court heard argument in 147 cases and issued 129 signed opinions and three *per curiam* opinions. The statistics for 1990 are similar, the Court hearing argument in 131 cases, and issuing signed opinions in 112 of those heard. *Statistical Abstract of the United States 1992* C3.134:992.

Koopmans, a European Court Judge from 1979 to 1990, underlined this recently, pointing out that, unlike national court systems, the EC court "cannot afford to be criticized for [its] lack of
ability to cope with [its] problems [as] the political and psychological basis of the institutional framework is still very frail."[33]
Second, the quality of the Court's decisions is bound to suffer.
And finally, the quantity of decisions issued by the Court may
overwhelm the legal community and possibly dilute the overall
prestige of the Court.[34] This will tend to exacerbate the problems
already facing the Community by decreasing respect for the
European Court of Justice as an institution, and, thereby, for the
pronouncements of European Community law that it makes.

A partial answer to this problem is to accord the Court some
kind of docket control. As it now stands, the Court is one of both
first and last instance on most matters of Community law. It may
hear cases of the utmost importance, or it may hear cases of the
most trivial nature. There is no *certiorari* procedure allowing the
Court to pick and chose; there is thus no real way for the Court
to control its caseload.[35] Cases that do not raise any significant
issues need to be siphoned off so that they do not reach the European Court of Justice.

This could be accomplished in any number of ways: Jacqué and
Weiler have suggested creating a system of Regional European
Courts of first instance;[36] another alternative is to increase the
jurisdiction accorded the present Court of First Instance. As
stated in Part II above, some progress in this direction was already
made last summer. This is likely to continue under the amendments to article 168a made by the TEU, which will permit the

---

33. T. Koopmans, "The Future of the Court of Justice of the European Communi-
    ties," *Yearbook of European Law*, 1991, p. 23.

34. Jacqué & Weiler, see above note 9, pp. 188-90.

35. Professor Rasmussen suggests that the Court should use other docket-control
    techniques (such as ripeness, justiciability, etc.) to restrict its docket, and con-
    sequently its activism. I am not using the concept of docket control in this
    manner, as I do not agree with his assessment that the Court is "too activist."

36. Jacqué & Weiler, see above note 9, p. 190.

Council to endow the Court of First Instance with competence not only over actions brought by natural and legal persons against the Community institutions, but over actions brought by member states and Community institutions as well. It remains to be seen whether this will suffice, given that preliminary references will still be within the exclusive jurisdiction of the Court of Justice.

Another solution (and these ideas are by no means mutually exclusive) would be for the Court to increase its efficiency by streamlining its procedures and availing itself to a greater extent (as the TEU would permit) of the use of Chambers. It is hard to believe that this would substantially improve its output, however. Moreover, any efficiencies thus gained probably could not overcome the even further increases in workload sure to face the Court as a result of further accessions to the European Community, the ECJ's participation in the European Economic Area Court, and the expansion of the Community into new substantive areas.

Geographic expansion brings with it, of course, the possibility of increasing the number of judges on the Court, as the member states have essentially insisted that at least one national from each member state sit on the Court. As a means to improve productivity, however, increasing the number of judges is hardly an ideal solution. It will cause the collegiality of the Court to suffer by increasing the Court's use of Chambers; and when the Court does sit in plenary session (as it is still required to do in many instances), discussions will become increasingly difficult as the number of judges increases from the current thirteen to seventeen with the accession of more states predicted for 1995.[37] Choosing judges on the basis of nationality, moreover, smacks of the kind of intergovernmental structures that the Community is trying to transcend in its struggle toward an "ever closer union." The Parliament's repeated suggestions for a Court chosen jointly by itself and the Council might, if appropriately implemented, represent at least a partial response to this problem.[38]

---

37. See, e.g., Koopmans, see above note 33, p. 24.

38. Under article 30(2) of the Draft Treaty Establishing the European Union, approved by the European Parliament on February 14, 1984, half the mem-

With respect to the other Community institutions, another important constituency of the Court, there appears to be less of a problem. The Court has been relatively responsive and has been a faithful umpire in their disputes. Thus it has sanctioned the Council for attempting to circumvent the legal processes in the treaties,[39] and it has protected the Parliament from incursions upon its prerogatives by the other institutions.[40] The TEU recognized and rewarded this and essentially "codified" many of the Court's decisions (i.e., by granting limited standing to Parliament in article 173). As stated above, the TEU would also allow the Council to expand the CFI's competence by granting it jurisdiction over cases brought by a member state or a Community institution.[41] This will, it is hoped, help to alleviate the current burden on the ECJ.

Finally, we come to the Court's relationship with the member states. This is perhaps the most controversial area of the Court's activities. Enforcement of the Court's judgments has been good — but not excellent — by member state governments, and needs to be strengthened.[42] Jacqué and Weiler have suggested two ways of doing this — using "hybrid" directives and permitting the Commission to bring actions directly before member state courts.[43] The Court itself has not stood by helplessly in the face

---

bers of the Court would have been appointed by the Parliament and half by the Council, with the Parliament appointing one more member than the Council in the case of an odd number of justices. 1984 O.J. C77/41. This proposal was apparently resuscitated in the Parliament's September 14, 1993 report. See *Eurowatch*, see above note 16, p. 1.

39. Commission v. Council (ERTA), Case 22/70, [1971] ECR 263, [1971] C.M.L.R. 335.

40. Parliament v. Council (Post-Chernobyl), Case C-70/88, [1991] ECR I-2041, [1992] C.M.L.R. 91; Parliament v. Council (Re Students' Rights), Case C-295/90, [1992] ECR ____, [1992] C.M.L.R. 281.

41. Treaty on European Union, article 168a.

42. The Commission counted forty-four non-implemented judgments in 1990. *1990 Commission Report on the Implementation of the White Paper*, Jacqué & Weiler, see above note 9, p. 197; Koopmans, see above note 33, p. 19 n.16.

43. Jacqué & Weiler, see above note 9, pp. 198-99. A hybrid directive is a directive with a clause providing that if the directive is not implemented by the end of the

of member state defiance, holding in *Francovich* that a member state's failure to implement a directive already sanctioned by the Court in an article 169 enforcement proceeding could entitle a person to claim compensation for damages sustained as a result of the member state's failure to implement EC law.[44] In addition, article 171(2) of the TEU would allow the Court, upon a request by the Commission, to impose pecuniary sanctions on a recalcitrant member state.[45]

Rather than adopting a "big stick" approach, Jacqué and Weiler would employ reverse psychology to win over noncomplying member states. They would reduce the Court's "activism" by encouraging its review of Community acts for compliance with the principle of subsidiarity, and propose adding another article 172*bis* that would be a grounds upon which a member state could bring an action against an EC institution for infringing upon its competences.[46] While the impulse is noble, query whether the concept of subsidiarity can be a justiciable principle: "From a legal point of view, the expressions and terminology are of a rare opaqueness, although their political meaning may be clear enough."[47]

---

period for its transposition into national law, it will become directly applicable (and thereby similar in legal status to a regulation).

44. Francovich v. Italy, Case C-6, 9/90, [1991] ECR ___, [1993] C.M.L.R. 66.

45. A penalty may not always be an appropriate sanction, however, as member states may fail to enforce judgments for reasons other than mere bad faith. Thus, it may be more appropriate to rely on strategies that would make implementation and non-enforcement more difficult. Jacqué & Weiler, see above note 9, p. 198. Parliament also apparently questioned the utility of this strategy in its recent report. *Eurowatch,* see above note 16, p. 8.

46. Jacqué & Weiler, see above note 9, pp. 204-05.

47. Koopmans, see above note 33, p. 20. The Council has opined that it would not have direct effect but would be justiciable. *European Council in Edinburgh, Conclusions of the Presidency,* Annex 1 to Part A, at 4. In an excellent analysis of the subject, George Bermann casts doubt on the practicableness of judicial review, although he considers it highly desirable that subsidiarity be considered a justiciable principle. George A. Bermann, "Taking Subsidiarity Seriously: Federalism in the European Community and the United States", *Columbia Law Review,* 94, 1994, 331.

But it is not only member state governments that play a role in applying and complying with the pronouncements of the European Court of Justice, it is national court systems as well, particularly through the preliminary reference proceeding of article 177. Article 177, which allows, and indeed sometimes requires, national courts to query the ECJ on points of EC law, has played a critical role in insuring the success of European integration. Although member states' courts may occasionally refuse to make references,[48] the preliminary reference has in general been highly successful. It has been the key to the uniform interpretation of Community law and essential to the success of the Community as a whole. It is also, aside from Commission enforcement actions under article 169, the only means by which the Court can control, albeit indirectly, the conformity of member state law with the Treaties and the secondary legislation of the Community.[49] It is thus a critical part of the legal edifice constructed by the Treaties and fleshed out by the Court.

The existence of the article 177 procedure, however, has implications for many of the would-be reforms suggested above. For example, the *certiorari* process one might envision to lighten the Court's load could leave national courts without guidance on many questions and thereby frustrate their cooperation with the European Court of Justice. And the creation of additional courts, whether regional or specialized, could destroy the uniformity of

---

48. See, e.g., Minister of the Interior v. Cohn-Bendit, [1979] Dall. June 155, [1980], 27 C.M.L.R. 543 (Conseil d'Etat December 22, 1978) and Re Value Added Tax Directives, Case VB 51/80 BFHE [1982], 33 C.M.L.R. 527, Bundesfinanzhof (the highest tax court in Germany) July 16, 1981.

49. The Court has no direct review over member state legislation to insure its conformity with the Treaties — only indirect review through the article 169 and 177 procedures (see, e.g., Trevor Hartley, Federalism, Courts and Legal Systems: The Emerging Constitution of the European Community, American Journal of Cooperative Law, 34, 1986 pp. 238-39. See also Mancini & Keeling, see above note 25, p. 8, quoting Oliver Wendell Holmes, "Law and the Court," in *Collected Legal Papers* 291, New York 1952: "I do not think the United States would come to an end if the Supreme Court lost its power to declare an Act of Congress void, but the Union would be imperilled if the Court could not make that declaration as to the laws of the several States."

interpretation that is today the hallmark of the article 177 process and add another step to what is already a slow process. Recognizing these pitfalls, the TEU did not grant jurisdiction over article 177 cases to the CFI; yet as the Community grows in size and scope, it will soon become impossible for the Court to keep up with the overload.

Conclusion

Although "blue-prints for a European edifice are out of fashion,"[50] let me nevertheless state the conclusion that I have drawn from my research on the role of the Court of Justice: the problem with the Treaty of Maastricht was not that it went too far, but that it did not go far enough, at least insofar as its provisions on the European court system go. This is not surprising; after all, the Court has been one of the Community's great successes and, as the saying goes, "if it ain't broke, don't fix it." There is a certain wisdom in proceeding slowly, even gingerly, as far as reforms of the Court are concerned. But if Maastricht was meant to symbolize the flowering of a new Europe, then the Court, like the other institutions of the Community, needs some new tools with which to tend the garden. That the Treaty of Maastricht faced difficulties in ratification is no reason to hesitate; as Jean Monnet himself stated:

> Resistance is proportional to the scale of the change one seeks to bring about. It is even the surest sign that change is on the way.... To abandon a project because it meets too many obstacles is often a grave mistake: the obstacles themselves provide the friction to make movement possible.[51]

---

50. Koopmans, see above note 33, p. 32.

51. Jean Monnet, *Memoirs,* pp. 61-62 (trans. Mayne 1978).

11
Multilateralism and Re-Nationalization
European Security in Transition

♦ ♦ ♦ ♦ ♦ ♦ ♦

Dieter Dettke

Introduction

Following World War II, Europe went through a long and successful phase of multilateralism. In spite of many setbacks between 1949 and 1992, Europe experienced an extraordinary intensification of economic, political, and cultural cooperation. Two factors in particular carried Europe beyond the nation-state: the experience with a self-destructive form of nationalism in the twenties and thirties and the threat of communism in the forties and fifties. NATO and the European Community (EC) were the main pillars of this multilateralism. In addition, the Council of Europe played a significant role in the legal and political realization of human rights.

The results of over forty years of multilateralism in Europe are impressive. To an extent previously unknown, Western Europe was able to improve its standard of living, establish an elaborate welfare system, and maintain domestic stability and external peace. Even more importantly, this development coincided with the building of democratic institutions in formerly totalitarian societies and with the triumph of human rights. Not surprisingly, however, there were also drawbacks and contradictions: the tacit tolerance of fascist regimes in Spain and Portugal for strategic reasons; the weak criticism of the Greek military junta resulting from a fear of communist advances; and the intolerance and anti-liberalism in Western societies for ideological reasons.

Multilateralism was never and will never be a cure for all social ills. Therefore, we should not pin all our hopes on the concept. However, as an engine of growth and as an instrument to balance interests and reconcile conflicts, multilateralism has become indispensable. In a traditional nation-state system, the impressive modernization that occurred in Western Europe after World War II would have been impossible.

European Multilateralism and the East-West Conflict

In many respects, West European willingness to cooperate on a multilateral basis after World War II was the result of a unique situation. At its core was a fundamental European weakness—Europe's dependence on the U.S. and the threat from the Soviet Union. Although weakened from the Second World War, the Soviet Union was still powerful, at least militarily. Europe's deep fall after the Nazi megalomania resulted almost inevitably in the perception of the Soviet Union as a threat.

European multilateralism was also the best answer to the German question. Germany could be accepted into the European family as an equal partner, with the multilateral structures in turn providing an element of assurance and security to its European neighbors. True enough, the European schism and the German partition were integral parts of this European order. No serious attempt was made to challenge that order because the system was based on bipolarity and a stable overall military balance. Though many people at the end of World War II pinned all their hopes on a one-world concept, their dreams were quickly shattered by Cold War realities.

Under these circumstances, European multilateralism could be only regional in scope. It could not reach beyond the respective borders of the two blocs. In addition, it was only in the West that integration was based on democratic principles. In the East, multilateralism was not founded on public support but almost exclusively on military control and forced ideological unity.

An all-European dimension was first added in the seventies, with multilateral arms control negotiations and the Conference on Security and Cooperation in Europe. While West European integration was thus supplemented by an all-European dimension, fundamental differences in quality and character between all-European cooperation and European Community (EC) and NATO integration remained. Genuine, authentic multilateralism was limited to Western institutions. At the all-European level, the fundamental differences between the two systems could not be obliterated. Security maintained borders and borders maintained security. Europe was divided into blocs, and bloc systems were the basis of European security in the postwar period.

The Revolution of 1989-90

This nexus disappeared with the anti-communist revolution of 1989-90 and the collapse of the Soviet Union. Nothing illustrates the full drama of these epochal events better than German unification, which was not the result of persistent efforts of the West German government or the Western alliance to achieve unification. It was serendipity—a byproduct of the collapse of the Soviet Union and other authoritarian power structures. By the late 1980s and early 1990s, non-Soviet style authoritarian regimes such as that in Chile were also drawn into the torrent created by the revolution in information technology. The worldwide proliferation of electronic media made it more and more difficult for totalitarian regimes to govern against the will of the people. Suddenly, changes that could have triggered another world war had they been a part of official Western policy came about by peaceful means. The eastern borders of the Western alliance were automatically extended to the Polish western border. Western values prevailed in all of Eastern Europe. Democracy and the market economy became the foundations for the new systems of government in Eastern Europe.

To use the words of Czech President Vaclav Havel, the end of Europe's division in the wake of the 1989 revolution was viewed in the East as a "return to Europe." From a different perspective, the importance of Europe's reunification lay in the restoration of cultural unity—or at least the restoration of severed natural ties and intellectual and cultural traditions that had once encompassed all of Europe.

In the West, these same developments were more likely to be viewed as an eastward extension of the Western system and its social and cultural values—a Westernization of Eastern Europe. Some even viewed them as the triumph of the West and the defeat of communism in the competition of the systems.[1] On an ideological level, there was even rhetoric about the victory of capitalism over communism. Whether or not Western victory theories of any kind contributed to the implosion of the Soviet system, there is no lack of theories that assert this view. One theory is that the West simply drove the East to its death by means of the arms race and that the non-workable SDI concept played a decisive role in this process.[2]

No matter how historians view this question in the future, the assumption that a process of self-destruction would have occurred even without Western assistance seems well founded. This process of self-shackling, and finally, self-destruction of the Soviet system has been best described by the late Sir Karl Popper:

> The road to serfdom leads to the disappearance of free and rational discussion; or, if you prefer, of the free market of ideas. But this has the most devastating effect on everybody, the so-called leaders included. It leads to a society in which empty verbiage rules the day; verbiage consisting very largely of lies issued by the leaders mainly for no purpose other than self-confirmation and self-glorification. *But this marks the end of their ability to think. They themselves become the slaves of their lies, like everybody else. It is also the end of their ability to rule. They disappear, even as despots.*[3]

1. See in particular Francis Fukuyama's essay "The End of History," in *The National Interest*, p. 3ff.

2. See Robert McFarlane, former security advisor to President Reagan, *The New York Times*, 24 August 1993.

3. Sir Karl Popper, "The Communist Road to Self-Enslavement," Address before the American Economic Association, New Orleans, January 4, 1992, printed in *CATO Policy Report*, May/June 1992, Vol. XIV, No.3, p. 10. Emphasis added.

Consequences of the 1989-90
Revolution for Security Policy

The crucial element of change for European security policy is the elimination of the East-West conflict as the decisive factor for alliance formation. Bipolarity and nuclear deterrence are no longer the key characteristics of international security, and the danger of an all-out military confrontation in Europe has disappeared.

The most positive aspect of this change is the now remote possibility of a nuclear war in Europe. The situation today is in many ways similar to that just after World War II and before the advent of the Cold War. The crucial question then was how to build the highest possible walls against aggression by using the concept of collective security in the framework of the United Nations. The experience with Nazi policies of territorial conquest in Europe and Japanese expansionism in Asia dominated the discussion. The lesson learned from that era was that a collective security system had to have at its disposal the most effective instruments available for the maintenance of peace. The creation of the UN Security Council was the result. Thus, the main weakness of the League of Nations—the lack of an effective executive body—was avoided in the UN system.

However, the high expectations of people at the time—an end to war and the dream of "one world" associated with the UN system—could not be met. Political-ideological and military blocs developed that did little to create a just international order. But they certainly provided a high level of external stability.

The new order in the wake of the 1989-90 revolution reflects the will of the people to a much higher degree. National movements that had long been suppressed can now develop freely after the collapse of the Soviet Empire. Above all, the personal freedom of the people has been reestablished: there is freedom of the press and freedom of expression.

At the same time, however, mechanisms that helped to inhibit conflicts have disappeared. Iraq's invasion of Kuwait coincided almost exactly with the end of the "Two plus Four" negotiations that put an end to the European East-West conflict, and the military campaign for the creation of a Greater Serbia began in the wake of the Gulf War. A Soviet Union with its old might would probably have prevented or at least controlled such encroachments in the interest of the stability of the system as a whole. A Russia struggling for survival and threatened by internal dissolution was not able to do so. As a result, while "America and its main allies were preoccupied with Iraq, Germany with unification, the European Union with the birth pains of its Maastricht Treaty and the Soviet Union with its own impending breakup,"[4] Yugoslavia began to slide into civil war in the winter of 1990-91.

The Conflict Potential of East European Nationalism

Because national independence movements were the main agents of the anti-communist revolution of 1989-90, nationalism was relegitimized in Eastern Europe precisely at the time when Western Europe was engaged in serious efforts to do away with nationalism for good through the Maastricht Treaty. West European multilateralism peaked at the same time as ethnic self-consciousness and national self-determination over communism triumphed in Eastern Europe.

What long-term effects will this asymmetrical development have on the process of West European integration, and to what extent and to what degree can European unity find its political expression under these circumstances?

The fact that democracy seems to have prevailed in Eastern Europe is a very significant and fundamental achievement for European unity. Most importantly, Russia is attempting a difficult transition to democracy. It is important that this progress continues, as the outcome is so crucial. Experience teaches that democracies do not engage in wars with one another.

But democracy is still faced with serious challenges in many countries—in Russia, Slovakia, Croatia, and the Ukraine, and to

4. See *The Economist,* 26 February-4 March 1994, p. 20.

some degree in Poland and Hungary as well—leaving aside the case of warring Serbia, the only overtly authoritarian regime remaining on the old continent. The recent rise of an almost imperialistic nationalism, manifested in Russia by Vladimir Zhirinovksy, is but one aspect of a problem that confronts all of Eastern Europe—the weakness of and lack of experience with the institutions of the civil society and democratic pluralism. The danger of a relapse into authoritarian forms of government—e.g., nationalist dictatorships—certainly persists.

The current political borders in today's Eastern Europe rarely coincide with homogeneous ethnic populations. There are exclaves (Kaliningrad), enclaves (Nagorno Karabakh) and minority problems in great numbers. Twenty-five million Russians live outside Russian borders in the territory of the former Soviet Union. In several countries they form strong minorities: the Baltics, Belarus, Ukraine, and the Central Asian republics. There is a Hungarian minority in Romania and Slovakia, a Turkish minority in Bulgaria, and an Albanian majority in Kosovo. Every single East European state has a minority problem within or outside of its borders. To use the wording of the 1992 German *Friedensgutachten*, the potential for conflict contained in this situation is "limitless and transcends borders."[5]

In today's world, it is impossible to enforce the principle of ethnic homogeneity on a nation-state level except by forced assimilation, ethnic cleansing, or even genocide.[6] Furthermore, migration creates ethnic diversity even in those nation-states where homogeneity is the official goal. In the past, this has all too often led to the ghettoization of minorities.[7] In Europe, the situation is complicated by the fact that the necessary economic reforms in all of Eastern Europe—in particular the privatization

---

5. *Friedensgutachten 1992*, edited by Reinhard Mutz, Gert Krell, and Heinz Wismann, Hamburg, 1992, p. 6.

6. See Eric Hobsbawm's paper presented at the conference "Toward a Civil Society: Common Dilemmas and Perspectives of the European and the American Left," Washington, D.C., September 1991 (to be published in Michael Walzer [ed.] *Toward a Global Civil Society* [forthcoming]).

7. Ibid.

of the huge public sector—will only be possible in the near future at the price of massive unemployment.

Therefore, the presence of minorities, the economic crisis, and the weakness of the institutions of the civil society all currently strengthen nationalist forces and tendencies in Eastern Europe. The dissolution of Czechoslovakia, tensions in Georgia, Tajikistan, and other former Soviet Republics, the war between Armenia and Azerbaijan over Nagorno-Karabakh, and the crisis in the former Yugoslavia all demonstrate the explosive force of nationalism and policies driven by ethnic rules of order.

The threat of war is likely to increase as a consequence of the ethnic, economic, and social tensions brought about by the demise of the Soviet Union. The situation in the former Yugoslavia demonstrates that war can just as easily be triggered by the attempt to preserve an existing federation as by the dissolution of an empire. If Europe were to be confronted in the former Soviet Union with a dilemma similar to the one it faces in the former Yugoslavia, it would find it much more difficult today to work toward containment of the conflict.

Russia's actions in Georgia, Moldova, and Tajikistan reflect a determination to play a special role in maintaining peace and security in the so-called "near abroad."[8] Furthermore, the Russian reaction to Estonia's citizenship law seems to indicate that Russia claims the right to represent the interests and intervene in favor of ethnic Russians living outside Russian territory.[9] There is even a noticeable change in tone of the rhetoric of the Russian foreign ministry—apparently driven by the increasing sentiment of those who identify reform with the disintegration of Russia. This new pattern of foreign policy behavior is not necessarily a new imperial policy. However, one should not overlook the domestic forces and pressures of the new Russia, too, to search for an identity that transcends the present Russian border. The West could eventually be confronted with a Russian version of a

8. See *The Economist*, 28 August 1993, p. 11.

9. Ibid.

Monroe Doctrine.[10] As a result, the West might not be able to avoid a kind of dual strategy toward Russia—a strategy with the overriding goal of seeking Russian partnership to maintain international stability that might nevertheless be accompanied by elements of competition in an effort to preserve the new political pluralism in the former Soviet Republics.[11]

In any case, the Ukrainian-Russian relationship is fraught with latent fears of a new Russian hegemony. Territorial disputes and the nuclear issue may lead to a heightening of tensions in the future. Although the Crimean peninsula was ceded to the Ukraine in 1954, the Russian government lays claim to Sevastopol,[12] and there is a very real potential for ethnic conflict in the Crimea, with its predominantly Russian population.

In all disputes between Russia and the former Soviet republics— who react rather sensitively to all forms of Russian influence— the West oscillates between its interest in forging a partnership with democratic Russia and its interest in containing Russian hegemonic inclinations by supporting and reinforcing the independence of the republics. In this context, the most far-reaching proposal has been to lend Western support to the Ukraine as a permanent nuclear power.[13]

Fortunately, this approach never became official Western policy. Consenting to the permanent nuclear status of the Ukraine would probably have meant the end of the non-proliferation regime in Europe and possibly even world-wide. A fulfillment of the Ukraine's commitment to renounce nuclear weapons by ratifying the Non-Proliferation Treaty is a crucial element for European security. A policy of the Ukraine seeking

---

10. Ibid.

11. See Zbigniew Brzezinski, "The Premature Partnership," in *Foreign Affairs,* March/April 1994, p. 67

12. See Gerard Holden, "Die russische Militärpolitik und die GUS," *HSFK-Report* 4/1993, p. 7.

13. See John Mearsheimer, "The Case for a Ukrainian Nuclear Deterrent," *Foreign Affairs,* Summer 1993, Vol. 72, Nr. 3, p. 50ff. For the opposite view see Steven E. Miller's article in the same issue, p. 67ff.

permanent nuclear status under the present circumstances could provoke precisely the conflict that all national and international efforts aim to avoid, namely, a military strike of Russia against the Ukraine.

The Ukrainian parliament's endorsement of the trilateral statement signed in Moscow by Presidents Clinton, Yeltsin, and Kravchuk, as well as its unconditional ratification of the START I treaty are both positive steps toward ensuring European security.[14] However, the establishment of a long-term basis for security in the region is contingent upon the ultimate entry of the Ukraine into the nuclear Non-Proliferation Treaty. Although President Kravchuk "reiterated his commitment that Ukraine accede to the Nuclear Non-Proliferation Treaty as a non-nuclear state in the shortest possible time,"[15] parliamentary ratification is still pending at the time of this writing.

The European Union and the Crisis in the Former Yugoslavia

The crisis in the former Yugoslavia, in addition to illustrating the explosive force of nationalism and policies driven by ethnic rules of order, has revealed the inability of the EU to prevent wars and settle conflicts. As a result, the crisis is not only a victory of violence and aggression but also a defeat for European unity.

Regional European negotiation and mediation efforts have failed miserably. For a long time to come, this failure will make it more difficult for European peacemaking efforts in the region to succeed. The European Union has to accept responsibility for pursuing a recognition policy without firm principles and for engaging in peace negotiations without adequate means and morality in the face of naked aggression. Experience has shown that successful peacemaking requires more than opposition to war; one also has to stand up to aggression.

---

14. See Robert Seely, *The Washington Post*, 4 February 1994, p. A1

15. See text of the Trilateral Statement in *Arms Control Today*, January/February 1994, p.21.

Europe's policy of granting early diplomatic recognition to Slovenia, Croatia , Bosnia, and Macedonia and then simply standing by while Bosnia as a nation was destroyed degenerated into a diplomacy that simply invited the Muslim leadership in Bosnia to capitulate to the claims of Serbia and Croatia.

Since the beginning, European peace policy in the former Yugoslavia has been a belated attempt to implement an old-style regional order policy based on nationalism. However, the main weakness of European mediation efforts has been the regional character of its approach, which provided the U.S. with a convenient excuse to stay out of the crisis. Had the United Nations engaged in a mediation effort from the very beginning—with the support and participation of the United States—the Serbian aggression might have been stopped. At the very least, a solution providing a better chance of survival for Bosnia and the Bosnian Muslims could have been found.

It is unlikely that the Vance/Owen—and later Owen/Stoltenberg—plan can be implemented without massive military involvement. Without adequate provisions for a military presence to enforce a future peace agreement, any attempt to preserve a territorially splintered Bosnia would amount to a de facto invitation for Serbia and Croatia to annex the Serbian and Croatian enclaves in Bosnia. The remaining Muslim territories would hardly be viable economically, and it would be extremely difficult to provide them with military security.[16]

When NATO finally and after long and agonizing deliberations issued an ultimatum in February 1994 to Serb military forces shelling Sarajevo, warfare came to a halt, and peace seemed to be at hand for the first time since the peace agreement of August 1993. Also, Bosnian Muslims and Croats moved closer to some form of understanding regarding a binational federation.

An agreement between Bosnian Muslims and Bosnian Croats to form a joint federation was reached in Washington in March 1994 with considerable American assistance and even pressure. If

---

16. See Morton Abramowitz, *Washington Post*, 29 August 1993, p. 7.

Russia is able to help secure Serb approval of a Bosnian federation, peace might indeed be established.[17]

However, there is little chance that the result will be an independent, multi-ethnic Bosnian State. The fact that the Bosnian Croats and Bosnian Muslims seek to create a joint federation on the territory of Bosnia-Herzegovina and that this federation will enter into a confederation with Croatia will increase the pressure on the Bosnian Serbs to ally themselves with Serbia. A confederation made up of Croatia and a Bosnian Muslim-Croat federation has a better chance of being economically viable, but for peace to prevail, Serbian cooperation is essential—and so is a Western commitment to provide aid and military protection.

The Crisis of Multilateralism in Europe

German unification, the revival of nationalist and ethnic principles of order in Eastern Europe, and the crisis in the former Yugoslavia constitute the most serious challenges European multilateralism has faced in its post-World War II history. At the same time, Western Europe may have reached a historic turning point.

While nationalism has been newly legitimized in Eastern Europe, the Treaty of Maastricht, with its federalist model, has triggered a wave of regional self-affirmation in Western Europe against an integration perceived as bureaucratic and imposed from above. However, in the EC it was actually the regions—not the nation-states—that gained ground from the excessive bureaucratic demands imposed by the political elites. One should not interpret this development as a wave of rejection directed against European unity as such. The EU regions identify with the goal of European integration, but they want an integration from below rather than from above.

It is for this reason that the distrust of unity by anti-integration movements in Western Europe is directed mostly against their own governments. As the example of the Lega Nord in Italy

---

17. See David B. Ottoway, "U.S. Bosnia Plan Relies on Russia's Help In Croatia" in *The Washington Post*, 21 March 1994, p. A32

shows, this involves a good shot of welfare chauvinism vis-à-vis the less wealthy neighboring regions.[18]

In Eastern Europe, multilateralism is threatened by ethnic self-affirmation. Furthermore, the rift between rich and poor divides Europe not only between East and West but also between North and South.

The most recent conflicts in economic policies and the monetary disturbances leading to wider bands of 15 percent on either side of central rates have basically halted the plans for economic and monetary union—despite the fact that the governments pretend almost religiously to adhere to the Maastricht schedule. The institution of a European central bank and a single currency are now no more than remote possibilities.

In addition, the unemployment rate in the EU is now more than 11 percent, compared to less than 7 percent in the U.S. and 2.5 percent in Japan.[19] Disappointment with Maastricht and the internal market program of 1992 is likely to increase as structural unemployment becomes a major domestic issue in all European Union countries, including Germany.

As a result, the new socioeconomic tensions are the most important reason for the crisis of multilateralism in Western Europe, and it is the new German question that is at the core of the dispute. The German question during the Cold War was essentially a territorial one. The new German question after unification is threefold: it is a question of economic competitiveness, domestic political culture, and foreign policy acceptance.

Germany's economy, in itself largely a product of the common market and of European integration, until recently also served as the engine of integration for the economically weaker members of the EU. The unification crisis has changed this constellation

---

18. See Udo Bullmann and Dieter Eißel, "Europa der Regionen — Entwicklung und Perspektiven," in *Aus Politik und Zeitgeschichte* B 20-21, p. 3ff, and Hans-Georg Betz, "Lega Nord — Ein Paradigma für Westdeutschland," in *Die Neue Gesellschaft / Frankfurter Hefte*, February 1993, p. 123ff.

19. See *The Economist*, 28 August 1993, p. 43.

for income distribution. From the point of view of Germany's partners in the EU, high German interest rates forced the rest of the EU to contribute to the financing of German unification. Considering the rules of the European Monetary System, the EU partners felt that they lost the capacity to stimulate their own economies when the German Bundesbank pushed up interest rates in an effort to fight inflation. On the basis of German monetary policy, Germany's EC partners concluded that the Germans put their own interests ahead of European interests.

In addition to this economic irritation, there is a more fundamental fear of the Federal Republic of Germany among the European partners—a fear that is no less disconcerting for proponents of European multilateralism. In the words of Connor Cruise O'Brien:

> When the transition is completed, the Germans are likely to feel a need to reassert themselves on the international scene as an independent force, and not as a mere component in a united Europe.[20]

If this perception of the effects of German unification becomes the prevalent view among Germany's EU partners, it could turn into a self-fulfilling prophecy and lead to a stalling of European integration even under the most pro-European conditions in Germany. Add to that an increase of Euro-pessimism in Germany and a paralysis of the integration process seems almost inevitable.

Apparently, the days of Euro-enthusiasm in German public opinion are over. Recently, only 17 percent of Germans believe that Germany draws a net benefit from its membership in the EU. Thirty-four percent believe that the disadvantages prevail, and 46 percent believe that the pros and cons are about the same.[21] Germans give the Single European Market equally negative marks: 58 percent of Germans (56 percent in the West and 66 percent in the East) view it as predominantly negative.[22] Although 54 percent

---

20. Connor Cruise O'Brien, "The Future of the West," *The National Interest*, Winter 1992/93, p. 4

21. See *Politbarometer* 9/92 of the Forschungsgruppe Wahlen e.V., Mannheim.

22. See *Politbarometer* 12/92.

expressed support for the Maastricht Treaty in December 1992,[23] the polls on the internal market and the pros and cons of EU membership reveal a general skepticism with respect to Europe.

Finally, the new military structure of NATO has changed little with respect to the independence of the national armies in times of peace. In spite of its multinational structure, the newly formed Rapid Reaction Corps is not much more than the logical result of the general adjustment to a smaller number of divisions. All members of the Atlantic Alliance preserve their national command on the corps level. Therefore, within the Atlantic Alliance as well, one sees a certain trend toward renationalization.[24] The Franco-German Corps may even reinforce this process. Although it was conceived as a multinational force, it will not inspire a new European multilateralism in the area of security policy as long as a majority of France and Germany's European partners views it with reservations or even open opposition.

Future Dilemmas for European Multilateralism

The current transition phase of both NATO and the EU is not without inherent dangers for the future of Europe. Most striking is the lack of a new strategic concept as well as the lack of a general vision for a dynamic European multilateralism that transcends security issues. Drawing historical comparisons with examples such as the European nation-state system before 1914[25] in order to prove the necessity for a balance of power between Russia, Germany, France, Britain, and perhaps Italy is not very useful. This is particularly true if the old concept of balance of powers—based on conventional military capabilities—is indiscriminately applied to current nuclear conditions. History would then predict that neither integration, nor multilateralism, nor nuclear non-proliferation have a future, and that Europe's destiny

---

23. Ibid.

24. See Jan Willem Honig, "The 'Renationalization' of Western European Defense," *Security Studies*, Vol. 2, No. 1, Autumn 1992, p. 122ff.

25. See John Mearsheimer, "Back to the Future: Instability in Europe After the Cold War," in *International Security*, Summer 1990, Vol. 15, No. 1, p. 5ff.

is to relapse into a system of multiple rival powers—a system with all the inherent dangers of a new great war.[26]

Another variation of the same dilemma would be the revival of an occidental pessimism à la Oswald Spengler and the diagnosis that the end of the East-West conflict constitutes the collapse of the West as a strategic unit. According to this view, the historic task of NATO has been achieved and NATO itself has become obsolete.[27]

In order not to become insignificant, NATO and the EU must develop new tasks, a new mission, and a new vision. It would be a rather peculiar irony of history should NATO and the EU face their demise at the very moment of a great triumph of Western values and culture.

Today, NATO and the EU must strive to contribute to the political and economic stability of Eastern Europe. Both institutions must open their doors to the membership of Poland, Hungary, the Czech Republic, and Slovakia. In Poland, Hungary, and the Czech Republic, there have been widespread calls for NATO membership since the 1989-90 Revolution. NATO created the North Atlantic Cooperation Council to alleviate the feeling of isolation of the former members of the Warsaw Pact, and the European Community offered technical assistance and political dialog to the Visegrad countries through the so-called "Europe-Agreements."

Poland and the Czech Republic then indicated interest in full NATO membership beyond involvement in the North Atlantic Cooperation Council. This interest has been satisfied only partially by the recent Partnership for Peace Initiative—an American concept originally tailored more to avoiding new military commitments than to responding to central Europe's interest in an expanded NATO and European Union.

However, there are signs that the partnership process may in the future amount to more than a strategy of buying time. While

---

26. Ibid.

27. See, e.g., Owen Harries, "The Collapse of 'The West,'" *Foreign Affairs*, Sept./Oct. 1993, Vol. 72, No. 4, p. 41ff. Connor Cruise O'Brien, (see note 13) argues in a similar fashion.

U.S. Secretary of State Christopher emphasized during the NATO summit that "participation alone will not guarantee membership," President Clinton made clear during his January 1994 Prague visit that, "while partnership is not NATO membership, neither is it a permanent holding room."[28] According to President Clinton, "the question is no longer whether NATO will take on new members, but when and how."[29] So far, in deference to Russian strategic sensitivities, NATO has reacted with great caution to the requests for membership by Poland, Hungary, and the Czech Republic. Instead, the January 1994 NATO summit should have initiated a policy of enlargement in the context of a larger association including Russia and the Ukraine. An expansion of the EU and NATO should not turn into an anti-Russian alliance. Both institutions must seek a partnership with a democratic Russia[30] at the same time that they support the Ukraine in its efforts to form economic and political ties to the European Union.[31]

The long-term goal of the West must be a European-American Peace Community[32] that includes a democratic Russia rather than limiting itself to ensuring a military balance with respect to the Russian military potential. NATO must now adjust its former, primarily regional multilateralism to the new global political conditions. The limitation of alliance activities to the boundaries of the Cold War makes little sense. If NATO should prove itself incapable of expanding its own area of responsibility and unable to take on new members, it will soon become obsolete. NATO is presently very limited in its ability to provide direct security guarantees; that is more a role of the United Nations. To the extent

28. News Analysis by Jack Mendelsohn, "Clinton Initiatives Find Success in Europe—For Now," *Arms Control Today*, Jan./Feb. 1994, Vol. 24, No. 1, pp. 17-18.

29. Ibid., p. 18

30. This is the suggestion of Ronald Asmus, Richard Kugler, and Stephen Larrabee, "Building A New NATO," *Foreign Affairs*, Sept./Oct. 1993, Vol. 72, No. 4, p. 28ff.

31. Ibid.

32. See Eckhard Lübkemeier, in *Transatlantic Relations in Transition*, Oliver Thränert (ed.), Bonn: Friedrich-Ebert-Stiftung, 1993.

that the Atlantic Alliance is able to combine its activities with the United Nations and to put its military potential and considerable multilateral experience at the service of the UN, NATO multilateralism will have a future.

Just as NATO must now coordinate its tasks and objectives with the United Nations, the EU needs to develop new horizons and a vision that will lead it beyond its current structure and objectives. In the so-called Visegrad memorandum, Hungary, Poland, and Czechoslovakia clearly emphasized their interest in full European Union membership in the future—a membership on the level of integration that the European Union will have reached at the time of their entry. This would include membership in the Western European Union, for example.

As difficult as the process of enlargement may be—in many respects, membership in the European Union, because of the detailed nature of regulations in economic, social, and political matters, is more difficult than the treaty accession to the North Atlantic Alliance—it is impossible for the European Union to reject the unmistakable wish of these countries for admission without jeopardizing its own future. In an ideal world, both EU and NATO membership could occur simultaneously, and sooner rather than later, in order to avoid taking this step under crisis conditions and to minimize the appearance of drawing new lines in Europe.

12
Europe Agreement
Economic Opportunities and Threats for Poland

♦ ♦ ♦ ♦ ♦ ♦ ♦

Andrzej Stępniak

Introduction

The collapse of the communist system in Central and Eastern
Europe has markedly redrawn the political map and political
situation of the European continent. The collapse took the European Community, the Commission, and other Institutions totally
by surprise. Nobody was really prepared, no one had a blueprint
for dealing with the new situation.[1] But it was quickly understood
in Brussels that an opportunity to unify the European continent
had just appeared, and a decision was made to support the former
communist countries' "return to Europe." An important element
of this hoped for return was the so-called "Europe Agreement."

The Europe Agreement constitutes both an opportunity and a
threat for Poland as well as for other countries such as Hungary,
the Czech Republic, and Slovakia.

The possibility of reintegrating with Europe represents the
opportunity; the threat can be defined as the possibility of not fulfilling the provisions of the Agreement. The provisions of the
Agreement (despite the so-called "asymmetry," which will be

---

1. Heinz Kramer, "The European Community Response to the 'New Eastern
Europe,'" *Journal of Common Market Studies*, vol.31, No. 2, June 1993.

described later) must be fulfilled within the period of internal transformation of the Polish economy. One should not forget that this is a twofold threat: first from the side of the EC (integration), and second from the side of the Polish economy (transformation). The EC must support the reform efforts of CEE (Central and Eastern Europe), and the most effective way for the Community to do so would be to involve itself in the building of institutions and to provide access to markets.[2]

Liberalization of imports from CEE countries must include those sectors that have remained heavily protected to date, but those sectors are potentially more competitive in the transitional economies. Since 1989-90, the Community economy has plunged into one of the deepest post-war recessions. Starting in the UK, concealed for some time by the reunification of Germany, it has now engulfed the whole of the Community. This has brought rising protectionist tendencies in the member states and has made the EC even more open to sectoral pressure group influence. At the same time, the economies in Central and Eastern Europe have been undergoing a far deeper depression. Such an economic climate is not conducive to great ideals or magnanimous gestures.[3]

Because the Community is peculiarly open to sectoral pressure group influence in a way that member state governments are not, pressure groups can more easily obtain protection for their interests at the Community level than at the national level. In deep recession this becomes particularly clear.

On the other hand, some member states regard the entry of Poland into the Community as negative for their political and economic position in the Community. These countries see Poland as a potential competitor for both influence and finance. This is especially true of the "cohesion member states."

2. Renzo Daviddi, "From the CMEA to the 'Europe Agreements': Trade and Aid in the Relations between the European Community and Eastern Europe," *Economic Systems*, vol. 16, No. 2, October 1992.

3. Alan Mayhew, "The Current State of the Relationship between Poland and the European Community," conference paper, Poznań, p. 6, May 1993.

These are only a few of the elements hindering the integration process of Poland into the EC. They are presented systematically (according to the subject areas and chapters of the Agreement) in the following text.

The Europe (Association) Agreement

The Europe Agreement is the most far-reaching (excluding European Economic Space) of all the agreements on establishing an association with the European Community because it regulates a wide range of economic cooperation.

The Association Agreement between Poland and the EC[4] is the most important document, providing a new legal framework for the development of cooperation between both parties. From a formal point of view, the Community elaborated a few variations from the Agreements on Associations:

- an "alternative to joining the Community" (on the basis of article 238 of the Treaty of Rome), established for the EFTA member states with strong economic links with the Community that fail to integrate for political reasons;

- association as the initial stage leading to full integration, worked out for those European states that wished to enter into the Community, but whose level of economic development did not meet that of the Community (e.g., Greece in 1967, Turkey in 1964, Malta in 1970, Cyprus in 1972);

- para-association agreements, the so-called *de facto* and *de jure* agreements on assisting development (they are agreements on establishing associations in name only) — these concern agreements with the ACP countries;

- agreements on economic cooperation (for instance, the former Yugoslavia and Israel);

- agreement on establishing the European Economic Space with EFTA.

---

4. Signed on 16 December, 1991.

The Association Agreement between Poland and the EC, signed on 16 December 1991, belongs to the so-called "second-generation agreements" concluded by the Community with third countries. This agreement is called the Europe Agreement to stress the particular importance given by the EC to cooperation with the newly emerging democracies in Central and Eastern Europe. The Europe Agreement has a much wider range and broader objectives than other association agreements signed by the EC. It provides for liberalization of trade, tightening of economic and technological cooperation, financial assistance, scientific exchange, political dialog, and Poland's participation in the internal life of the Community. Among the main objectives of the agreement with Poland is the setting up of an appropriate framework for Poland's gradual integration into the Community. Gradual integration should be built around the mutually recognized objective of Poland's future membership in the Community.

The Agreement provisions deal with the following elements of political and economic cooperation between Poland and the EEC:

a. political dialog;

b. movement of goods;

c. movement of workers, establishment and supply of services;

d. current payments and movement of capital;

e. harmonization of laws, including competition law;

f. economic and financial cooperation;

g. cultural cooperation;

h. institutional involvement.

The above provisions are to be accomplished in the "transitional period," which is to last at least ten years, divided into two five-year stages. The commercial part of the Agreement entered into force on 1 March 1992 as an "Interim Agreement." The whole document will enter into force subsequent to its ratification by thirteen national parliaments and the European Parliament. The Agreement has been concluded for an unlimited period of time. Each of the parties may renounce it by notifying the other party.

Political dialog constitutes an important objective of association. The aim of this dialog is to establish new links of solidarity between Poland and the EC that might result in better understanding of their respective positions and greater political convergence. Political dialog should maintain security and stability in Europe, as well as foster democracy and market-oriented transformation in Poland.

The *movement of goods*, workers, services, and capital, combined with the right of establishment, represent provisions focused on gradual liberalization and creation of *four freedoms* between Poland and the EC. Liberalization of trade and capital movements (plus establishment) are strong concessions aimed at establishing a free-trade area in industrial goods, as well as removing all restrictions to foreign investments. The process of liberalization envisages a certain amount of asymmetry in favor of Poland, as well as a possibility of applying protectionist safeguards. Safeguards applicable in Poland would affect infant industries, industries undergoing restructuring, and industries facing serious difficulties. Market disruption is another argument for protectionism. The European Community, in turn, can make use of general safeguard clauses consistent with GATT.

On the issue of movement of workers the Agreement provisions are very limited and concern the recognition of the status quo rather than granting new concessions. The scope of liberalization can be broadened through bilateral agreements with particular member states of the EC.

The *harmonization of laws* is an important objective of association. The Agreement emphasizes a need for the approximation of Polish laws to Community legislation. This approximation is recognized by both parties as a major precondition for Poland's integration into the Community. The following areas of approximation are specified by the agreement: customs law, company law, and banking law; company accounts and taxes; intellectual property; protection of workers in the workplace; financial services; rules on competition; protection of the health and life of humans, animals, and plants; consumer protection; direct taxation; technical rules and standards; transportation; and the environment.

Economic and financial cooperation: the agreement defines the main areas of cooperation and assistance that are essential to economic and industrial reconstruction in Poland. They are as follows:

- industrial cooperation aimed at strengthening the private sector, restructuring of individual industries, promoting new setups and small- and medium-size enterprises;

- investment promotion and protection;

- cooperation in science and technology, education and training;

- cooperation for the restructuring of agriculture and the agro-industrial sector, the electric and gas sector, telecommunications and transportation;

- protection of the environment;

- technical assistance in the field of customs systems, statistics, standardization;

- financial cooperation covered by:

    a. the PHARE measures,

    b. the European Investment Bank loans,

    c. financial assistance within the IMF supported programs, focused on maintaining the convertibility of the zloty, medium-term stabilization, and balance of payment support.

The Agreement does not include a separate financial protocol on EC aid.

Institutional provisions: the Agreement provides for the establishment of common institutions that are to supervise and monitor the implementation of the association provisions. The Association Council is a major institution that consists of the members of the EC Commission on the one hand and of members of the government of Poland on the other. The other common institutions are the Association Committee (its task is to assist the Association Council), and the Association Parliamentary Committee (a forum for meeting and exchanging views among members of the Polish Parliament and the European Parliament).

Future progress in Poland's integration with the EC will depend on the fulfillment of the necessary conditions by Poland (Article 1, p. 2); this entails a long-lasting process of approximating legal and administrative regulations as well as creating instruments for economic restructuring and macroeconomic stabilization.

The Potential Opportunities

In view of the titles, chapters, and articles of the Agreement, it may be stated that the Agreement covers a wide range in a variety of fields. It encompasses industry, transport, commerce, tourism, services, employment, social and monetary policies, protection of the environment, and much more. An analysis of all the regulations enables one to state that in each of them there is an asymmetry of benefits. As the party on a higher level of economic development, the EC commits itself to giving assistance in technology, management, organization, accounts, systems, training, education, culture, and tourism. This extensive aid is intended to foster the economic development of Poland and to decrease the disparities between Poland and the Community.

Poland, in accordance with article 1, p. 2, "will provide an appropriate framework for its integration with the Community. To this end, Poland shall work towards fulfilling the necessary conditions." The approximation of laws is one of the most important parts of the Agreement. While it will require great efforts, it will enable Poland to integrate into the Community's legal system. The Polish Parliament will have to prepare new legislation to replace the old laws, which are incompatible with those of the Community. Poland will have to apply these regulations and accede to several conventions that it has not yet ratified (e.g., on according favorable treatment to companies and nationals by both parties); acceding to these conventions will automatically entail their subsequent adoption.

All these changes may contribute to establishing in Poland an area of more security and easier access to the market for foreign investors. Poland, in which the principle of "aquis communataire" is in force, may offer many more investment opportunities than are currently available.

Furthermore, approximation of law to that existing in the Community will help to establish a stabilized legal system and will preclude swift, short-term, and transitory changes. Thus a stable and enduring legal framework for promoting the expansion of the economy will be established, and entrepreneurs will no longer need to fear unjustified (from their point of view) and arbitrary changes. The Agreement provides for a timetable for implementing these changes, and therefore no companies will be taken by surprise.

Adapting the Polish standards to the European ones, putting into force new documents in Poland, and modifying accounting systems are all changes aimed at establishing a free-trade area and ultimately making Poland a member of the Community. This will considerably facilitate trade and decrease the costs of services (applying mutual standards will be associated with initial high costs). It will enable cost assessment and calculations of enterprise profits.

It should be stressed that the Europe Agreement creates a free-trade area (as specified in article 24 of GATT), and not a customs union (as in the case of Association Agreements with Turkey and Greece). Moreover, the contracting parties may undertake unusual measures to protect their markets (with some limitations). Poland may use special instruments of trade protection if this is justified by the protection of new industries, the protection of sectors that are undergoing restructuring, or the elimination of important social problems.

The most important advantages accruing from the creation of a free-trade area will include a drop in import prices, better access to substantial EC markets, better use of specialization, and an increase of trade.

The Agreement safeguards the stability of the Polish economy. The European Community supports the stability program and measures aimed at maintaining the rate of exchange of the Polish zloty and establishing its full convertibility. Convertibility (although only internal) makes it possible to compare the costs and operations of Polish companies in relation to foreign ones.

Thus the real state of Poland's economy was revealed, enabling an estimation of the distance that separates Poland from the Community. The Community, aware of this distance and the high social costs of implementing the reforms, has accorded a transitional protective period to some industrial sectors, which are either newly set up, undergoing restructuring, or would involve high social costs if the protective measures were not applied.

Granting concessions entails making changes in the timetable with regard to the right to reduce customs duties and to impose new ones (both in imports and exports). The Community's concessions state that the total value of imports covered by protective measures cannot exceed 18 percent of the import of industrial products, the customs duties on imports should not exceed 25 percent ad valorem, and the protective period resulting in a complete abolishment of customs duties should last no more than five years at the most.

Aiming at abolishing protective measures in a relatively short time (five years) is justified by the general tendency of liberalization to have positive effects, the first of which is an increase in competition. Polish enterprises would be deprived of taking part in this competition, which might bring about modernization and restructuring of Poland's economy. Moreover, since the Agreement provides for the establishment of companies by Polish nationals during the first stage following the Agreement's entry into force, Polish companies have to face direct competition with European firms. Poland may regulate the establishment of these companies, depending on the branch in which they function (either in five or ten years from the date the Agreement goes into force).

Granting access to the Polish market may create favorable conditions for investment and ensure the free movement of capital, thereby improving the situation on the labor market and reducing unemployment, which has become a serious social problem. Some Polish enterprises may feel threatened with regard to their competitiveness by the future inflow of capital. However, the movement of capital can only accelerate restructuring by introducing new technologies that may improve the effectiveness of the entire economy. For the time being, Poland may take advantage of the unilateral protective clause. The low level of interest of foreign capital in investing in Poland accounts for the liberalization of the policy concerning movement of capital. Striving for protection might exacerbate this lack of interest.

Poland is interested in the approximation of its laws and in taking measures to protect the environment. Protection of the environment and combating its deterioration should be taken into consideration in making decisions regarding new foreign investments. Polish enterprises ought to take all possible measures to avoid devastating the environment.

The next objective of the Polish government's activity, which may be assisted by the Community, is the stabilization of the Polish economy. In view of Poland's limitations in currency turnover, Poland may receive financial assistance from Group 24 — coordinated by the Community — from the Community itself, and in the form of credits granted by the European Bank for Reconstruction and Development. The monetary policy should adhere to that conducted within the framework of the European Monetary System. Financial aid granted to Poland by the Community will be disbursed through special programs; its granting and continuation will depend on progress in creating a market economy in Poland.

The Community's assistance goes beyond financial support. Each part of the Agreement includes exchange of information, training, exchange of experts, and collaboration in reforming Polish education. The fact that a separate article of the Agreement has been devoted to appropriate information testifies to the importance of the role it plays in relations between the parties. Initially, priority will be given to programs providing essential information on the Community, along with specialized information, to a large circle of recipients. The Agreement provides for cultural exchange and exchange of information among societies of Europe as a whole by means of joint actions such as the development of tourism.

Relations between Poland and the Community are to be institutionalized, meaning that special organs will be established to supervise the process of integration. At the same time, Poland should accede to numerous organizations and conventions in order to cooperate in many different fields and to increase its participation in the activities of the specialized European institutions (e.g., European Environment Agency — article 80, European Education Fund — article 74).

Rapprochement between Poland and the Community is to be accompanied by political dialog, which will contribute to better understanding and will ensure increasing convergence of positions on international issues.

The Community's concessions to Poland are not unconditional. Many articles mention granting aid and support, but this is subject to progress in introducing a market economy.

In return for building a homogenous market, adopting the provisions of the Maastricht Treaty, and increasing integration with the Community of highly developed European countries (e.g., Sweden, Austria), Poland would become a country of minor importance in the world economy.

Possible Threats of the Agreement

Negotiators of the Agreement stated that Poland could not obtain more concessions during the negotiations because it was the party most interested in concluding the Agreement. Poland's situation is far more difficult because it is Poland that must integrate into the Community, not the reverse. Due to the fact that Poland's economic, commercial, agricultural, and social policies are not yet fully established, they are not up to the standards of the Community and therefore incompatible.

Lawyers underline that the Preamble of the Agreement is too general. The part concerning the future objective of Poland's membership in the Community is too vague. This membership is to be preceded by the adaptation of Poland's economy and the establishment of an institutional framework. The Agreement provides for a transitional period of ten years for accomplishing this aim. It includes the Community's promise of assistance during this difficult period. It should be emphasized that the Agreement on establishing an association does not guarantee Poland's membership in the Community. Its eventual membership seems implicit, yet it is not specified in any comments concerning the establishment of an association.

The Agreement mentions that there are differences in the economic and social levels of development of the two parties. Poland's membership will depend on the rate of approximation and the leveling of these differences. It should be noted that the Community granted Poland ten years to achieve all that it took the Community thirty years to accomplish.

Although the Community commits itself to financial aid during the transition period, it does not specify the amount of that aid. The assistance will depend on Poland's particular needs and the difficulties it will face on its way to integration. The drawback of the Agreement is that — unlike the previous agreements on establishing associations concluded with such states as Greece, Turkey, and Cyprus — the Agreement with Poland does not include the so-called financial protocol, which specified the amounts that constituted the assistance to an associated state in the form of donations and loans. Poland presented a proposal for such a protocol, but it was rejected by the Community. Furthermore, this proposal underlined the need for receiving long-term aid, claiming that only then would rational allocations of assets be possible; it would also enable the donor to participate in decisionmaking. The final provisions in Title VIII (articles 95-100) state that after the PHARE program expires, a new system of long-term aid will be introduced. Beginning on 1 June 1993, credits from the European Investment Bank may be granted to Poland; however, under the Agreement financial assistance depends on the particular needs and difficulties Poland may encounter. The provisions of the Agreement concerning coordination of this support with the policy of the member states of Group 24, the International Monetary Fund, and the European Bank for Reconstruction and Development are unfavorable to

Poland (article 101). The above-mentioned institutions state that assistance to Poland depends on the implementation of the economic programs. Since in many cases these programs were imposed from outside, their implementation was not always feasible, and sometimes they were unfavorable even if applied for a longer period of time.

While the Agreement gives Poland great chances for entering into Europe, the question may be asked whether Poland will be able to take advantage of this opportunity. It is a sizable challenge to its industry, agriculture, and trade. It should be kept in mind that in Poland's case, access to the Community must be accompanied by considerable economic reforms. If the process of liberalization and integration into the Community is more rapid than the increase in the competitiveness of its products and companies, the Agreement may become a "trap" to the whole economy.

The provisions concerning asymmetry are not too optimistic. Asymmetry means that the Community's producers will enter Poland's market later on; however, in view of the gap in development, the structures of trade, and the slight differences in granting concessions, this may not be advantageous to Poland. Asymmetry may serve as an argument for achieving political and publicity aims. The Community provides 45 percent of Poland's imports and receives 35 percent of its exports, whereas Poland's commodities comprise 1.1 percent of the Community's imports and 1.2 percent of its exports. That is why a realistic view of the clause concerning asymmetry should be taken. The share of each partner in global turnovers ought to be taken into consideration. The so-called transition period of opening the Community's market to Poland cannot compensate for Poland's backwardness or account for the lack of competitiveness of its products. Moreover, the transitory period will last only a few years whereas Poland's underdevelopment has lasted for decades.

A liberal trade policy introduced by Poland will have to face constructive measures for protecting the market worked out by the Community as far as so-called sensitive goods are concerned. At present those goods account for 51 percent of Poland's exports to the Community. Almost all market protective measures such as subsidies, a system of qualitative limitations, quotas concerning diversified customs duties and voluntary limitations of exports, anti-dumping procedures, and an outflow clause are steps that may be taken by the Committee responsible for supervising the Community's trade policy and protecting its domestic market. In such a situation, considering the existing protective measures, the provisions mostly concerned with trade barriers do not touch the problem. After Poland had eliminated the state monopoly in foreign trade, customs duties remained in force as an essential instrument of protection.

As already stated, the commercial objective of the Agreement is establishing a free-trade area (apart from agricultural products). Implementing these provisions will probably result in a quick import of more competitive goods (in price and quality) than the Polish ones. Such a situation satisfies Polish consumers (as has already happened), but not the producers. Poland is practically granting free access to its market for all industrial goods that are not produced within its borders. From the Community's point of view, this market is important because it has no competitors and it has the capacity to absorb a large volume of goods. On the other hand, access to the Community's market for Polish industrial goods cannot be increased because of their poor quality, their structure, and the lack of tariff limitations. Costs are very often an important element limiting competitiveness (e.g., energy-consuming products). It should be underlined that the danger of a quick inflow of goods from the Community member states, replacing domestic production, will be strengthened by the external aspect of the Agreement with regard to its effects on the third countries. As a result of establishing free trade, a deterioration of the conditions of sales on the Polish market for suppliers from third countries will occur. In this connection their demands for the granting of certain concessions by Poland to balance their losses in this new situation are likely to be put into effect. An example is the U.S. demand for the reduction of Poland's rates of customs duties within the framework of negotiations with GATT; the U.S. argues that the duties adversely affect access to the Polish market for American products.

The cost of adapting to the Community with respect to establishing a free-trade area will be very high, particularly for producers who have a high cost of production and low economic performance. Because of the lack of industrial policy in Poland, these producers have no chance of survival. The Community's industrial policy objectives are clearly defined, and its means and instruments enable it to realize these objectives. Confrontation between Poland's industry and the well-organized, well-managed, and technically superior industry of the Community does not forecast a prosperous future for Poland. The negotiated terms of the Agreement allow three years for industry to adapt.

The most difficult issue involves agricultural products (constituting about 20 percent of Poland's overall exports to the Community), not only because of the contradictory opinions of the parties, but also because of the complicated system of protection in the Community. This system includes four kinds of barriers — customs duties, quotas, levies, and tariff ceilings — which are applied according the share of agricultural raw materials in processed goods. Liberalization accorded to Poland is only partial and diversified in relation to six groups of commodities. Once the Agreement enters into force, a 50 percent reduction of levies with regard to meat and potato products will be most noticeable. With reference to the other group (fruit and vegetables), where quantitative restrictions do not apply, customs duties have been lowered as much as 100 percent but with the retention of minimum prices, which are unfavorable for Polish exporters. For the remaining groups (which also play an important role in the structure of exports) the timetables specify annual reductions of customs duties or levies, tariff ceilings, and an increase of small quotas. For instance, the quota for beef for the year 1992 amounting to 4,000 tons is lower compared to export in former years.

Generally speaking, the Community opens its market for those products in whose production Poland is not competitive. It should be stated that there will not be considerable profits in the export of agricultural products and the breeding of animals. Polish exporters of agricultural goods need time to get acquainted with the mechanisms of such selective liberalization, but they cannot delay export if they want to be included in the special limitations and quotas. In return for this doubtful liberalization, Poland has pledged to lift customs duties for about 1,500 products, comprising about 27 percent of its imports from the Community member states starting 1 March 1992; this takes place in a situation where export subsidies for agricultural goods exported from the Community total 40 percent. Poland does not subsidize export in this field. Under these conditions, liberalization of imports of agricultural products will ruin Polish agriculture. Lack of agricultural policy, small farms, poor standard of soil cultivation, low productivity, and the collapse of the home market leave no chance for saving Polish agriculture. Furthermore, Polish farmers do not know to whom to turn in case of damage or loss caused by export of agricultural products; no procedure for this eventuality has yet been worked out.

On the day the Agreement enters into force, the Community grants Polish companies the same rights to establish enterprises in the Community as are in force in the mutual relations among the member states. The problem for Polish companies willing to benefit from the "right of establishment" are the "national treatment" and "reciprocity" rules. These principles may prevent the process of developing the activities of Polish companies in the EEC countries (as long as there are restrictions in Poland regarding foreign investments, like closed sectors).

Profits resulting from the provisions of the Agreement on the movement of services, workers, and capital are questionable. The movement of workers and the supply of services are under the member countries' supervision. The Agreement does not contain any "revolutionary" articles, which is unfortunate, as Poland expected some benefits in this area. Because Poland is not competitive, the so-called non-discriminatory treatment of workers of Polish nationality is therefore not profitable for Poland.

Conclusions

Most of the conclusions are included in the final parts of this paper. It should be added that during the transitional period it will be necessary for Poland to implement financial and organizational facilities to ease the modernization and restructuring of the most jeopardized branches of industry. It will also be necessary to implement flanking instruments (for example, import policy and non-tariff measures) aimed at protecting industry branches against foreign competition, e.g., domestic textiles and electronics. "A lot of Polish producers have already got or will have in the future problems with keeping the competitiveness of their products on the present level."[5]

It should be realistically presumed that in the transitional period of the Agreement, Poland will not achieve the level of economic development of the EC countries. Moreover, these countries will still benefit from financial facilities provided by the Community, unavailable to Poland, thereby deepening the inequality in economic development. The equalization process will begin after Poland's accession to the Community.

In the period of the Europe Agreement the Polish government should aim at deepening the scope of privileged economic relations with the EEC countries. Since the effects of macroeconomic policies (budget policy, inflation, and employment) will constitute the criteria of Poland's accession to the EEC, curbing inflation, lowering the unemployment level, and reducing the budget deficit should be the main objectives of its macroeconomic policy.

In conclusion, it should be emphasized that the principle of asymmetry in the ratified Agreement is not new. It was applied by the Community in the sixties in relation to ACP countries. The Community always aims at developing trade with the less-developed countries and in thus gaining significant profits for its member states. In the modern world less-developed countries can export few unprocessed or semi-processed goods to balance their imports of high-technology goods from the Community. Upon implementation of the Agreement, several problems connected with insufficient competitiveness of the Polish economy will surface in the near future in connection with balance of trade, currency exchange rates, stagnation, and unemployment.

---

5. Wyrzykowska E. Kawecka, "Implications of Poland's Association with the European Communities for Poland's Economy; Preliminary Assesment," discussion Papers, Foreign Trade Research Institute, No. 35, November 1992.

Selected Bibliography

Daviddi, R., "From the CMEA to the 'Europe Agreements': Trade and Aid in the Relations between the European Community and Eastern Europe," *Economic Systems*, vol. 16, No. 2, October 1992.

Europe Agreement, EC-Poland, Original Text (Warsaw/Brussels), Article 55.

Falk, Evans A., ed., *Transformation and Integration, Polish-Swedish Perspectives*, Center for Economic Community Law & International Trade Law, University of Umea, Sweden, 1992.

Gawlikowska, Hueckel K., and A. Stępniak "The Association Agreement between Poland and the European Economic Community, Advantages and Threats," Working Paper No. 2-3/1992, University of Gdańsk.

Gawlikowska, Hueckel K., A. Stępniak, and Gęrbocka A. Zielińska, *Polska — EWG, Wybrane aspekty dostosowań w świetle Rynku 1992 i Umowy o Stowarzyszeniu*, Gdańsk, 1993.

Kawecka-Wyrzykowska, E., "Implications of Poland's Association with the European Communities for Poland's Economy; Preliminary Assessment," Discussion Papers, Foreign Trade Research Institute, No. 35, November 1992.

Kramer, H., "The European Community Response to the 'New Eastern Europe,'" *Journal of Common Market Studies*, vol. 31, No. 2, June 1993.

Mayhew, A., "The Current State of the Relationship between Poland and the European Community," Conference Paper, Poznań, p. 6, May 1993.

Mayhew, A., "PHARE: The European Community's Programme of Assistance to the countries of Central and Eastern Europe," Working Paper No. 2/1992, University of Economics, Poznań.

13
Economic Cooperation between Russia and EC Countries
Obstacles and Prospects

◆ ◆ ◆ ◆ ◆ ◆

Yuri V. Fedotov and Sergei F. Sutyrin

Introduction

The problem of economic relations between Russia, and the European Community and other Western countries is both controversial and comprehensive. Today it is clear that in the field of economic cooperation between the Western countries and Russia there are enormous untapped possibilities. Political leaders of both Russia and the Western countries have declared many times that they are committed to "integrating Russia into the world economy," "development of economic relations with Russia," and so forth. Recent political changes in Russia have established all — or at least most — political prerequisites that will eventually enable bridging the gap in economic relations between Russia and the West. However, at the current stage of development existing opportunities on both sides are under-utilized in relation to the scope and scale of our national economies.

For one, Russian political reforms and, to a certain extent, economic reforms are particularly attractive for Western businessmen who wish to start and run their own businesses in the country. Because of the weak economy in Western Europe, penetration of this market might seem very alluring. For another, under the present economic circumstances Russian enterprises, free from state monopoly and rigid central planning, should be very interested in almost any kind of international activity that yields hard currency. Nevertheless, there have been no overwhelming efforts to link Russian and Western economies. This leads one to ask why this is so and what the prospects are for the future.

These are the issues we will address in this paper. Inasmuch as these questions are relevant to economic relations between Russia and all the West, we will refer mostly to economic cooperation between Russia and the West rather than between Russia and the EC. There are two other reasons for doing so.

First, one can find hardly any official documents that would clearly illustrate the economic policy of the Russian government toward the EC;[1] therefore we may conclude that there is no well-defined strategy toward interacting with the EC. Current, short-term economic and political goals prevail in economic cooperation between Russia and EC. However, this is typical for all West-Russian economic relations and, moreover, the problems facing Russian-EC cooperation are just the same as those existing in economic relations with the other Western countries.

Second, current economic cooperation between Russia and the EC countries is in the form of economic assistance from the EC governments to promote Russian economic reforms. Actually, it is more relevant to speak about G-7 assistance to Russia than about direct EC support. On the governmental level, today, this "consists of a complex matrix of bilateral and multilateral initiatives under the jurisdiction of several different international organizations and funded through a myriad of means."[2]

---

1. The persistent attempts of the Russian government to get an agreement with the EC on free trade is the only exception. However, the same policies are carried out toward other Western countries, as the appeals of the Russian government for GATT membership illustrate.

2. Barton Kaplan, "U.S. Assistance to the Former Soviet Union: A Status Report," Occasional paper No.3, Center for Russian and Eurasian Studies, Monterey Institute of International Studies, 1993, p.1.

Obstacles

Many Western businessmen find the Russian business environment (legal, economic, psychological) unusual, obscure and even threatening. This makes them feel uncomfortable in running their businesses in Russia.

Russia is presently undergoing fundamental changes. This transformation is confusing for outsiders. At least some "long-time sovietologists" find themselves in a position similar to that of their colleagues in 1917 when, as Walter Laqueur observed,

> the Russian experts were quite unprepared to explain to the non-Russian public the meaning of the events in Petersburg and Moscow. Pares, Hoetzsch, and the other experts had been accustomed to dealing with a Russia that bore hardly more resemblance to the new Soviet Russia than did China to Brazil; the fact that the new rulers spoke the same language as the old was about the only helpful feature in an otherwise chaotic situation in which all the familiar landmarks had disappeared.[3]

Thus, with due respect to the opinions of Western experts in financial institutions and management, taxes, antitrust legislation and other fields, one should bear in mind that their expertise is in developed Western-type market economies. Although many Russian economists and politicians consider this economic system the ultimate goal of current reforms, the present state of the economy in terms of both technological and organizational development obviously does not fit the desirable pattern. This seems to be an important obstacle to West-Russian economic cooperation, although a short-term one.

Moreover, the situation is not insurmountable. In this respect, George F. Kennan in his memoirs greatly overestimated the importance of the so-called "mysterious Russian soul" arguing that

> the apprehension of what is valid in the Russian world is unsettling and displeasing to the American mind. He who would undertake this apprehension will not find his satisfaction in the achievement

---

3. W. Laqueur, *The Fate of the Revolution: Interpretations of Soviet History*, London, 1967, p. 8.

of anything practical for his people, still less in any official or public appreciation for his efforts.[4]

Today, it is precisely this lack of knowledge that is unsettling to Western businessmen and to some experts.

The prospects of West-Russian economic cooperation both depend upon and are hindered by many interrelated factors, several of which we will discuss briefly: (a) the economic crisis in Russia; (b) political and social instability in the country; (c) the qualifications of Russian managerial staff and new businessmen.

Economic Crisis in Russia

Executors and proponents of the current reform declared that their intention was to achieve a wide range of economic and social reforms in order to solve many of the acute problems the country faced at that time (1991-92). The most important among these were to reduce the rate of inflation and the budget deficit; to replace the bureaucratic and politically dominated system of administrative planning with efficient market regulation, based upon economic rationality and socially oriented. This was to take place after a short period of shock therapy, which was to stabilize the main economic indicators and secure prosperity for the country and the majority of its citizens.

In fact, just the opposite has resulted. In 1992 prices had risen 2500 percent. In December 1992, the Central bank of Russia printed money equal to three-fourths of that month's GDP. In January 1993 one week's inflation was 50 percent. Now, according to official figures, it is about 20 percent per month and, according to less optimistic estimates, 1.5 percent per day. In September 1993, the reported inflation rate was 16 percent.

At the same time, the output of both industrial and agrarian sectors as well as investments dropped sharply. From the beginning of 1991 until April 1993, the decline in industrial output was 40 percent. This may be compared to a 23 percent decrease in

---

4. George F. Kennan, *American Appraisals of Soviet Russia, 1917- 1977*, ed. by E. Anschl, New York, 1978, p. 344.

respective output during the first two years of the Second World War (1941-42), and in Western history it compares with a 40 percent decline in the U.S. during the Great Depression. As for investments, the situation is even worse: in 1992 the decline was 48 percent.[5]

Political and Social Instability in the Country

In addition to the current economic crisis, the general business environment in Russia is quite unfavorable for international economic cooperation on the whole, mainly due to the political and social instability in the country. There are several aspects of this problem, but the one most relevant for international economic cooperation is the lack of credibility of the policies of official bodies at the federal, regional, and local levels. Policymaking depends to a large extent on the personalities of the top officials. Political parties, though they are numerous now, are not developed. They lack clearly defined political goals and a social base, and they have not elaborated their respective economic programs. As institutions, their influence upon government policies at all levels of state bureaucracy is negligible. For the most part, the top officials of the state execute the policies of "temporary teams," which they themselves were able to create because of the current political situation. Changes in short-term policies and reform strategies are the result of constant hirings and firings.

One instance of this is the foreign trade policy. The ministry started to tighten controls over foreign trade substantially after Mr. Glaziev came into office, though the liberalization of foreign economic relations had been officially proclaimed as one of the main means to ensure Russia's transition to a market economy. In this regard foreign economic relations are not an exception; more or less the same situation prevails in Russia's foreign policy, which lacks a comprehensive strategy. Numerous fluctuations in policy in many areas are inspired by powerful individuals on President Yeltsin's team.[6] Recent accusations of corruption of

5. V. Ryazanov, "Posle shoka," *Sankt-Peterburgskie Vedomosti*, 25 June 1993, pp. 1, 4.

6. I. Panovko, "Dva MIDa Rossii," *Sankt-Peterbugskie Vedomosti*, 21 August 1993, p. 3.

top political leaders such as Alexander Rutskoi and Vladimir Shumeiko brought to light the ongoing political struggle for power among different teams and hence, for the strategies of reforming the Russian economy. Thus, it is understandable that modern Russia is not the safest place to invest.

It is also worth saying that both the instability and the inadequacy of Russian commercial legislation create barriers to economic cooperation between Russian and Western businesses. A stable legal environment today is precluded by the extreme political struggle in the country. The chaotic changes in the economy do not favor the creation of stable and efficient commercial legislation to promote market-type reforms. Adjustments in the legal system (not only laws or acts, but also decrees, instructions, and other sublegal papers issued by different ministries and committees) are happening too often and too fast. As a result, national and foreign enterprises and other businesses are often unfamiliar with the "rules" by which they have to operate. Under these circumstances even mutual trade (to say nothing of more sophisticated forms of cooperation such as joint ventures and long-term investments) is rather difficult.

The increasing corruption may be viewed as the result of both the weak law and the lack of institutions able to execute the policies of official bodies at every level of authority. Thus, corruption has become an important obstacle to Western businesses in Russia. It damages the Russian economy on the whole and destroys many of the transactions with foreign companies. Shleifer and Vishny's observation that "the menu of both consumer and producer goods available in the country is determined by corruption opportunities rather than tastes or technological needs"[7] sounds very plausible at the moment. Their assertion that "to invest in a Russian company, a foreigner must bribe every agency involved in foreign investment," as well as their conclusion that "the obvious result is that foreigners do not invest in Russia" are not far from the truth.

---

7. See "Officials on the Take Damage an Economy," *The Christian Science Monitor*, 8 October 1993, p. 9.

Finally, it is not surprising that the scale of Western firms' operations in Russia does not meet existing opportunities. The average size of authorized funds of joint ventures in Russia today is 2.3 million rubles, whereas three years ago it was 3.5 million rubles (in current prices). This shows that foreign companies do not intend to broaden their activities in Russia under present conditions.

Professional Level of Russian Managerial Staff and New Businessmen

Under the old system a relatively narrow substratum of professional civil servants was in charge of developing and executing most of the economic relations with the outside world. Today the situation has changed drastically. Managerial staff and new businessmen have much greater access to foreign markets. However, to be successful in these markets they need to meet certain requirements in relevant qualifications and skills, which very few of them possess. When the state monopoly of foreign trade was abandoned and almost every enterprise got access to foreign markets, they were enthusiastic about export and especially import transactions. However, most of these new managers lack competence in buying and selling abroad and, as a result, they pay more and get less. According to some estimates, Russian losses resulting from foreign trade liberalization in 1992 alone were in the range of $20-40 billion.

One may distinguish two categories of managers who are especially relevant to our discussion: (1) top- and, to some extent, medium-level managers of "old" (i.e., state-owned) enterprises, which now may be both state-owned and privatized; (2) senior managers of big and successful "new commercial structures," e.g., commercial banks, joint ventures, associations, and foundations.

As for the managers of the first group, usually they are rather well-qualified, though they retain their old-style manner. They were trained to work under the conditions of central planning, i.e., they were mainly responsible for implementation of decisions made by superior party bodies and state agencies. For the most part, they had to deal with engineering problems. Basically they are engineers and, hence, their "modus operandi" is technical rather than in the line of business. They do not know much about financial management, international trade, business ethics, and other relevant disciplines. Their lack of qualifications creates problems for their partners, both foreign and domestic. However, having been in power since the late 1980s, these managers have accumulated considerable business experience. According to some economists,[8] in the near future they may turn out to be the most promising group of managers.

The second group consists to a large extent of former party officials. These people attained their current top-level business positions due to their careers in either the administrative or party hierarchy; they are barely qualified for the positions they hold. They neither know much about market economies, nor can they appreciate the value of professional knowledge. Besides being incompetent managers, often they do not have strong commitments to their business partners. There are many stories in the press on how such managers have destroyed contracts with foreign or domestic partners.

Prospects

The basics necessary for a market economy are completely missing under the present situation of the Russian economy. The economy lacks the proper institutions to ensure market regulations. Property rights are still inadequate. There is no rule of law to govern business and economic transactions. Corruption is spreading. Large areas are still under the control of monopolies and state trading organizations. The ruble is only partly convertible. The process of privatization still has not induced drastic changes in the economy.

All these circumstances, in conjunction with the economic crisis and political instability, have complicated economic coopera-

---

8. I. Boiko, "Predprinimatel'stvo v sovremennoi Rossii," *Herald of St. Petersburg University*, Economics series, forthcoming 1994.

tion between Russia and the Western economies. Nevertheless, since it is rich in natural and human resources, Russia remains an enticing potential partner, at least for the long run. According to the World Development Report estimates of GDP at purchasing power parity, in 1991 Russia was the sixth in the world, after the U.S., Japan, China, Germany, and France). However, it was only the ninth according to GDP per capita estimated at purchasing power parity.[9] Another reason that Russia could be attractive for Western businesses is the potential of its consumer markets. The Russian economy, which has undeveloped manufacturing and agricultural sectors, provides an enormous market for a wide range of commodities produced in the West.

It is well-known that foreign trade is the basis for other forms of international cooperation. In order to understand the changes in foreign trade now taking place and their implications for Western countries, one should know the basic features of foreign trade in the Soviet economy in the past. Pekka Sutela and Jukka Kero[10] observed three important features: (1) Foreign trade was regarded as a tool for dealing with shortages of domestic production. Imports were needed to overcome the bottlenecks of domestic supply and for technological innovation. Imports were not allowed to compete with domestic production. Exports were mostly designed to be the source of hard currency to pay for imports. (2) In order to maintain control, concentrate expertise, and exploit economies of scale, foreign trade was the legal monopoly of state-owned foreign trade enterprises. Their activities were closely monitored and directed by foreign trade and planning authorities. (3) Domestic enterprises were effectively isolated from the direct effects of trade by separating foreign trade prices from domestic prices by means of vast commodity- and country-specific coefficients and by applying a highly arbitrary system of rates of exchange.

---

9. *The Economist*, 10-16 July 1993, p. 63.

10. See P. Sutela and J. Kero, "Russian Trade Policies with the West: 1992 and Beyond," in *The Russian Economy in Crisis and Transition*, ed. Pekka Sutela, Helsinki, Bank of Finland, p.114.

Russia accounted for probably 70 percent of the ex-Soviet Union's $4.8 billion surplus in trade with the EC in 1992. The present state of foreign trade is to a great extent influenced by the ruble's exchange rate for foreign currencies; the extremely low rate currently is a powerful incentive for Russian companies to export their products. This brings negative consequences both for the Russian and the Western economies. The Russian budget suffers a great loss of currency inflow because enterprises are selling their products abroad for very low prices. These low prices provide them with competitive advantages in the West on the one hand, and with large incomes as compared to those derived from selling products in Russia[11] on the other.

Russia is persistent in its appeal to be treated according to GATT rules, which include safeguards against dumping. However, political leaders in the West are very cautious about free trade with Russia, although the Russian government insists on being treated as an equal partner. Most of the Western experts in international trade think that it will be a long time before the EC and the U.S. are ready for free trade with Russia.[12] In July 1993, Moscow asked for membership in the GATT and for official inclusion in the near future in the Group of Seven in order to facilitate access to the markets of the European Community. However, it is very unlikely that this demand will be met soon, since the Russian economy is very far from the standards of Western economies. In the opinion of GATT officials, it will take at least two years to negotiate Russia's membership.

Russia is interested in getting an agreement promising to make the EC a free-trade area for its products. However, Euro-

---

11. The exchange rate of ruble for foreign currencies does not reflect its purchasing power in Russia. According to the purchasing power parity in some specific products the exchange rate of dollar per ruble was: machinery — 70-90 rubles per dollar; oil and gas — 100-110; metals — 130-140. These estimates were published in February, 1993 when the exchange rate of dollar per ruble was around 600. (V. Shprygin, "Pod pressom infljatcii," *Ekonomika i Zjizn*, February 1993, n. 8)

12. See R. Dale, "Advice for Russia: Not So Fast," *International Herald Tribune*, 20 July 1993, p. 9

pean manufacturers frequently complain that Russia is guilty of dumping exports.[13] Thus, it is unlikely that this request will be granted by the governments of the EC's member countries, even though at its summit held in Copenhagen in June 1993, the EC promised "to continue and enhance its support for the Russian reform process." The current economic difficulties — e.g., high unemployment and budget deficits — do not favor opening their markets for Russian products. As mentioned by the *Economist*,[14] "The EC's apologists say that Russia at least has most-favored-nation trading status (the Soviet Union had not) and that 83 percent of Russia's exports to the EC face no tariffs at all. True, but most of those tariff-free exports are oil and gas. . . ." Actually, the Western countries close the doors to those Russian manufactured goods and services that can compete with their own. There are several instances of this, including the satellite launching service, which Russia can provide at half the price of Western Europe's Arianespace, but where Russia has agreed to voluntary quotas and price floors.

Russian government officials have repeatedly expressed their deep concern about the fact that while Western states proclaim the need to help Russia, they do not give Russia the opportunity to help herself. As reported by the *Financial Times*, the former minister of foreign trade, Sergei Glaziev said that "revenues from uranium exports could help finance the conversion of defense plants to civilian uses. Just think how the U.S. could save budget expenditures by not giving us credits [for this purpose] but giving us market access."[15]

Besides this political issue, there are many other obstacles impeding efficient foreign trade in Russia. An intrinsic feature of

---

13. Aluminum exports give an instance of this sort. Aluminum exports from Russia undermined the competitiveness of West European manufacturers whose industry now faces certain hardships. Ultimately, in August 1993 aluminum exports from Russia to the EC countries were sharply restricted.

14. See *The Economist*, 3 July 1993, p. 30.

15. Leyla Boulton, "Russian calls for greater market access," *Financial Times*, 2 April 1993, p. 4.

Russian foreign trade is a high share of barter. Due to the regulations of foreign trade, Russian enterprises widely practice barter trade because they have to pay less customs. According to some estimates, about 40 percent of foreign trade in 1992 was carried out through barter transactions.

The other factor, which has been mentioned above, is the incompetence of Russian managers, especially in the field of foreign trade, which appears to be a serious obstacle to the current development of international cooperation. However, there are relatively easy ways to overcome this, of which the Russian-American commodity exchange Rusamex is an illustration. It was established to overcome this barrier in a Russian-American business partnership and to promote Russian-American trade and business contracting. According to the estimates of some independent experts on Russian-American trade, in 1992 the value of trade and financial operations between Russia and U.S. was at least 3.5 billion U.S. dollars. It is worth mentioning that many of the deals negotiated failed to be settled because of the incompetence of the enormous number of mediators involved. The headquarters of Rusamex are in Washington, DC, and it also has offices in New York and Moscow.[16] The first transaction carried out through this new commodity exchange was a contract on the delivery of the ferrous metals to the U.S., valued at $2 million.

It is interesting that despite all the difficulties of doing business with Russia, Western companies have started activities to develop infrastructure and communications in Russia. The reconstruction of existing airports and the building of new ones that would meet modern standards present good prospects for attracting Western investments in the near future. The Transport Ministry of Russia and Lehman Brothers have signed an agreement according to which the American side will elaborate technical and financial issues of the project on the reconstruction of four airports in Moscow. Boeing has developed a general project for the reconstruction of the international airport in the city of

---

16. See *Izvestya*, 1993, N19, p. II.

Novosibirsk. Twenty-six American companies have submitted twelve applications for participation in that project.[17]

Poor communications in Russia create enormous difficulties for doing business both inside and outside the country. The respective market is large and undeveloped, so it is not surprising that a world-famous company like AT&T has started to operate in Russia to develop communication networks.

The shortage of consumer goods always has been and still is an intrinsic attribute of the Russian economy. This factor makes Russia attractive to Western manufacturers of consumer goods because of the capacity of its prospective markets. The willingness of these companies to supply their products to Russia depends to a great extent on the level of competition in their respective industries and the current situation in the world market. Two examples support this assertion.

The Russian cigarette market, believed to be the third largest market in the world, is attracting Western tobacco firms, which are among those companies that are rapidly expanding their activities in Russia. Rothmans International plc announced that it would invest $79 million[18] to build a joint venture cigarette factory in St. Petersburg. The plant is expected to start production by the middle of 1995. Rothmans will own 75 percent of the joint venture, Rothmans Nevo AS; the rest will be held by its partner, Nevo Tobacco Ltd.[19]

On 29 June 1993, Philip Morris said it would invest more than $60 million in the Krasnodar Tobacco Factory (Southern Russia) and acquire the majority stake. Philip Morris will acquire the interest from the regional State Property Fund, initially buying a 49 percent stake and taking the majority after the investment is completed.[20] Currently Philip Morris produces

---

17. See *Izvestya*, 1993, N19, p. II.

18. The Russian press reports a higher value for the English investment, namely $90 million (see *Izvestya*, 1993, N19, p. IV).

19. See *International Herald Tribune*, 6-7 March 1993.

20. See *International Herald Tribune*, 30 June 1993, p. 16.

cigarettes at its factory in the city of Samara and plans to build a factory in St. Petersburg.

Another market in Russia that is of certain interest to Western producers is the automobile market. According to some experts, the annual shortage of cars on the Russian market is about 1.5-3.0 million units. The potential demand is confined by the present low purchasing power of the majority of the population. Nevertheless, there exists persistent demand for cars, not only of domestic production but also foreign-made. Official statistics state that during the first 9 months of 1992, 98,000 cars were imported into Russia, with a total valuation of $504 million. Most of the dealers working for foreign automobile companies forecast a 50-100 percent increase in import automobile sales for the year 1993.

The Russian automobile market is rather specific in several aspects. The competition between foreign and domestic producers is relatively weak due to the very asymmetric distribution of welfare in the society. The prices for cars — even the cheapest ones — are so high compared to household incomes that people cannot afford to buy them.[21] At the same time, those people who may be regarded as relatively wealthy and thus can afford to buy a reasonably good car prefer foreign cars because of their superior quality. Despite some of the difficulties of owning foreign-made cars, there is a steady demand for them, both second-hand and new. Second-hand cars are purchased mostly by individuals not wealthy enough to buy a new foreign car; prosperous companies and organizations and wealthy individuals demand new cars. It is an interesting fact that two years ago new foreign-made cars were sold mostly to companies and organizations. Now the shops that sell foreign cars focus their activities on sales to private buyers, the number of which is growing steadily.

Another specific feature of the car market in Russia is that it is divided into relatively closed geographical zones. Car manufac-

---

21. It is worth mentioning here that maintaining a car also takes a lot of money. Maintenance of foreign-made cars is especially expensive, because the network of service stations is rather poor and usually one has to pay in hard currency either for the services or spare parts.

turers from the EC, Sweden, and the U.S. dominate the market in the European part of the country, developing networks of shops to sell and service their cars. Japanese companies have a relatively small share of the market in the European part of Russia. They are mostly represented in the Far Eastern part of Russia, though they are trying to penetrate the European part of Russia through their European affiliates (Toyota is good example of this).

Volvo holds the strongest position in Russia among Western carmakers. It has sold 15,000 cars and expects to sell 3,000-5,000 annually. It has seven service stations in Moscow and two in St. Petersburg. Mercedes-Benz has five firms in Russia selling their cars and will have ten to twelve by the end of 1993. Another German carmaker, BMW, has also displayed some interest in selling its cars in Russia; currently, BMW cars are sold in Moscow and in St. Petersburg. The French producers Peugeot and Renault are also represented on the Russian market. Renault expects to sell about 3,000-4,000 cars within the next five years.

The American producers are represented by General Motors, Ford, and Chrysler. Ford has a network of nine dealers who are quite successful in selling cars manufactured in Europe. GM has two dealers in Moscow and one in St. Petersburg and is going to start selling cars in the southern part of Russia (Stavropol, Volgograd, Rostov na Donu). Chrysler, though it has not opened an office in Russia, sells its cars through three dealers in Moscow and one in St. Petersburg; they expect that the Jeep Cherokee will be successful on the Russian market.

Even though the volume of cars traded in Russia is not impressive, one should keep in mind the present economic situation in the country and the disadvantageous rules for trading foreign-made cars, which stipulate that the foreign car sales outlet has to pay 80 percent of the car's price in taxes.

Being one of the richest countries in the world in the amount and the variety of natural resources, Russia is in a favorable position to obtain investments from the West to exploit the deposits of natural resources. The oil and gas industry is one of the most attractive for foreign companies in Russia. Despite all the risks of political instability and deep economic depression, they are keen in their efforts to get access to the oil and gas fields. This is confirmed by the fact that Gasprom (the branch company that extracts gas and builds all the facilities needed to transmit it to consumers) is very much favored by Western companies and banks. According to the data reported in the Russian press, it is the world's largest supplier of gas, controlling about 40 percent of the world's gas extraction.

This state company appears to be the object of competition for Western companies, as witnessed by a recent loan of $86.2 million to this company from the Eximbank of the U.S., given for five years with an annual interest rate of 5.93 percent. This sum was designated to buy the 295 Caterpillar tractors needed for constructing new pipelines in Russia. As was reported in the press,[22] the decision to grant this loan was influenced by fears that the contract would be signed with the Japanese producer of Kamatcu tractors. This happened previously when American companies failed to ensure financing of a similar contract.

One of the largest contracts signed early this year is between Gasprom and the Italian state company ANI. This is a long-term contract for the delivery of gas to Italy. The amount of gas transmitted from Russia to Italy annually will increase from 13.7 billion cubic meters to 20.0 billion cubic meters (an increase of approximately 70 percent). The contract is valued at $2.0 billion.[23]

France's Elf Aquitane had started its activities in the former Soviet Union in 1987 by establishing an office in Moscow. In 1991 they had accomplished negotiations on the exploration of oil fields in the Volgograd and Saratov regions of Russia. According to the contract, Elf will explore oil fields in these regions for a period of nine years. Elf has also signed a similar agreement with Kazakhstan.[24]

---

22. See *Izvestya*, 1993, N25, p. II.

23. See *Izvestya*, 1993, N19, p. IV.

24. Chevron is leading a group of Western companies seeking to tap the rich oil and gas deposits of Kazakhstan. It started the activities on the Tengiz fields in the Soviet Union, and now it is very close to completing the bargaining

Environmental protection is a field in which the EC and other Western — primarily European — countries have especially strong incentives to cooperate with Russia. The importance of this kind of cooperation increased substantially during the last decade as the pollution produced by Russian industries grew steadily.[25] Another factor relevant to these issues is the nuclear technology operated by Russian nuclear power stations and some plants. At the last Rio de Janeiro Congress (1992) Russia, along with other post-communist states, was given the status of a country with a transitional economy. This status reduces Russia's obligations to cooperate with international agreements on the environment. This decision illustrates the willingness on the part of the world community to support environmental protection in Russia and recognizes this field as a high priority of international cooperation.

With regard to conventional industrial pollution, there are several factors that contribute greatly to the deterioration of the environment and increase the risks of ecological catastrophes. The first is the slowdown of technological change in industries that produce investment goods. There has been a substantial increase in industrial pollution due to the combination of insufficient capital and lack of qualified financial institutions as well as an expansion of manufacturing that uses poor technology.

The second factor is the over-utilization of existing manufacturing facilities. These facilities are old, on a low technological level, and rarely repaired. They have deteriorated badly and thus the pollution they produced substantially exceeds the levels one might expect according to their initial technical specifications.

There are many instances of this sort, especially in the case of metallurgical works, which consume enormous amounts of coal for energy. Almost all the cities in the former Soviet Union where

---

process. By the end of March, 1993 the only problems to be solved were those of taxation (*IHT*, 23 March 1993, p. 11).

25. Although the present situation with pollution is not worsening in absolute terms, in relative terms it is. According to some estimates the 40 percent decline in production in the last two years was accompanied by inadequate decline in pollution.

these plants are located were recognized as regions of ecological disaster. The best-known of these are the cities of Magnitigorsk, Ekaterinburg (former Sverdlovsk), and Tcherepovetck in Russia; Donetck, Zaporojie and Mariupol (former Zjdanov) in the Ukraine; Rustavi in Georgia.

Chemical, oil, and gas extraction industries have contributed greatly to the pollution. The utilization of inefficient technologies that are far below environmental protection standards has had a terrible impact on the health of the people living in these areas. One of the most blatant examples of this is the fact that oil refining plants still do not use the gas from oil drilling and therefore the gas is burned, polluting the surrounding areas. Poor technologies directly endanger the health and safety of the people living in these areas, as exemplified by the city of Astrakhan, where there is a gas extraction plant.[26]

The Western countries, especially those neighboring Russia, are very concerned with the industrial pollution encroaching upon their territories from Russia. Therefore, they are eager to develop cooperation to improve the ecological situation in those industrial parts of Russia that are relatively close to them. Most active in this respect are the Scandinavian countries. One example of this approach to cooperating with Russia is an investment by the Norwegian Government in reconstruction and in changing equipment at a nickel plant. This plant is located in the northwest part of Russia not far from the Norwegian border in the city named Nickel and, thus, a large part of the pollution produced is carried by winds to Norway. The Baltic countries are also doing research on preventing the pollution of the Baltic sea.

Nuclear safety is an issue with which both the EC countries and the U.S. are especially concerned. One of its significant aspects is the safety of nuclear power stations. This problem was

---

26. It is worth mentioning here that during the first years of Perestroika there were a great number of press and TV reports concerning these catastrophes. But now, because of the severe economic problems and political tensions they are mostly out of the public discussion. One can now find few publications of this sort and they do not pretend to demand government action.

adequately recognized by the world community after the Chernobyl accident (1986). Today, it has become even more important. Despite numerous conclusions on the safety of Russian nuclear power stations submitted both by national and international inspections, the stations are still in operation employing techniques that are not safe enough according to international standards. This fact encourages the Western states to cooperate with Russia in order to ensure an acceptable level of safety at the nuclear power stations. During the July 1992 summit the G-7 came up with a five-year action program designed to increase the safety of Soviet-built nuclear reactors in Eastern Europe and the former Soviet Union. The assistance program focuses on five basic elements: improving operational safety; reducing risk; improving regulatory regimes; finding alternative energy sources; upgrading more modern plants. Programs like this one inevitably create new areas of economic cooperation between Russia and Western countries.

On 27 August 1992, Eximbank signed three contracts designed to improve safety at nuclear power plants. The agreements were as follows: (1) Russia will buy six mainframe computers at a cost of $32 million from Control Data Systems to analyze the safety features of its reactors; (2) a St. Petersburg power plant will buy a training simulator worth $12 million from General Physics Corporation; (3) Simulations, Systems & Services Corporation will design and install two training simulators at other power plants for $4 million.

The EC has undertaken independent initiatives targeted to improve the safety of nuclear energy in Russia. It has its own anti-nuclear program: TACIS. In 1991 TACIS designated 40 million ECU for the purposes of studying the safety of all Russian nuclear reactors. About half of this sum has allegedly been given to the International Science and Technology Center (Moscow), but there the ultimate decision is still pending.[27]

The importance of international cooperation in this field was confirmed by the accident that took place in 1993 at the plant in

---

27. See *Nevskoe Vremya*, 17 June 1993, p. 5.

Tomsk-7. This issue should get higher priority, since Russia has started a program of disarmament that necessitates storing a large amount of nuclear waste in its territory.

Conclusion

The above discussion of the current state of the Russian economy and the prospects of economic cooperation with the West, although not complete, may be summarized as follows.

1. Despite the present economic crisis and political instability, Russia remains an attractive partner for the West. The growth in both the scale and the scope of cooperation between Russia and the West proves this assertion. Western economic assistance needed to overcome the economic problems in Russia, such as financial stabilization, appears to be an important aspect of establishing the basis for efficient economic cooperation between Russia and Western countries.

2. However, there are two controversial issues with regard to economic assistance from the West. First, there are too many stipulations by international organizations for actually sending funds to Russia. Only 44 percent of funds promised to the former Soviet Union in 1990-92 has actually arrived (according to the General Accounting Office a total of $91 billion was pledged, of which only $39.9 billion has been received). The same has happened with the $24 billion aid package assigned to Russia by the G-7. And as Jeffrey Sachs, economist from Harvard University states, only about $10 billion of that sum has found its way into Russia.[28] These stipulations vary across countries. Thus, while the U.S. is the main contributor to the international funds provided by G-7 to assist Russian economic and political reforms (about 20 percent of G-7 total), Germany has contributed 60 percent of all Western aid that has arrived in Russia (in terms of actual assistance the U.S. share is approximately 10 percent).[29]

---

28. Jeffrey D. Sachs, "Russia Needs Real Aid — Now," *Washington Post*, 4 December 1992, p. A30.

29. Barton Kaplan (cited in note 3), pp. 2, 15.

The second controversial issue is Russia's trade status in the Western markets, and the EC in particular. While the Russian government is very keen on getting wider access to Western markets (it considers this a kind of economic support that is, at least, no less important and efficient that the various forms of financial assistance delivered through international organizations), the Western states and EC, in particular, are very cautious about this. In many markets Russia may have a competitive advantage, and this is likely to be the reason that the Western governments are not in favor of accepting Russia as an equal trade partner.

3. Russia's economic cooperation with the West is substantially complicated because of the political instability in the country, which results in the absence of clear foreign and internal policies. The latter undermines the nation's credibility to the reformers and impairs the international reputation of the government.

4. The lack of appropriate political and economic institutions is an essential obstacle to the efficient development of West-Russian economic cooperation. It appears that establishing proper economic institutions may offer a potential for cooperation between Russian political and governmental bodies and their Western counterparts.

5. Cooperation in particular fields, e.g., industries, will be determined to a great extent by the economic situation in the Western countries and the competition in the respective world markets.

6. Environmental protection is an important area of West-Russian cooperation and it is likely that in the near future it will receive higher priority, beginning with the European countries. The implication is that sound economic cooperation in this field will emerge.

14
Environmental Policy in Europe
The Greening of Europe?

♦ ♦ ♦ ♦ ♦ ♦

Michael Strübel

Environmental policy in Europe cannot be separated from international politics. Global warming, trans-boundary acid precipitation, ozone depletion — these and other key topics of the ongoing debate before and after the Earth Summit 1992 in Rio de Janeiro indicate a high level of international interdependence. Such international interdependence, however, cannot always be viewed positively; an unsuccessful international policy may multiply ignorance and may lead to apathy at the national level. Thus, the role of intermediate organizations located between the nation-state and worldwide organizations, such as the United Nations Conference for Environment and Development, are of considerable importance.

There are many and various organizations in Europe that are concerned with environmental issues. The European Community, with jurisdiction in environmental matters, acts as a supranational organization. Many international regimes, such as the Convention on Long-Range Trans-boundary Air Pollution (LRTAP) in the framework of the UN Economic Commission for Europe (ECE), the Baltic Sea Commission (HELCOM), and others responding to pollution of the Mediterranean and North Seas address certain aspects of environmental concerns. Moreover, the Council of Europe speaks to problems of cultural heritage and urban development, and the Organization of Economic Cooperation and Development (OECD) effects a plausible and practical symbiosis of economy and ecology. In addition, there is a network of bi- and multinational treaties on many different environmental concerns, from nuclear safety to pollution of the Rhine, Lake Constance, and the Elbe. Finally, the agendas of the Conferences for Security and Cooperation (CSCE) in Europe as well as meetings of the Group of Twenty-Four (G-24) countries, the European Investment Bank, and the World Bank often address environmental issues.

Since a description of the work, failures, and successes of these organization exist (Strübel, 1992), more specific questions need to be examined. One such question involves an examination of the environmental policy in the European Community (EC) before and after Maastricht, focusing on decisionmaking procedures and the transformation or deformation of national interests in the process of policy formulation. Yet, the "Greening of Europe" is more than just a problem of supranational institutions and decisionmaking. It also entails informal and formal organizations, such as environmental groups and Green parties, that have sprung from increased environmental awareness on the part of the citizens of the European Community. Other important points of interest include a discussion of the problems that have arisen from the demise of the Cold War, the need for an all-European policy, and ecological demands, all of which the European Community must face.

Environmental Policy
and the European Community

For a long time environmental policy was a peripheral issue in EC politics. Although it was not directly mentioned in the Treaties of Rome and other constitutional frameworks, in 1973 the Commission began formulating environmental principles and guidelines, policy directives, and propositions with support from the European Parliament. From a strictly judicial point of view, however, it was the Single European Act (SEA), signed in 1985, that constituted the major step toward a common European environmental policy. Previous, dissimilar policies of the European Community

produced many of the environmental problems that it is now trying to solve. Agricultural policies provoked the use of numerous
pesticides and other chemicals, which indirectly led to acidifica-
tion of the soil and rivers as well as nitrate pollution of the soil and
ground water (Conrad, 1991). Regional and structural policies
directly stimulated the destruction of natural parks and landscapes, especially in Southern Europe. Energy policies almost
exclusively favored nuclear energy, and there was little support
for research and development of alternative non-fossil and non-
nuclear energy sources. Trade policies demonstrated a contradiction between free exchange of goods, services, and capital on
the one hand and high norms of emission standards and consumer protection in several member states on the other hand.
Moreover, by exporting toxic chemicals (many of which were
prohibited for use in Europe) to developing countries and import-
ing poisoned products from these developing countries back to
Europe, the EC found itself entangled in a number of scandals.

With horrifying nuclear accidents like Chernobyl and chemical accidents emanating from Basel and other cities in the Rhine
valley, which poisoned drinking water for 20 million people in
Germany and the Netherlands, a political strategy of damage-limiting became a necessity. In turn, experiences from this political
strategy — including a lack of political leadership, a lack of effective control and implementation of rules and guidelines, and high
costs of damage-limiting actions or end-of-the-pipe technologies
— provoked a new type of political strategy: preventive measures.
These preventive measures were "soft" in the sense that they
implied low-risk probabilities and decentralized energy use. It
became popular to encourage environmental awareness in large
segments of the population, hoping for a "snowball effect" that
would change the lifestyle and behavior of the society as a whole.

Policies were created that advocated the following:

- avoiding trash and waste rather than collecting and recycling it;
- using better and more efficient sources of given energy rather
  than producing more energy (i.e., with nuclear power plants);

- using public transportation with its low energy costs and low emissions instead of private cars or trucks;
- encouraging the automobile industry to produce cars that minimize noise and gasoline and oil consumption;
- stimulating environmentally sound agricultural production wherever possible, instead of paying subsidies for overproduction and storage of agricultural products; and
- minimizing the risks inherent in the process of nuclear energy production by developing non-fossil and non-nuclear energies.

These and other policy demands have characterized the programs of the European Community since 1972. Let us now look at the problems arising from the decisionmaking and the implementation of such policies, beginning with a brief presentation of the European Law before and after Maastricht.

The conflict between ecology and economy is evident in at least two different articles of the Single European Act. On the one hand Article 100a introduced as a norm "a high level of protection in the fields of health, security, environmental protection and consumers protection." On the other hand Article 130r limited these high levels of protection by "taking into account the economic and social development of the Community, especially the development of regions." According to the decisionmaking procedure outlined in Article 130s, it was proposed that the Council could only make decisions according to a rule of a qualified majority and only if the Council settled upon this rule unanimously — all in all, a very unusual practice of using the majority vote in a democratic institution.

An innovative aspect was introduced in Article 130r: "All demands of environmental protection are part of the other policy fields of the Community." In addition, the principle of prevention was strengthened and unilateral measures by member states were allowed explicitly "in accordance with other articles," which referred especially to free trade and non-financial limits on trade. In case of conflicts the European Supreme Court gave priority to environmental and consumer interests over supposed values of free trade. Hence, unilateral, environmentally sound measures by a single or a few nation states often did not conflict with European Law and allowed the member states to make further policy advancements in relation to those offered by the Community. Another important point is that the SEA strengthened the influence of the European Parliament: with a quantitative majority of the Parliament in the second reading, the Council could only reject laws unanimously. The European Parliament successfully used this advantage in cases of emission standards and catalytic converters for new cars and the general introduction of environmental impact statements.

After the Maastricht Treaty (1991), the legal situation became more complicated. After the introduction of a mediation committee, the decisionmaking procedure outlined by Article 189b became more problematic in terms of judicial clarity and public support. Because less power was given to national and European parliaments, a democratic deficit was created that accelerated the crisis of the Community. This could be seen in the referendums in Denmark and France as well as in the battle over Maastricht in the British House of Commons. Finally, a new point regarding environmental policy was introduced in Maastricht by Article 130s, which advocated using a cohesion fund for environmental projects and policy in more needy regions and member states, such as the Mediterranean area.

All in all, the integration of environmental policy into other policy fields of the Community, as demanded by the SEA, is far from realization. Quite often conflicts arise among member states or between member states and important institutions of the Community. At times these conflicts lead to strange coalitions and dubious bargaining positions. For instance, Spain will only accept stronger environmental standards if it gets more money from the new cohesion fund; Italy will only agree to build more purification plants in its northern industrial triangle if Germany introduces a strict speed limit on all highways; Denmark will only accept the political union if France does not export any more mineral water in pet bottles; Germany will only contribute more funds to the EC budget if the Netherlands adopts German regulations on hormones in calves and if Belgium brews its beer in the tradition of the "Deutsches Reinheitsgebot" (without adding chemicals); Greece will only accept strict air emission standards if the EC rejects the membership of Turkey and the acknowledgment of Macedonia; Great Britain will only support Community policy if it does not have to ratify the Social Charter or accept common control of pollution in the North Sea area. These are just a few examples that demonstrate how linkages between policies on a high level (mostly inside the Council of Ministers or summits between heads of state) produce systematically inefficient and often counterproductive policies because of the "decisionmaking trap" (Scharpf, 1985). The linkage between different policy fields, which essentially have nothing to do with each other, shows that the policy process follows national interests rather than ecological imperatives. Moreover, this dilemma is not a specific characteristic of environmental policy; it afflicts most of the Community's policies.

In addition, the financial and personnel resources of the Commission are insufficient to implement and control the norms and guidelines for environmental quality. The budget of the EC allocates only 1 percent of its resources under the title "environment" (and for many years less than 1 percent) compared with more than 60 percent for "agriculture" and more than 10 percent for "regional policy" (Weidenfeld and Wessels, 1991: 218). Also, more than 2,000 employees of the commission deal with agricultural policy and more than 600 are occupied with new information technologies, whereas only 300 — including external experts — deal with ecology, nuclear safety, and consumer protection.

A remarkable democratic element in the political system of the Community is the fact that every EC citizen can send complaints to the Commission, and the Commission has the responsibility of asking officials and agencies in the member states about the validity and seriousness of the accusation. Examples include the quality of drinking water in Germany, the control of air pollution in Great Britain, the quality of bathing water in Italy, and the destruction of natural parks and biotopes in Spain. In extreme cases the Commission can (and in fact has) initiate a legal proceeding against member states. Quite often this procedure takes some time, sometimes even two or three years, but none of the EC member states relish being considered an "outlaw" and therefore often try to avoid violation of the EC Law by introducing new environmental protection policies.

Environmental Awareness, Green Parties, and Environmental Organizations in the European Community

The "Greening of Europe," if it indeed exists, is more than the policy of the Community. It is the summary of environmental policies inside the member states and their neighbors, like Poland, Sweden, Austria, and Switzerland. Many Western countries can present a remarkable list of successes on different issues such as air and water pollution, public transportation and traffic systems, recycling, noise reduction, and energy conservation. Comparative research shows that ecology and modernization of the economy in highly industrialized societies are not mutually exclusive (Jänicke, 1992; Prittwitz, 1993). In the long run an environmentally sound policy saves state expenditures for health care, reconstruction of decrepit infrastructures, and the preservation and restoration of cultural heritage, among others. It also reduces consumers' costs for the use of energy, and it preserves the public good of nature for present and future generations.

More importantly, the impact of ecology introduces a new dynamic in society and smaller communities — it provokes serious debates about the behavior of "outlaws," both individuals and states. The important question in this context is the following: how have new ecological thinking and value orientations significantly changed political actors and institutions? In the European arena parties, party systems, and interest groups are central to our concerns. Their advancement, compared with previous decades, can be understood only in the context of a general change in environmental awareness.

Studies from the eighties about environmental awareness in the countries of the European Community (Commission, 1983, 1986, 1988) show a significant change in value orientation by citizens in nearly all member states. In surveys employing the "Eurobarometer," the broad majority of Europeans considered environmental problems and the protection of nature a "very important" or "important" issue. In a list of priority issues, concern for the environment placed second only to worries about unemployment or economic crises. But these studies also showed a significant discrepancy between value orientation on the one hand and individual capacity for actions and changes in behavior on the other. In Mediterranean countries such as Italy, Spain, Greece, and Portugal, high sensitivity was expressed for environmental issues such as problems caused by traffic; air and water pollution; devastation of natural parks, landscapes and beaches; noise; and trash. But the samples also showed a low willingness to change individual behavior or participate in environmental organizations or concrete actions of protest.

The environmental awareness of people in the Netherlands, Germany, Belgium, and Denmark was quite high as well on certain issues. And, unlike some of their counterparts in other European countries, they demonstrated a strong will to support environmental groups or to make changes in their own behaviors and lifestyles that would support the environment. These tendencies can be verified if we look at the active or electoral support of Green parties in elections and the overall strength of environmental organizations in these countries. Green parties are active in almost every Western European country (Müller-Rommel, 1989). Their common characteristic is that they are very often one-issue parties (e.g., anti-nuclear). Green membership is often quite heterogeneous. Many of the members and militants are young and occupy positions in academic and educational institutions. Green parties try to keep close tabs on new social movements, such as the environmental and peace movements and they often choose unconventional forms of extra-parliamentarian protest, sometimes instigating large and spontaneous mobilization for rallies.

The German Green party was one of the first and, for a number of years, most successful Green parties. The German Greens received 5.6 percent of the vote in the 1983 national election, winning entrance to the national parliament (Bundestag). In 1987 they received 8.3 percent of the vote. Many different types of young voters were attracted to the Green Party: environmentalists, peace fighters, feminists, gray panthers, gays and lesbians, non-violent civil rights groups, ex-communists, libertarians, and even indirect supporters of terrorism. The involvement of this last militant group for a long time precluded any possibilities for strategic coalitions with democratic parties.

The Green party conventions looked like a circus of freaks. The fights between "Fundis" (fundamentalists) and "Realos" (realists) are legendary. It was difficult to find a common platform for the different currents of these new social movements. And it was also difficult to form a professional party with a stable and continuous membership large enough to participate in political functions on all levels, with expertise on a number of political issues besides "environment and disarmament," and with fundraising strategies and public relations outside the green spectrum (e.g., invitations to talk shows, access to TV channels and business dinners).

Soon enough the Greens began to experience a crisis in which the programmatic and organizational aspects of the crisis were empirically obvious (Raschke, 1993). The Green faction in the national parliament did not survive German unification. Obtaining only 4.8 percent of the vote in the 1990 national elections, the West German Greens, at that time unable to coalesce with the East German civil rights movement of "Bündnis '90," lost their seats in the Bundestag. The complicated position of being a party and a movement at the same time, the never-ending internal fights between the factions, and the oscillation between "protest and power" (Frankland and Schoonmaker, 1992) accelerated the decline of the Greens, at least on the national level. But still, on the level of the states (Bundesländer), where the Greens were partners in a coalition with the governments of Hessen, Niedersachsen, Brandenburg and Bremen for many years, the Greens fared better. In city governments with strong Green electorates, like Berlin, Bremen, Hamburg, Frankfurt, and Munich or university cities like Freiburg, Tübingen, Heidelberg, Marburg,

Göttingen, and Gießen, there was indirect or direct support for "red-green" coalitions with the Social Democratic party (SPD) or "traffic-light-coalitions" ("Ampelkoalition") with the Social Democrats and Liberals (whose official party color on posters is yellow).

In the last election for the European Parliament in 1989 — just before German unification — the German Greens were not the most successful party. They won only 8.4 percent of the vote in Germany, while Green parties in other countries of Europe won greater percentages in their own countries: Great Britain (14 percent), Belgium (13.9 percent) and France (10.6 percent). Because of different national voting systems — such as Britain's strict majority vote, Italy's proportional representation, and Germany's mixed system — the representation of Green parties in parliaments is not always a valid indicator of their real strength. The Green faction has 29 out of 518 representatives in the European Parliament. Disregarding the large variety of different political approaches and programmatic orientations of the Green parties, compared to the Socialists and Social Democrats (180) and the Christian Democrats (122) the "Greening of Europe" is nearly a non-event in the European Parliament.

But the main function of Green parties in Europe is found outside of representation in Parliaments. In Germany, France and Italy the Green parties forced others, mostly left-wing parties, such as the German SPD, the French Socialists, and the former Italian Communists, to integrate ecological issues into their programs. Yet, the very existence of Green parties and the positive feedback from the public sphere has been an important element for increased environmental awareness. The diversity of their policy stances explains why young voters have been fascinated by the Greens, but at the same time this diversity may cause obsolescence. The more other parties integrate Green issues into their policies and the more successful environmental policy appears in general, the more the Greens as a party become irrelevant.

International environmental groups and organizations such as Greenpeace, World Wildlife Fund, Friends of the Earth, and others also represent challenges for the Greens as well as other parties. There are about 8.5 million members of such groups and organizations in the countries of the European Community, which is about 4 percent of the voting population. In specific countries the percentage of the population that actively supports environmental groups is much higher, e.g., in the Netherlands (17 percent), Denmark (10.9 percent) and Germany (7.5 percent) (Krohberger and Hey, 1991).

Also it seems that there is an immense north-south difference in the organizational strength and public influence of environmentalists. In all the Mediterranean countries environmental organizations are very small, mobilizing only low support and typically have weak organizational structures. With great idealism the small staff of the European Environmental Bureau in Brussels, the umbrella organization of most of the environmentalist groups, tries to manage lobbying. But compared with other more powerful interest groups, such as the chemical industry or the agro-industrial lobbies, their influence is marginal at best. Often the environmentalists on the European level seem to be paralyzed by debates between different groups on extra-parliamentarian actions and strategies, fund raising, and diplomatic activities. Other interest groups, e.g., trade unions occupied with topics such as "health and safety conditions at work," have priorities other than the environment as they lobby and participate in the Council for Economy and Social Affairs.

Concluding Remarks

As awareness of environmental issues increased in the general populace, environmental issues were integrated more and more into the agenda of the European Community. Significant modifications were made in the programmatic orientation and the organization of the Commission. But the standing of the Directorate of the Environment inside the Commission is still quite weak; other departments have a stronger influence on the policy outcome. This inequality became obvious with the resignation of the Commissioner for environmental affairs, Ripa di Meana, after the Rio Summit, when his line of mediation between developing countries and highly industrialized Western countries was not supported by the President of the Commission, Jacques Delors. Apart from this conflict on the highest political level, it is primarily the scientific community, with support from the Commission's Directorate General for Research and Technology (DG XII), that brings innovations by presenting studies, documents, and declarations on issues such as global warming, energy reduction strategies, and public traffic. But even this fact did not help initiate the foundation of a European Environmental Agency. The creation of such an agency has been blocked for years by an endless debate in the Council on its place, competence, and budget. Some of the potential functions of this agency, e.g., data gathering and monitoring, have meanwhile been adopted by the Statistical Office of the EC.

In summary, the environmental policy of the Community can still be characterized as "too little, too late, too slow" (Christie, 1988). This state of affairs is even more distressing when we consider the tremendous pollution in the former communist countries and the environmental demands after the breakdown of the wall between Western and Eastern Europe.

Many of these problems can be analyzed by examining the case of unified Germany. It is the "magic triangle" — economic growth, social security, ecological modernization — that initiates new conflicts and leads to unknown dilemmas. It is nearly impossible to eliminate on a short- or mid-term basis all of the destructive and dangerous environmental damage caused during more than forty years of communist rule. Examples include the highly polluted areas of Halle, Bitterfeld, and Leipzig and the problems in Greifswald's nuclear power plants. Furthermore, because the East Germans use high amounts of brown coal that is notorious for its high CO_2 emissions, the patterns of energy production and consumption in that area must be changed fundamentally. The installation of new public and private heating systems will take a lot of time and money. In addition, in order to limit the damage of the pollution of ground waters and the contamination of soil, the construction of purification plants and advanced nuclear safety measures need high levels of public investment for long periods of time. Since many private investors shun any participation in

environmental conservation expenditures, the federal government is often asked to fill this monetary gap as well as to encourage new investments in the East. Social uncertainties, such as the
threat of unemployment for millions of people, complicate the
introduction of homogeneous environmental policy. It is especially difficult to garner widespread social support for some policies that imply the closing of major polluting factories and the
loss of thousands of jobs, such as the chemical factory Leuna-
Werke in Halle.

But it is not only domestic politics in the former GDR that prevent radical changes or more ecological orientations in environmental policymaking. The rapid "Westernization" of the new
"Bundesländer" has had quite a negative impact on the different
fields of environmental policy. The strict free market economy
has destroyed a well established system of recycling bottles and
other domestic waste. Without financial support from the state,
the decentralized collecting points were no longer affordable, and
after 1990 the lack of economic resources forced the closure of
the entire recycling system. Without any substitute, the amount
of waste has increased enormously.

A second point has to do with energy policy. The big West German electric power companies controlled the electricity supply,
excluding the authorities of towns and cities. These cities are now
highly dependent on Western monopolies and have lost an important source of income that is urgently needed. The ecological and
social costs, risks, and charges of waste management are
absorbed by the state, whereas profits are made exclusively by
the more-or-less private companies. Thus, democratic control,
which exists partially in municipal companies, is not possible.

The last issue covers traffic problems, both private and public.
In the private field the massive rush to buy Western cars and the
high mobility in the East has increased the volume of traffic,
especially on roads and highways to and from Berlin. In the public field the partly decayed railway system of the "Reichsbahn,"
the lack of money for modernization of equipment, and a dump-
ing-price policy by West German carriers led to an immense

increase of truck traffic as compared to the transport of goods by rail, which does not have such negative effects on the environment and on the use of energy.

Regarding the actors, a tragic situation occurred. Environmentalists in the former GDR, among others, accelerated the transition to democracy, the breakdown of the Berlin wall, and the peaceful revolution. The open discussion of environmental issues became a vehicle for "Systemkritik," a more explicit and general debate of the whole political system (Hager, 1992: 106). The so-called "civic movements," spontaneously organized in different parties, were mostly unsuccessful in founding elections in East Germany and in other countries. With the exception of the CSFR (which later became untenable because of nationality conflicts), Green parties were unable to mobilize support in Central and Eastern European countries, even though most citizens were quite aware of catastrophic environmental damage and the need for direct action. The historic achievement of the environmentalists, then, was bringing attention to the relationship between state and civil society and successfully placing environmental issues on the agenda of public policies.

All these tendencies dramatically demonstrate that, in the process of cleaning up the environment by using the modernization of the economy for ecological goals, the transformation of socialist economies does not follow ecological priorities. This fact is relevant not only in the analysis of East Germany; similar developments are apparent in all Central and Eastern European countries, which often have even less external financial support than East Germany. Yet, the number of projects planned by the EC, the ECE, OECD, the World Bank, and other organizations (Levy, 1993) is impressive, even in a time of recession. Without broad participation of civil society and the integration of NGOs in the process of policy formulation, implementation, and control, however, the dream of a "Marshall Plan for the environment" (Gore, 1992) is far from realization. Whatever the results of future "big politics," summits, and international conferences, the "Greening of Europe" remains a challenge for the people of Europe.

References

Beck, U., *Die Erfindung des Politischen*, Frankfurt, 1993.

Bergedorfer Gesprächskreis, *Energiesicherheit für ganz Europa?* Hamburg, 1992.

Christie, I., "Cleaning up a Continent: Environmental Policy in Eastern and Western Europe," *Policy Studies* 2/1988.

Commission of the European Community, *The Europeans and Their Environment*, Brussels, 1983, 1986, 1989.

Conrad, J., *Options and Restrictions of Environmental Policy in Agriculture*, Baden-Baden, 1991.

Frankland, E.G. and D. Schoonmaker, *Between Protest and Power: The Green Party in Germany*, Boulder, CO, 1992.

Gore, A., *Earth in the Balance*, Boston, 1992.

Haas, P.M., R.O. Keohane, and M.A. Levy (Eds.), *Institutions of the Earth*, Cambridge, Mass., 1993.

Hager, C.J., "Environmentalism and Democracies in the Two Germanies," *German Politics* 1/ 1992, pp. 95-118.

Hurrel, A. and B. Kingsbury (Eds.), *The International Politics of the Environment*, Oxford, 1992.

Inglehardt, R., *The Silent Revolution: Changing Values and Political Styles among Western Publics*, Princeton, 1977.

Jachtenfuchs, M. and M. Strübel (Eds.), *Environmental Policy in Europe — Assessments, Challenges and Perspectives*, Baden-Baden, 1992.

Kaltenthaler, K., "Coping with the Legacy of the East-German Environmental Policy," in C. Anderson, K. Kalthenthaler, K.and E. Luthardt (Eds.), *The Domestic Politics of German Unification*, Boulder, CO, 1993, pp. 187-204.

Kitschelt, H. and S. Hellemans, *Beyond the European Left: Ideology and Political Action in the Belgian Ecology Parties*, Durham, N.C., 1990.

Krohberger, K. and C. Hey, "Die Beteiligungschancen der Umweltverbände auf europäischer Ebene," EURES-discussion paper 11, Freiburg, 1991.

Levy, M.A., "East-West Environmental Politics after 1989: The Case of Air Pollution," in R.O. Keohane, J.S. Nye and S. Hoffmann (Eds.), *After the Cold War*, Cambridge, Mass., 1993, pp. 310-341.

Meadows, D. and D., and J. Randers, *Beyond the Limits*, Vermont, 1992.

Müller-Rommel, F. (Ed.), *New Politics in Western Europe: The Rise and Sucesses of Green Parties and Alternative Lists*, Boulder, CO, 1989.

Prittwitz, V.v. (Ed.), *Umweltpolitik als Modernisierungsprozeß*, Opladen, 1993.

Raschke, J., *Krise der Grünen — Bilanz und Neubeginn*, Marburg, 1993.

Scharpf, F.W., "Die Politikverflechtungsfalle," in *Politische Vierteljahresschrift* 1985, pp. 323-356.

Strübel, M., *Internationale Umweltpolitik — Entwicklungen, Defizite, Aufgaben,* Opladen, 1992.

Strübel, M., "Nationale Interessen und europäische Politikformulierung in der Umweltpolitik," in M. Kreile, (Ed.), *Die Integration Europas.* Politische Vierteljahresschrift Sonderheft 1992, Opladen, 1992, pp. 274-291.

Strübel, M., "The End of the East-West Conflict and the Ecological Challenge for Europe," in Jachtenfuchs and Strübel (Eds.), Environmental Policy in Europe, pp.241-266.

Strübel, M., "Klimawandel und Treibhauseffekt: Von der Reformbedürftigkeit des internationalen Systems," in B. Meyer (Ed.), *Umweltzerstörung: Kriegsfolge und Kriegsursache,* Frankfurt, 1992, pp. 273-298.

Task Force Report on The Environment and the Internal Market: "1992" — The Environmental Dimension, Bonn, 1990.

Urwin, D.W., "The Wearing of the Green: Issues, Movements, Parties," in D.W. Urwin and W.E. Paterson (Eds.), *Politics in Western Europe Today,* London, 1990, pp. 116-137.

15
The Other
"Democratic Deficit"
Women in the European Community before and after Maastricht

♦ ♦ ♦ ♦ ♦ ♦

Joyce Marie Mushaben

> *I think it is the duty of governments and the Commission to practise what they preach and I have seen in the latest appointments to the Commission that somebody is not practising what is being preached in the field of equality for women.*

—Dame Shelagh Roberts, MEP, January 1981

The "Europe of the Twelve" encompasses some 327 million residents, of whom more than 167,700,000 (51.3 percent) are women. While women do account for more than half of the citizens in Western countries ascribing to "majority rule," their share of seats in national parliaments during the early 1980s generally fell between 2 and 6 percent. Women appear to fare much better within the parliamentary chambers of the Community than they do on their home turf. By the mid-eighties, female delegates accounted for 18.9 percent of the total EP mandates, with proportions among individual member states ranging from 8 percent to 37 percent. By contrast, their share of seats in the national legislatures averaged 10.7 percent, from a low of 2.5 percent in the

French Senate, to 6.5 percent in the British House of Commons, to a high of 30.7 percent in the Danish Folketing.[1]

At first glance, the Danish rejection of the Maastricht Treaty in May 1992, coupled with near-misses in Britain and France, appear to reflect growing citizen vexation with "government" in general. Those with a deeper comprehension of the Treaty's extensive provisions, however, fear that further steps toward European political unification will reinforce a preexisting "democratic deficit." While East European leaders struggle to institutionalize long-awaited democratic freedoms, their Western counterparts seem to be ceding many comparable rights to ever more remote, highly bureaucratized decisionmaking structures, impervious to direct citizen control. The one EC body subject to direct popular election, the European Parliament (EP), has been and remains the very institution bestowed with "undefined powers and little importance."[2] It is also the only organ of the Community in which women account for one-fourth (an all-time high) of those directly capable of influencing Community policy.

This essay offers a preliminary assessment of diverse Community directives and initiatives aimed at gender equality that came into being prior to the 1992 Treaty on European Union. In addition to reviewing "authorizing" clauses found in the 1957 Treaty of Rome and key equality directives initiated by the Commission, it explores the potential impact of the Single European Act (SEA) on female-dominated employment sectors. The broader question raised is whether more active engagement by women in European Community politics might result in better European policies regarding the advancement of women's rights.

Accounting for Women in European Community Politics

At least three societal factors are commonly seen to account for low levels of direct female participation in national political

---

1. *Women in Statistics*, Women of Europe supplements, No. 30, December 1989, published by the Women's Information Service in Brussels.

2. Elizabeth Vallance and Elizabeth Davies, *Women of Europe: Women MEP's and Equality Policy*, Cambridge/London/New York, 1986, p. 9.

institutions.[3] First, there are the pressures of everyday life, rooted in the traditional belief that women are not only primarily responsible for bearing children but also for rearing them, while ensuring the smooth operations of the household. A second factor related to the dearth of women in government is the perception that politics was and remains a male pursuit; the image of toughness, competitiveness and a high degree of self-confidence is at odds with female socialization patterns. Last but not least, there is the recognition that politics constitutes an upper-middle-class occupation that draws its participants from the intellectually oriented or "articulate professions," i.e., university teaching, law, or local politics.[4] Restrictions on women's access to higher education prior to the 1960s meant that few were judged to possess the "credentials" necessary to comprehend complex sociopolitical and economic processes.

While traditional constraints on women's political activism persist, there are a number of countervailing trends with respect to EC office holding. First, members of the European Parliament (MEPs) are less directly involved with a particular "constituency" than is true of their national counterparts. MEPs are more likely to interact with lobbyists from major interest associations, allowing them to conduct their business during "normal" working hours. Another factor derives from the status of European seats vis-à-vis other government posts. Though well-paid and prestigious, the "burdens of office" ascribed to Community parliamentarians are deemed less important than positions in the national legislatures. A third variable affecting women's desire to run for European office entails questions of style and method. Emphasis on committee work in Brussels and Strasbourg means less

3. This is by no means a comprehensive listing of these variables. For a broader sampling, see Joni Lovenduski, *Women and European Politics: Contemporary Feminism and Public Policy*, Amherst, Mass., 1986; Lois Lovelace Duke, *Women in Politics: Outsiders or Insiders?*, Englewood Cliffs, NJ, 1993; Virginia Shapiro, *The Political Integration of Women*, Chicago, 1983; and Council for the Status of Women: *Women — Partners in Policy-Making: Regional, National and European Perspectives*, Dublin, 1992.

4. Vallance and Davies, p. 43.

grand-standing, less media exposure and, hence, less "confrontation for confrontation's sake ... with an opponent whose words one may have to wait to hear on the translation service!"[5]

Turning to structural variables, there is the impact of the electoral process itself. With the exception of Britain, national governments have relied on proportional representation in selecting their European parliamentarians. Procedural changes have moreover led to a greater share of seats being occupied by candidates from minority parties (21 percent for the Communists, versus 12 percent for Conservatives in 1984, for example). Fifth, many new parties that have entered the EP as a consequence of proportional representation also afford women candidates a very different "political opportunity structure." Women currently account for one-fourth of the mandates controlled by the Ecology Party, which includes the goal of gender equality in its official platform. This stands in stark contrast to a mere 6 percent among the ranks of the Conservatives, who neither favor a "deepening" of the Community nor any form of "reverse discrimination." Finally, there is the relative youth of the Community organs; in particular, of the Parliament itself. Less visible under the old system of appointment by the national legislatures, women's presence in the EP grew significantly with the first direct elections of 1979, largely because they faced no long-entrenched incumbents.

Whatever weights one might assign to individual variables, the cumulative impact of this second set has been a significant rise in the number of female MEPs, from a "high" of 11 out of 198 under the old appointment system, to 66 out of 410 by 1980, to 75 out of 434 in 1984 (see Tables 1 and 2). Before addressing the prospects for a further expansion of women's influence over EC governance after Maastricht, let us consider the nature and scope of Community policy toward women as it has evolved since the 1970s.

---

5. Ibid., p. 8.

Table 1: Women in the European Parliament 1979/84

	Total Membership (1984)	Women Members				Women in National legislature	
		1979	1984	1979	1984	1979	1984
Belgium	24	2	4	8%	16%	8%	5%
Denmark	16	5	6	31%	37%	23%	25%
France	81	18	17	22%	21%	4%	6%
Germany	81	12	16	15%	19%	8%	10%
Greece (1984 only)	24	—	2	—	8%	—	4%
Ireland	15	2	2	13%	13%	4%	8%
Italy	81	10	8	12%	10%	8%	8%
Luxembourg	6	1	1	17%	17%	10%	14%
Netherlands	25	5	7	20%	28%	14%	19%
United Kingdom	81	11	12	14%	15%	3%	3%
All (1979)	410	66	75	16%	17%	9%	10%
(1984)	434						

Source: Vallance and Davies, op. cit., p. 7

Table 2: Women in the European Parliament (actual figures and percentages)

Member States	1979 Actual Figures	%	1984 Actual Figures	%	1989 Acutal Figures	%
Belgium	2/24	8.3	4/24	16.6	4/24	16.6
Denmark	5/16	31.2	6/16	37.5	6/16	37.5
France	18/81	22.2	17/81	20.9	18/81	22.2
Germany	12/81	14.8	16\81	19.7	25/81	30.8
Ireland	2/15	13.3	2/15	13.3	1/15	6.6
Italy	11/81	13.6	7/81	8.6	8/81	9.9
Luxembourg	2/6	33.3	3/6	50.0	3/6	50.0
Netherlands	6/25	24.0	7/25	28.0	7/25	28.0
United Kingdom	11/81	13.6	12/81	14.8	11/81	13.6
Greece (1984)	—		2/24	8.3	1/24	4.2
Portugal (1986)	—		—		3/24	12.5
Spain (1986)	—		—		9/60	15.0
Total	69/410	16.8	76/434	17.5	96/518	18.5

Source: *Femmes d'Europe*
Reprinted in: Ailbhe Smythe, with Anne Roche, *Strategies pour la Promotion des Femmes en Politique. Sondage dans les Etats membres de la EC pour le Lobby Europeen des Femmes, Dublin, October 1992.*

Legitimizing European Policies
on Gender Equality

The EC has pursued a very gradual course with respect to equality issues, despite the fact that its justification for addressing these questions is as old as the Community itself. The key to all forms of EC action on this front rests with Article 119 of the 1957 Treaty of Rome, which specifies members' obligation to uphold "the principle of equal remuneration for the same work as between male and female workers."[6] When the de Gaulle government announced its plan to mandate a national minimum wage, along with equal pay, prior to ratification of the EEC Treaty, French industrialists feared they would be undercut by external competition; i.e., as long as other member states could continue to pay female workers less. Hence the Community's "founding fathers" (read: there were no "founding mothers") attempted to circumvent the problem of unfair competition by adopting the equal pay clause. Rendering the goal of equal pay for equal work a binding one for all would-be members, the Treaty set a four-year deadline but left implementation up to the discretion of the member states.

The binding character of Article 119 is reinforced by Articles 100, 177, 189, and 235.[7] While its actual scope is quite narrow — i.e., limited to a particular facet of work-place relations — Articles 100 and 235 grant wider implementational powers, if necessary, to achieve the Community's fundamental, long-term objectives. As

6. Cited in Ibid., p. 73.

7. For a more extensive treatment of the legal parameters, consult Leila Sadat Wexler's chapter in this volume. Article 100 grants the Council of Ministers power to issue directives "for the approximation of such provisions . . . as directly effect the establishment or functioning of the common market." Article 235 enables it to "take the appropriate measures to attain, in the course of the operation of the common market, one of the objectives of the Community when this Treaty has not provided the necessary powers." Article 177 allows national courts to refer matters to the COJ for a *preliminary ruling*. Article 189 permits supplementary or secondary legislation, in addition to specifying the binding or non-binding nature of all forms of Community action. *Treaty of Rome*, as cited in Vallance and Davies, p. 88.

many national jurists now recognize, it is the secondary legislation foreseen by these articles "which forms the real body of European anti-discrimination law."[8] In theory, these provisions place a formidable instrument at the disposal of equality advocates. Their utility is restricted in practice by a key procedural barrier: all decisions deemed critical to "national interests" require unanimity, under the terms set by the 1966 Luxembourg Accord.[9]

The European Parliament has emerged as the primary mobilizer around women's issues; therefore it is worth examining its functions in greater detail. It began as the Common Assembly of the ECSC, consisting of 78 delegates designated by and generally simultaneous members of the national parliaments. It was renamed the European Parliament in 1962, although its 142 delegates continued to stem from the national legislatures. The accession of Denmark, Ireland, and Britain in 1973 raised the number of MEPs to 183. The Parliament sought further legitimacy in its turn to direct elections as of 1979. With the addition of Greece in 1981, EP membership grew to 434; its final expansion followed German unification, bringing the total to 518 representatives to date.

The EP is chaired by a president, who is assisted by a Bureau, twelve vice-presidents, and five quaestors. The Bureau's primary duty is to coordinate plenary sessions and to administer the affairs of the EP's eighteen permanent committees, to which delegates are assigned for five years (one electoral cycle). Specialized according to policy areas, committees develop "a symbiotic working relationship" with Directorates pursuing similar issues.[10] EP women evince the usual concentration with respect to their committee memberships (e.g., consumer protection, education, health, child welfare, social affairs, women's rights) and domi-

---

8. Ibid., p. 74.

9. The veto power inherent in this "compromise," at the insistence of France, reinforced the power of the Council of Ministers: the "vital interest" of any single state cannot be overruled — even if that "interest" contravenes the needs of a majority of that member's citizens.

10. B. Guy Peters, "Bureaucratic Politics and the Institutions of the European Community," in Alberta M. Sbragia, ed., *Euro-Politics: Institutions and Policy-Making in the "New" European Community*, Washington, D.C., 1991, p. 91.

nate the staff as secretaries and interpreters.[11] The mid-eighties found 230 women situated in the lower administrative grades, vis-à-vis 2,695 men: they held 10 percent of the posts in Staff Category A, and 62-90 percent in the lower grades of B and C.[12]

Concentration camp survivor Simone Veil (France) is the only woman to have served as president to date; five women functioned as vice-presidents between 1979 and 1984. In 1983, only four women, out of eighty-two officials, were situated at the highest levels of the Directorates. By 1990, only one woman had held a seat in the Council of Ministers beyond British Prime Minister Margaret Thatcher, namely, Foreign Minister Colette Flesch of Luxembourg. Two women joined the ranks of the EC's seventeen Commissioners in early 1989: Vasso Papandreou (Greece) became responsible for Social Affairs, while Christine Scrivener (France) was placed in charge of Taxation Policy; Papandreou left the Commission in 1991. As of this writing, women head two of the twenty-two Directorate-Generals. They are similarly underrepresented among the many interest organizations that seek to influence Community operations at the member state level, e.g., in national employers' associations and labor unions.

The Parliament's duties are regulated under Art. 137 of the Rome Treaty, but few actually involve legislating.[13] One increas-

---

11. Vallance and Davies, pp. 66-67. Further, Sabine de Bethune, ed., *PANORAMA, Statistical data concerning the participation of women in political and public decisionmaking*, under the auspices of the European Network "Women in Decision-Making," Brussels, 1992.

12. Figures derive from a self-study cited in Vallance and Davies, p. 143.

13. **Supervisory powers** include the right of "question-time" vis-à-vis Commissioners and their representatives; formal inquiries relating to women's concerns rose from 12 interventions in 1978 to 45 after the 1979 elections. **Motions of censure** may result in the dismissal of the Commission but do not guarantee parliamentarians influence over the appointment of a new one. The EP has become increasingly vocal with respect to budgetary decisions, over which it does possess a veto, but the discretionary portion of the EC budget is limited to 15 percent; it is routinely "consulted" about Regulations and Directives proposed by the Commission. Once approved by the Council, **regulations** become immediately binding and must be upheld by all; **directives** are binding with respect to the specific goal to be achieved but leave the

ingly significant role rests with its ability to publicize Community actions, or the lack thereof, regarding issues near and dear to members. The first EP able to claim a more "democratic" base established an ad hoc committee on the situation of women in Europe in October 1979. Twenty-five women and ten men worked to produce an extensive report (called the *Maij-Weggen Report*, after its primary *rapporteur*) in 1981. The plenary debate on 10-11 February was "at times a turbulent affair," even though participants were primarily female.[14] The resulting resolution led to the creation of a Committee of Enquiry on the Situation of Women in July 1981, focusing on eighteen topics for investigation; its status became permanent in 1984 as the Committee on Women's Rights (CWR). On 17 January 1984, the CWR presented a 116-point Resolution for plenary debate, eventually approved by 125 members, opposed by 17, with 55 abstentions (less than half of the MEPs bothered to vote).[15] The Commission later established its own Advisory Committee on Equal Opportunities for Women and Men.

Formal responsibility for issues affecting women rests with the Directorate General on Social Affairs (DG V). Interestingly, the so-called "Eurocrats," the Commissioners, have assumed an obvious advocate role. Indeed, "without pressure from the Commission and its continuing interest in the development of the

---

choice of methods up to each member (affording many opportunities for circumvention and delay). Governments are obliged to pass national laws addressing the substance of all directives within a specified time-period if none exist. The power to issue **decisions**, binding upon the individual organs or states to whom they are addressed but lacking general applicability, rests solely with the COM. Weaker still are **resolutions,** which usually derive from reports issued by relevant EP committees after they have assessed pending legislation; the EP may propose amendments but the Council is not obliged to adopt these modifications.

14. One conservative, Mr. Forth of the United Kingdom, discounted the report as "a bulky document making utterly unrealistic demands . . . seeking commitments of resources which would cause us to cut back on other programmes" [author's note: probably of greater value to European males]. Vallance and Davies, p. 79.

15. Some 59 paragraphs of the Resolution found their way into the Commission's New Action Programme of 1982. Ibid., p. 79.

equal pay clause in the Rome Treaty, the three directives on women's rights would probably never have been drafted."[16] This is not to underestimate the mobilizing role of the new generation of EP representatives. Former Commissioner Ivor Trevor (1980-84) testified that it was feminist pressure emanating from the directly elected Parliament that gave rise to the First Action Program. One example of EP activism centers on the European Social Fund, which allocated resources for female training projects in 1978; when funding expired in 1983, the EP countered member states' failure to reappropriate by proposing to stop all ESF monies to governments denying a balanced distribution to women and men.

To date, neither the Council as a whole nor any individual member state has demonstrated a willingness to fight unreservedly on behalf of women's issues. In the sardonic words of one British official, "There is no problem here, and the problem that there is not is best solved by voluntary agreement."[17] National leaders are particularly averse to any proposition that might require domestic public spending. Global recession, coupled with rising unemployment, has rendered all governments unwilling to undertake any action not absolutely compelled by law.

Community Case Law, "Standing" and Evolving Legal Principles

The Commission may initiate "infringement proceedings" against a particular government, as it did in August 1989 when Germany refused to factor child-rearing years into the pensions of Belgian, French, and Luxembourgian women who had accompanied their mates to the FRG. Eurocrats have moreover engaged in direct court battles with the member states for failing to implement equality directives fully within prescribed deadlines.[18]

---

16. Ibid., p. 31. Ironically, this did not stop those same enlightened officials from successfully attempting to protect their own turf against "preferential hiring" in the 1987 case of *E. Delauche v. Commission of the European Communities.*

17. Dipak Nandy (UK), in Vallance and Davies, p. 112.

18. This was demonstrated in two COJ rulings featuring the *Commission of the European Communities v. French Republic* (June 1988 and October 1988,

Described by Shapiro as the "forward-thrusting element of the Community," the Court of Justice has ruled that obligations specified in the 1957 Treaty "directly bind private citizens and enterprises of member states. Thus, in the course of regular lawsuits in national courts, individuals may claim their legal rights under those treaty provisions. . . ."[19] The COJ has played an active if unintentional role in broadening the framework for EC equality policy; the qualification is that the provision in question must be unconditional or *directly effective*.[20] Insofar as all provisions in the Rome Treaty supersede national law, Article 119 requires no independent, intervening action on the part of national legislatures, as elaborated in two cases brought to Luxembourg during the early sixties.[21]

Belgian women in the Hersatl region were the first to put Article 119 to the test, when workers in the defense industry went on strike to protest pay discrimination. Their claims having been rejected at the national level, they appealed to the European Court on the basis of Article 119, winning a substantive right to equal pay in 1966. The first case involving an individual's charge

respectively), as well as by the suit involving the *Commission of the European Communities v. Kingdom of Belgium* (pertaining to unemployment benefits and invalidity allowances, May 1991).

19. Martin Shapiro, "The European Court of Justice," in Sbragia, p. 127.

20. That is, "if the directive is clear, precise and unambiguous and leaves no discretion to the member state." The principle was defined in the 1974 case of *Van Duyn v. Home Office;* Vallance and Davies, p. 21.

21. Under *Van Gend en Loos v. Nederlandse Administratie der Belastingen* (1963), law promulgated in the name of the EC "not only imposes obligations on individuals but is also intended to confer upon them rights which become part of their legal heritage. These rights arise not only where they are expressly granted by the Treaty, but also by reason of obligations which the Treaty imposes in a clearly defined way upon individuals as well as upon member states and upon the institutions of the EEC." *Costa v. ENEL* (1964) held that EC law "could not, because of its special and original nature, be overridden by domestic legal provisions, however framed, without being deprived of its character as Community law and without legal basis of the Community itself being called into question." Both cited by Vallance and Davies, pp. 89-90.

of pay discrimination was filed by Gabrielle Defrenne in 1968.[22] It was not until the second Defrenne case of 1976 that Article 119 was turned into "real law," that is, decreed directly effective and hence binding on member states.[23]

Defined in the 1979 *Cassis de Dijon* verdict, the concept of *mutual recognition* obliges "receiving nations" to accept the standards of the "producing nation." In the context of the SEA, this ruling could incite a "race to the bottom" if the country with the lowest standard is eventually able to prevail. The COJ has already blocked a least-common-denominator approach to environmental policy and has further declared that this will not obtain in cases of overt sexual discrimination.[24] Mutual recognition has yet to be replaced or supplanted with a "best practice" orientation, which puts a new spin on the initial Danish "no" to Maastricht. In addition to offering the most progressive legislation among the Twelve, Denmark displays the highest rates of female participation in top-level governmental/administrative posts. MEP Bodil Boserup observed in the early eighties that, in contrast to conditions in her own country, the Community's equality directives "are thirty years out of date."[25] It is thus conceivable that women differ from men in their reasons for rejecting the idea of European political union. Why should Danish women settle for less under Maastricht?

---

22. A stewardess for SABENA Airlines, Defrenne was forced to terminate her flying career upon turning forty, a condition not required of men. She appealed to the European Court in 1968, regarding her subsequent ground job, which paid significantly less than in-air service. The Court required the payment of damages and equal pay for the alternate position but rejected the claim that she was entitled to a higher pension to compensate losses incurred by her displacement.

23. The case of *McCarthys LTD. v. Smith* broadened the base for individual standing, finding that a complaintant need not supply as evidence a man employed under comparable circumstances at exactly the same time. Another significant victory was scored in the May 1990 verdict of *Douglas Harvey Barber v. Guardian Royal Exchange Assurance Group*. The COJ declared in a preliminary ruling that occupational pensions are an integral component of worker remuneration, henceforth falling within the scope of Art. 119 TR.

24. Shapiro, pp. 140, 132.

25. Cited in Vallance and Davies, p. 113.

Many women lack easy access to information regarding their legal status and rights as Community citizens. They have not made sufficient use of the Equal Treatment Directive — perhaps discouraged by the fact that merely one-fifth of the suits filed along these lines secured favorable verdicts during the first five years after its issuance.[26] Nor do they possess the financial means to pursue a case, since most national systems of jurisprudence deny free legal aid to persons in paid employment (in *Catch-22* fashion, women unable to afford legal representation cannot fight against unequal pay). COJ rulings do little to deter and rectify employer behavior; until recently, victorious plaintiffs received only symbolic compensation. Penalties are not "directly effective," compelling a reliance on national law; this explains the frequency of the so-called "postage stamp awards" witnessed in the FRG, for example. In *Von Colson & Kamann v. Northrhein-Westphalia* (1983) the Court finally decreed that sanctions must stand in relation to the amount of damage or harm caused.[27] Recent cases have highlighted the need for a further harmonization of legal systems and proceedings.[28] MEPs want employers made accountable for maintaining detailed records on pay, training, and promotion according to race and gender categories.[29]

---

26. Ibid., p. 122.

27. The Court awarded Colson and Kamann six months' worth of salary, in addition to their so-called *Bewerbungskosten* (stamps and xeroxing), for having been passed over as the most qualified applicants; they were not accorded the jobs they deserved as social workers in a Northern German prison. Hortense Hörburger, *Europas Frauen fordern mehr. Die soziale Dimension des EG-Binnenmarktes am Beispiel der spezifischen Auswirkungen auf Frauen*, Marburg, 1990, p. 30.

28. Two existing models, Anglo-American style case-law and the system of codified or Roman law, afford differential access to would-be grievants in terms of "test cases" and the judiciary's ability to "fill in the gaps."

29. Another stumbling block is a lack of legal expertise. Discrimination law is nationally subsumed under industrial relations law; few judges or lawyers are conversant in both fields, at the national *and* the EC level. There now exists a specialized community newsletter informing jurists in the member states of pending resolutions and final rulings relevant to women. *The Law Network Newsletter* is published by the Directorate-General on Employment, Industrial Relations and Social Affairs.

Expanding the Conceptual Framework
for Legal Action

Since the seventies the Commission has issued five directives pertaining to gender equality, grounded in the precepts outlined above, that should have already compelled the national governments to take effective implementational action. Their contents can only be briefly summarized here.

The *Equal Pay Directive of 10 February 1975* embodied a substantive reiteration of Article 119, mandating "equal pay for equal work." It gave members six months to enact effective measures and to devise methods that would protect female workers filing a job-related discrimination complaint. Years after its promulgation, the directive fell quite short of its goal of warranting the same hourly wages for women and men. Women's salaries in Great Britain, which amounted to 77 percent of their male counterparts in 1977, dropped to 73 percent in 1980; females in Ireland saw their pay rise from 61 percent in 1975 to 68 percent by 1982. Italian women also witnessed an increase in their wages, from 79 percent to 87 percent of men's pay, while proportionate earnings in the FRG remained constant.[30] Since employers adhere more to the letter than to the spirit of the law, Commissioners began to focus on moving women out of lowest-paid job categories and occupations per se.

The *Equal Treatment Directive of 9 February 1976* was a great leap forward, expanding the concept of equality beyond the limited question of pay actually received, although "unequal treatment" remained tied to the situation of women-at-work. The ETD not only broadened access to new careers, training and promotion, it also laid a foundation for improving the work environment, e.g., eliminating sexual harassment. Member states were given thirty months to meet its main objectives (1981 for Greece, extended several times beyond accession). West German and Italian Ministers argued that their constitutional guarantees of

---

30. Vallance and Davies, p. 119-20. Further, Pippa Norris, *Politics and Sexual Equality: The Comparative Position of Women in Western Democracies,* Boulder, CO, 1987.

equality sufficed as implementational legislation, although neither state had fully operationalized those provisions at home. When the Commission threatened to initiate infringement proceedings, the FRG sought to limit its application to the private sector.[31] Others attempted to circumvent the directive's requirements linguistically, i.e., by utilizing the term "like work" in national statutes.

The ETD first raised the problem of *indirect discrimination*. Grounds for excluding women from specific jobs are not subject to uniform, objective criteria, hence much is left to the discretion of employers. Cases later based on the ETD paid damages to those facing discrimination or dismissal but did not compel hiring or reinstatement. The "burden of proof" originally rested with the woman alleging unequal treatment; in 1988 EP delegates successfully reversed "proof" requirements, at least subsequent to presentation of prima facie evidence in the domestic courts. The first report assessing the ETD's impact was made public in 1981, compiled from questionnaires to governments, employers' associations, and workers' organizations: all actors were found sorely negligent in their efforts to implement its provisions.[32]

Assessments of earlier directives brought the realization that equal treatment must also apply to social security programs (for illness, accident, disability, old age, unemployment, and welfare aid). "Positive discrimination," as advocated in the *Social Security Directive of 19 December 1978*, aims to have years devoted to child bearing and rearing included in calculations of women's "contributions." Initially the SSD's reach was limited to statutory programs, neglecting supplementary employer-provided schemes, since the COJ had excluded social security as a component of

---

31. The Kohl Government argues that the state cannot engage in "positive action" or preferential hiring because the Basic Law (Art. 3GG) prohibits "reverse discrimination" — hence it must protect the "equality" of men.

32. The 1975 and 1976 directives obliged member states to nullify existing collective agreements, laws and regulations that were overtly discriminatory (e.g., "head of household" allowances paid only to husbands). Both likewise outlawed "victimization," though this applied only to grievants who might be fired, not to colleagues who might be called as witnesses.

"equal pay" in the 1971 Defrenne case. Commissioners allowed six years for implementation, in view of the extraordinary diversity characterizing national programs. It inferred that women rely more heavily on social security benefits than men, as a function of existing wage inequalities — and as a consequence of their relative longevity (outliving men by six to eight years). Recession brings the need to safeguard a complex web of cumulative benefits.

The three directives fostered recognition that "equality at work" must begin with equal treatment in the separate but related spheres of education, hiring, promotion, and retirement. They further impelled each member state to establish a national oversight body on women's rights. As EC women interviewed by this author nonetheless attested in May 1992, national leaders should not rely on these bodies to do all their work, since they are typically understaffed, underfunded, and usually outside the mainstream of portfolio positions. Member governments have repeatedly evinced "a distinct lack of political will toward equality."[33]

National governments offered the recession of the 1980s as a justification for not proceeding further with the effective implementation of women's rights. The "freeze" on advances is moreover rooted in the unanimous vote rule invoked over issues affecting important "national interests." Mindful that directives lack the clout of such decisions at the ministerial level, the Commission has sought to educate national leaders concerning a wide array of implementational strategies and mechanisms. Foremost among its enlightenment devices have been three multi-year "Action Programs." The *Social Action Program of 1975* was introduced at a time when feminist groups were on the march throughout the West and interest in European integration had waned considerably. The SAP complemented a 1974 Council Resolution as well as a memorandum on "Equal Treatment for Male and Female Workers" in February 1975.[34]

---

33. Vallance and Davies, p. 100.

34. Space constraints prohibit a review of further directives and resolutions issued by the Council of Ministers per se. They include: Directive 86/378 of 24 July 1986 (on equal treatment with respect to employers' voluntary or self-imposed

Its successor, the *Community Action Program on the Promotion of Equal Opportunity for Women, 1982-85* sought to strengthen the individual rights of European the citizeness. It advocated "positive action" against indirect discrimination and assessed progress toward occupational desegregation (finding that it had been quite limited). Initial reactions from the national governments were "predictably cool"; the Council of Ministers resisted efforts to establish common regulations in most areas covered by the program. The interim report of January 1984 was unabashedly pessimistic; it cited employers' general reluctance to initiate special training programs for women, reinforced by official notions (reflecting a paucity of women in government) that "hard times" impose other priorities.[35] From the Ministers' perspective, women's rights are relative, only to be pursued in times of plenty.

The second or *Medium Term Community Programme, 1986-90* centered on the legal rights of individuals, coupled with "positive action" as a way of removing non-legal barriers to equal opportunity.[36] The *Third Medium-term Action Program, "Equal Opportunities for Men and Women," 1991-95* aims to consolidate measures and capitalize on Community experiences to date; it stresses employment and training initiatives sensitive to structural problems in less developed areas and urges the development of partnerships among actors inside and outside the EC. It advocates the idea of "work of equal value," calls for a study of payment systems and promotion as well as legal monitoring in member states.

As this telegraphic review of directives and action programs illustrates, the Commission, the Parliament, and the Court have

---

social security schemes); Directive 86/613 of 11 December 1986 (on equal treatment for women in the self-employed or "independent" sectors, including agriculture).

35. Ibid., p. 128.

36. See Directorate-General for Employment, Industrial Relations and Social Affairs, *An Evaluation Study of Positive Action in Favor of Women*, Commission of the European Communities, Brussels, 1990. One study attempted to sample 2,700 individuals and 28 companies — the rate of valid responses was less than 13 percent (n=346). See also Evelyne Serdjenian, *12 European Programmes for Equal Opportunities*, Brussels, 1990.

all accorded equality issues a prominent place on their agendas. In addition to supporting numerous official initiatives, the EC has provided a forum for substantial self-mobilization over the last decade.[37] One result has been the compilation of a formidable set of data-banks involving a wide array of occupational fields.[38] The chief stumbling block to implementation remains a lack of political will among national governments, embodied in the Council of Ministers. The question is whether the changes foreseen by the Single European Act and the Maastricht Treaty will induce a significant redistribution of power among the policymaking organs of the Community as a whole.

Women, the Market, and Maastricht

Experts point to at least five processes that will significantly affect women in conjunction with SEA implementation. They are: (1)

---

37. Organizational offshoots include the Women's Information Bureau, the Center for Research on European Women (CREW), the Women in Employment Network, along with Networks on "Diversification of Occupational Choices," "Positive Action in the Private Sector," and "Local Employment Initiatives"; more recent formations are the Working Group on Higher Levels of the Public Service, the Steering Committee on Equal Opportunities in Broadcasting and Television, and the IRIS Network (focused on vocational training), inter alia.

38. Among the many specialized studies sponsored by the DG-V (all printed in Brussels) are: Caroline Turner, *Women's Local Employment Initiatives in the European Community*, 1989; Marie-Laurence Delacourt and Jacques A. Zighera, *Woman's Work and Family Composition — A Comparison of the Countries of the European Community*, September 1988; Jane Millar, *The Socio-Economic Situation of Solo Women in Europe*, 1991; Dina Vaiou, Zoe Georgiou, and Maria Stratigaki et al., *Women of the South in European Integration: Problems and Prospects*, October 1991. On training, see Frederique Deroure, *Accompanying Measures in Women's Training — Vocational Training for Women*, June 1990; Monique Chalude, with Margaretha Lisein-Norman, *The Re-Insertion of Women in Working Life; Initiatives and Problems*, 1986; Rosemary Crompton, Linda Hantrais et al., *Women in Professional Occupations in France and Britain*, September 1990; Evelyne Sullerot, *Diversification of Vocational Choices for Young and Adult Women*, Final Consolidation Report, 1987; and Jill Rubery and Colette Fagan, *Occupational Segregation amongst Women and Men in the European Community*, October 1992. For a treatment of their political progress, see Margaret Page, *Women Change Decisions — Final Report on Women, Decision-Making and Local Strategies: Some Comparisons between Italy and the UK*, November 1992.

the restructuring of a wide variety of industrial branches and service sectors; (2) the creation of a transnational core of social rights; (3) the redefinition of mobility and residency rights (dividing women as well as men into two classes, EC- and non-EC "nationals"); (4) the harmonization of norms, especially in reference to matters of health, hygiene, and occupational safety; and (5) the reconceptualization of "equality" per se.[39]

The COM Resolution of 21 May 1991 decreed that "women must be in a position to benefit on equal terms from the achievement of the single market and to contribute fully to such achievement." In this document, the Council "*invites the member states* to implement the relevant measures" and "*invites both sides of industry* [my emphasis] to make equal opportunities and equal treatment an element in collective bargaining, in particular by endeavouring to implement positive action programmes in occupational branches and sectors as part of a cohesive policy of staff management." Whether the Ministers will accept their own invitation depends on the extent to which they can henceforth agree to decide such issues on the basis of majority rule.

As of January 1993, the Single European Act has opened the door to greater use of the qualified majority vote. The addition of Article 118A to the 1957 Rome Treaty does subject questions involving the "world of work" to majority decisions, though it simultaneously upholds "the rights/interests of employers" under the unanimity principle. The heart of the SEA, Article 8A seeks to turn the common market into a realm without internal frontiers, typified by the free flow of goods, personnel, services, and capital. The "free movement of persons" entails at least one critical qualification, however: to date, the Act provides no independent residency rights for relocated family members of the employed party, e.g., in the event of divorce or a spouse's death.[40] Many gaps remain with respect to the transfer of social benefits;

---

39. For a detailed treatment of the social-policy ramifications of the open market, see Hortense Hörburger, op. cit; also, Beverly Springer, *The Social Dimension of 1992: Europe Faces a New EC*, New York/Westport, Conn./London, 1992.

40. Hörburger, p. 12ff.

areas requiring further reform include supplemental pensions based on child-rearing years and gender-biased taxation structures. The advantages of mobility will accrue to workers with the highest professional qualifications, leaving female workers to "catch up" for many years to come.

Women will not be particularly affected by restructuring in the industrial sectors, where only 20 percent of their kind were gainfully employed in 1987 (men: 42 percent). Rather, the greatest impact on their employment status will stem from efforts to rationalize the service sector, which provides jobs for 73 percent of their ranks.[41] Between 1979 and 1982, the total of registered unemployed in Western Europe rose from 6 million to 11 million; women accounted for $2\frac{3}{4}$ million in 1979, and for $4\frac{1}{2}$ million of the jobless by 1982. Comprising 35.9 percent of those engaged in paid labor in the late seventies, they constituted 41.8 percent of those lacking (yet actively seeking) jobs; as the number of female workers rose to 36.8 percent of all wage earners in 1980, their proportionate share among the registered unemployed also increased to 45 percent.[42] According to the Community's own studies, women experienced a larger percentage increase than men with respect to entry into the paid labor force between 1982 and 1987, albeit mostly in part-time or non-secure positions; 70 percent of those entrants were concentrated in the service sector. Not all of these trends can be attributed to the ratification of the SEA per se. The Act has not caused, only accelerated industrial changes already underway, e.g., increasing employer reliance on "temporary" or "atypical" forms of employment.

Out of the EC's total population, over 70 million are women in their child-bearing years, aged fifteen to forty-four; they are primarily responsible for roughly 40 million children under the age of ten (36 percent under the age of four in the FRG, 74 percent under seven in Denmark). The phenomenon of part-time work sustains a gendered division of labor for women as a whole, but at least it helps to ease the "double" (actually "triple") burden for the

---

41. Ibid., pp. 8, 22.

42. Vallance and Davies, p. 123.

individual employee. Only a significant restructuring of the "normal" working day, coupled with bona fide *parental* leave options, will alleviate their burden. The SEA has yet to "harmonize" the minimum number of hours (ranging from zero to eighteen) that must be worked in order to qualify for standard national benefits.

According to medium-term projections, the "opening" of the EC market will generate a minimum of 1,800,000 jobs.[43] Yet the goal of regional "competitiveness" carries the risk of declassification for many segments of the labor force. Community analysts are skeptical regarding short-term or medium-term SEA payoffs for women; trends toward new forms of "homework," coupled with an increasing emphasis on "flexibility" through part-time work (to the benefit of employers) will reestablish workplace segregation and segmentation. Under the rubric of "new technologies," the tasks assigned to women will continue to fall into the low-wage, routine "processing" category.

Consider trends projected for the banking sector. Mounting competition means increased risk for European financial markets, which, in turn, will place new emphasis on "profitability." One likely outcome will be an effort to squeeze production costs by replacing the variable human with reliable new technologies (e.g., electronic banking, telecom marketing, and automatic teller machines). With the exceptions of Italy, Portugal, and Spain, the banking sector tends to be more heavily "feminized" than other branches of the economy.[44] Prior to 1988, the banking sector was not a major utilizer of either part-time or temporary labor.

Internal experts on "Women in Employment" offer a rather pessimistic assessment as to a potential rise in demand for skilled laborers in this particular job market,

> and this pessimism is deeper for the long term than the short term when only slower growth is forecast. . . . The so-called traditional functions, mainly administrative tasks, will be sacrificed in favor of

43. Francois Jortay, Daniele Meulders, and Robert Plasman, *Evaluation of the Impact of the Single Market's Completion on Women's Employment in the Banking Sector*, Brussels, 1991, p. i.

44. Jortay et al., p. 37.

functions such as commercial activities and customer counseling. . . . Women are up to now underrepresented in the areas that are headed for expansion. By contrast, they account for a majority of the staff in areas where extensive rationalisation measures will take place.[45]

New technologies may, at the same time, enable more women to create their own businesses, albeit subject to other forms of economic insecurity. Jortay and company urge member states, and the industry itself, to pursue vigorous "positive discrimination" policies, e.g., in the context of collective bargaining agreements.

Ranked second only to the United States, the EC's textile and clothing markets currently account for 34 percent of the world clothing exports, against 42 percent of the world clothing imports.[46] The preferred strategy for restructuring the textile branch lies in "reducing as much as possible wage share in production costs through introduction of automation," a trend not as pronounced in the clothing market, where consumer interest in quality often outweighs price concerns.[47] In both sectors, part-time work is more prevalent among women than men (the latter make up at most 15 percent of the total). The clothing industry serves as the top provider of domestically based labor; it accounts for 10 percent of all homeworkers in the Netherlands, for instance, where female wages in clothing only reach 59 percent of the male wages (not including an estimated 6,000 in underground or sweatshop operations).[48]

A high level of product differentiation makes it difficult to predict the overall impact of the open market on female textile workers in the member states. Table 3 attempts to sketch the types of restructuring likely to occur. At a minimum it can be argued that these sectors will prove increasingly vulnerable to low-wage competition from lesser developed countries.

---

45. Ibid., p. 96.

46. Daniele Meulders and Olivier Plasman, *The Impact of the Single Market on Women's Employment in the Textile and Clothing Industry*, Brussels, 1991, p. 19.

47. Ibid., p. 27.

48. Ibid., pp. 50-52.

Table 3: The 1992 Perspective and Employment

Belgium	The hosiery and clothing sectors are threatened and have high female employment rates
Denmark	9% drop in Danish textile-clothing-footwear by 1992 and 20% drop in clothing, which employs more than 90% women.
Spain	Initially, female jobs will be threatened by reconversion, but the high rate of enrollment in textile job-training centres and high presence in new business allows for moderate optimism.
Greece	Fall of employment consecutive to shutting off of indebted businesses. Sector experiences hardship competing with low-wages countries
Ireland	For the Irish textile-clothing sector, heavy dependency on the British market whose opening creates risks. Probable job losses in heavily feminised clothing.
Italy	Pressure on labour costs in production costs will cause deconcentration toward low-wages countries, thus job losses, mainly in hosiery and clothing. Phasing-in of technological advances will cause requalification and hit lowly skilled personnel.
Luxemburg	Growth in floor-covering.
Netherlands	Possible growth in textile employment; especially in subsectors with only very few female workers. Negative effects on employment in the clothing industry.
Portugal	Women's employment threatened by reconversion in textile-clothing: • business closures; • introduction of new technology works against the less skilled, often female, jobs and leads to deskilling of women. In clothing, employment becomes increasingly unstable.
FR. Germany	Delocalisation operations and production in low-wages countries, much used in the FR. Germany, negatively influence textile-clothing employment. Reliance on crew-work and night shifts endangers female employment.
United Kingdom	Developments in employment depend markedly on retailers' policy.

Source: Meulders and Plasman, *The Impact of the Single Market on Women's Employment in the Textile and Clothing Industry,* Brussels, 1991, p. 74.

Institutional changes foreseen by the two treaties can provide an important antidote to the immobilism of national governments regarding gender equality policies. Acting as a brake on national action is the realization that change costs money; yet the very existence of a law can change attitudes, which eventually induces changes in behavior. The hope is that the industrial interplay of "positive action" and the "human resources approach," on the one hand, and entrepreneurs' self-interested promotion of the open market under the Single European Act, on the other, will produce its own multiplier effect, adding substance to the Vallance and Davies conclusion that "Europe is good news for women."[49]

The actors most committed to advancing European political integration and the internal democratization of the Community are those who have worked hardest to put women's rights on the European agenda. Correspondingly, member states most intent on preserving "national sovereignty" or protecting "national interests" have become the greatest impediments to that process, viz., the United Kingdom and, somewhat paradoxically, the Federal Republic of Germany. Less developed countries have taken big steps forward thanks to the equality directives, notably Ireland and Greece (although abortion remains a touchy subject).

Thus far the strongest, most consistent champion of women's rights has been the directly elected EP itself, hence an enhancement of its powers and proportional increases in the number of female delegates will ultimately serve the equality cause. Created in 1987, the European Women's Lobby (now under the direction of Barbara Helfferich) has scheduled a concerted pro-women campaign for the EP elections of 1994.[50] This electoral united front may help many women — and men — to overcome the long-standing perception that the EC is a bureaucratic monolith "that doesn't affect my life." The focus on Europe's *citoyenne* will add a "human face" to what has long been perceived as "an industrialists' club" following a purely self-interested course.

---

49. Vallance and Davies, p. 114.

50. Ailbhe Smyth, with Anne Roche, *Strategies pour la Promotion des Femmes en Politique. Sondage dans les Etats members de la CE pour le Lobby Européen des Femmes,* Dublin, 1992.

The real problem for women of the European Union, after Maastricht,

> probably lies not so much in the small number of men who are overtly hostile but in the great majority who are apathetic. They may not make sexist remarks, it is no longer socially or politically acceptable to do so, but they will not put themselves out to support women's rights, or to help their female colleagues to do so.[51]

Equality is not a once-and-for-all affair. National governments, as well as Community institutions, must deliver financial means and effective sanctions along with their Sunday sermons. Hard times are exactly the occasions when women most require the enlightened moral and material support of men.

---

51. Vallance and Davies, p. 63.

16
European Cultural Policy after Maastricht

♦ ♦ ♦ ♦ ♦ ♦

Robert Picht

Cultural policy and, to a greater extent, cultural realities play an important and difficult role in Europe's progress toward unity or toward even further fragmentation. Before we can determine why culture is so crucial, we must first agree on what we mean by this concept. Since this paper tries to analyze European integration or disintegration from a sociological perspective, the concept of culture is used in a broad sense, similar to the approaches applied by cultural anthropology to exotic societies. Thus European culture is perceived not merely as philosophy, the arts, and other spiritual, artistic, and intellectual manifestations with their corresponding popular forms of expression; it is seen as a system of structures, choices, and interdependencies that have developed historically in specific ways in the different nations of Europe. The question here is: "What are the cultural conditions for European social, economic, and political cohesion?"

To what extent is what Talcot Parsons called "a core system of shared meaning" common to all Europeans? Parsons considered this the psychological, spiritual, social, and political precondition for any human group to be able to live together and to interact in a meaningful way. "Shared meaning" constitutes social identity.

As groups grow into larger units, they need institutions in order to be able to function and to establish continuity. Jean Monnet insisted that institutions alone assure structured social memory.

However, the efficiency and legitimacy of these institutions depend on "shared meaning." Like medieval monarchies, institutions can become atrophied, unresponsive to changes in reality, and they can lose shared meaning; hence they have the power either to generate or to destroy symbolic cohesiveness. This systemic and historical approach to cultural cohesion gives a better understanding of the difficulties entailed in the process of European unification and progressive integration.

The United States of America faced the challenge of integrating individual Europeans (as well as other nationalities), their families, and sometimes entire religious groups. To a certain degree they were able to do so, creating a melting pot around one common language and some very simple hopes, symbols, and elements of "shared meaning" for all American citizens. Education plays a very important role in this process of assimilation. It appears that American society is actually in some danger of cultural disintegration; similar phenomena of growing anomie are evident in Europe. But before we make hasty comparisons, it is important to understand the fundamental cultural differences between American nation-building and European integration, since these differences are at the heart of the redefinition of European cultural policy after Maastricht; they are centered around concepts such as national and regional identity, subsidiarity, and the dialectics between unity and diversity. Evidently unifying Europe entails more than integrating people and businesses, more than the difficult task of overcoming language barriers among groups that have no intention of abandoning their native traditions for a common idiom. Consequently, melting pot tendencies have been formally rejected by the Maastricht Treaty; diversity is the founding principle of the European Union.

But the problem of mutual understanding goes far beyond linguistics and the great expense for translation in Brussels and Strasbourg. It is directly related to our investigation of "shared meaning." Europe's multiple states and regions as well as its highly structured social entities such as churches, trade unions, and universities are institutions with secular traditions and constraints that shape the minds and behavior of their members. Traditions, institutional constraints, and interactions create ways of thinking and acting that may be perfectly appropriate and necessary in one European country but may sometimes be incompatible with the approaches of a neighboring nation.

A case in point is the current conflict on GATT and the Blair House agreements on the reduction of European agricultural subsidies and exports. Or consider the cultural GATT conflict on the film industry. The French — who, over the centuries, have built one of the most successful and brilliant European societies based on state intervention and a certain degree of protectionism — are perfectly justified in thinking that what is at stake in the GATT negotiations is not just quotas and prices but the future of the fragile rural society and cultural identity in the media. The West Germans — who, after Hitler, have recovered a measure of security, prosperity, and respectability through close association with the United States, through an open market economy, and through worldwide free trade — are perfectly right in considering that, in strictly economic terms, the two problems are relatively marginal with respect to the necessity of keeping the markets open. The invasion of private and — increasingly — public television by Hollywood B-series is not perceived as a danger to national identity. Compromises on GATT will again be reached; the Franco-German partnership is still functioning well. But the unresolved questions are basically cultural in nature.

The same could be shown for a number of other urgent problems such as unemployment, industrial policy, environmental issues, and international relations. If Europeans cannot agree on the kind of society, the sort of culture they envisage for their future or — as the cultural anthropologist Ruth Benedict defines culture — what should be their future project of life, then practical problems such as GATT negotiations will remain extremely difficult to resolve, and their solutions will often be incoherent and contradictory.

Mutual understanding is made more difficult by the fact that among European cultures, even the basic concepts are far from being identical. The fact that fundamental terms like state, economy, trade union, elite, nation, democracy, and friendship do not have identical meanings in the various European languages is due not only to semantics but also to deeply rooted historical experience. Political cultures are as widely divergent as social structures, family links, and educational systems.

Is European unification consequently condemned to the fate of the Tower of Babel or, in modern terms, of a gigantic and complex technostructure that will collapse with the breakdown of communication? I do not think so, even though it appears more difficult to achieve unity in diversity than to organize homogeneity along the lines of the traditional hierarchically structured nation-states. In fact, from a political and economic standpoint — and even more so from a cultural one — post-Maastricht Europe is a highly contradictory but nevertheless dynamic postmodern structure. It is beyond the scope of this paper to explain why the Maastricht Treaty is more a treaty on intergovernmental cooperation in a complex "variable geometry," progressing in different domains at different speeds and with different partners, than it is a treaty on full integration into a European Union. What matters here are the forms of communication that need to be developed to run this kind of structure successfully — the problems of mutual understanding and cooperation after Babel, that is to say, the problems of cultural policy after Maastricht.

What makes me relatively optimistic are the constraints of pure necessity. The establishment of the Common Market has already produced far-reaching economic interdependency, at least in the core of Europe: Western Germany, France, the Netherlands, and the Benelux countries. The market has created such a degree of complementarities that we already have the economic conditions that constitute a common European society. However, we do not have a government adapted to this society with all its problems of intercultural understanding and cooperation.

It is at this point that it becomes necessary for cultural policy and cultural practice to intervene. For the first time, the Maastricht Treaty officially gives some authority to the Commission in the areas of education and culture, although the Commission is severely restricted in its decisionmaking and enforcement ability in order to protect diversity and subsidiarity — i.e., the independence and sovereignty of the nation-states and the regions. Even prior to Maastricht, the European states and the Commission renounced all temptations to harmonize the various educational systems in the same way that the EC tried to standardize industrial norms and products; it is too difficult a task to negotiate in detail the equivalencies of diplomas. But long before Maastricht, some positive steps had already been taken. Countries such as France made large investments in promoting foreign language learning — at the elite universities. For obvious reasons, high-ranking business schools were the first to create integrated studies programs with a year abroad in three European countries. On a bilateral plane, youth exchange programs were created, such as the Franco-German Youth Office. National institutions like the German DAAD were active in developing special programs for Germanists, political scientists, historians, and economists — the strategic disciplines for mutual understanding. On the European level, the European Cultural Foundation created new forms of integrated joint studies ventures. These grew into what is today the Commission's biggest success: the ERASMUS program, an all-European student exchange system. Its ambitious aim is to raise the number of students who experience serious study abroad from the current level of four percent to ten percent.

The result is evident: we are educating a new generation of Europeans who are able to understand differences and to overcome cultural obstacles not by negating but by respecting and negotiating diversity. But these students constitute only a very small elite. Seldom do politicians speak foreign languages beyond elementary English. Even in business one does not frequently find real European managers. Although ambitious businessmen like to present themselves as global players, they generally possess no particular sensibility for the specific European conditions of their work. Consequently, in education, training, and professional success that is linked to more sophisticated international qualifications we also observe the phenomenon of varying speeds of European integration. As in former periods of European history, we are developing a small elite that is able to move among nations and cultures: new European leaders and new European clerks. There is a growing number of civil servants at national and regional levels who are confronted in some ways with European legislation and cooperation. But the vast majority remains essentially national or provincial in their outlook. Frequent travel by tourists and businessmen as well as more superficial programs intended to promote some European identity through rapid youth exchange, along with some new forms of elementary language learning, may stimulate some sympathy, but they are insufficient to promote deeper understanding of other cultures. Similarly, the impact of the media in this respect is highly overestimated. Without intense personal experience and training on the part of those who produce the media, they are unable to transmit knowledge that is durable and to influence changes in thinking and behavior on the part of their audience. Consequently, true "Europeans" constitute a small minority, even in relation to the mainstream of traditional national elites who think and act essentially in a national or regional context.

Thus, for the foreseeable future, European integration or disintegration depends not only on the superstructure of common European institutions and leadership but largely on the evolution of the diverse national societies. Will they be able to converge toward greater complementarity, allowing coherent common action, or will they — even against their own best interests — diverge into Babel-like incoherence?

The odds are uncertain. On the one hand we see in Europe (as in the U.S.) many worrisome signs of social, moral, political, and cultural disintegration of the traditional structures and values of our respective societies. The changes brought about by the so-called postindustrial age are associated with a progressive dissolution of fundamental elements of society such as family (with a 30 to 50 percent divorce rate in most European countries) and identification with a given profession as well as a stable social background. Unemployment has become a major problem, going far beyond the financing of social welfare. Violence and all the signs of anomie are appearing with greater frequency. The relative ethnic homogeneity of Europe is being further destabilized by increasing migration. Traditional identities are being undermined from many sides.

On the other hand, social and cultural changes are being accelerated by sheer necessity. New challenges are creating new consciousness, new elements of shared meaning. When traditional administrations and politics fail, society must seek new solutions. Western Europe — as well as the former communist countries in the East — must develop new forms of civil society on a transnational level. Postmaterialistic values are progressing rapidly. In a very concrete sense, a cultural reorientation of European societies must take place before any further progress can be made toward unification. The true criterion for European cultural policy after Maastricht should be its capacity to contribute to this process of cultural innovation. It is the intensity of the current crisis that entitles us to hope.

17

The Context of Tradition and Cultural Identity
Regionalism and Contemporary European Architecture

◆ ◆ ◆ ◆ ◆ ◆

Udo Kultermann

New Frontiers

In comparison with the political changes that have taken place in the past, the transformations in recent years have made a significant impact on the way architecture in Europe is conceived, constructed, and evaluated, specifically in regard to the existing national borders between the various countries and the crossing of borders in terms of cultural identity.[1]

The geopolitical reality of 1993 contains several new elements: countries that had been divided developed into new unified states; countries that had suffered from long-time domination became independent and able to express officially their own regional and cultural traditions — and, countries were created out of the collapse of a former political union that for a long time

---

1. U. Kultermann, "Diversity versus Uniformity: Tendencies in Architecture and Politics since the late 1980's," *Mass, Albuquerque*, Spring 1992; see also Paul Michael Lützeler, (ed.), *Europa, Analysen und Visionen der Romantiker*, Frankfurt, 1982.

had not allowed the self-expression of ethnic groups and their political agendas.[2]

Unification of parts and the particularization of wholes have to be viewed under multiple constellations, as was demonstrated in the USSR and the USA and as is still under negotiation in Europe. One crucial questions remains: how much independence is given to the individual units and how much responsibility to the whole? Small and large will have to be in a harmonious relationship that is specifically articulated in cultural matters. The goal is a proportional continuity between the parts and the whole, like that of the individual building and the city. Each part has to participate proportionally in the whole. Is this not also the essence of all individual social, political and cultural life?

This extraordinary geocultural change can best be exemplified by a comparison of two maps: one shows the established borderlines of the former Europe, and the other — a conceptual map created in 1991 by the French artist Ben Vautier — shows a situation in the United States where fictitious regional differentiations have resulted in ethnic divisions similar to the changes in Europe.[3]

European architecture is a unique symbol of contemporary transformations typical of our time and possibly of the near future. Herein an indication of the development of architecture in general can be seen that, in the larger context of the international scene, may be of specific importance. European architecture in this sense can serve as a signpost for a development that is in the process of overcoming the imperialistic tendencies of the two superpowers and their ideologies of style.

Both the International Style of Modernism, which dominated large parts of architecture in the Western world, and the International Style of Social Realism, which dominated large parts of the Communist world, are in the process of being transcended by

2. U. Kultermann, "Mit Zitaten bauen. Von der Gegenwart der Vergangenheit im architektonischen Historismus heute," *Neue Rundschau* 104, 1, 1993.

3. U. Kultermann, "La 'perestroika' anunciada. Europe Oriental en los ochenta," *Arquitectura viva* 13, July/August 1990.

regional independent manifestations that no longer adhere to political domination. As the power base in America and in the Soviet Union was founded on style, power and style were intertwined to such an extent that alternatives in architecture that did not follow official doctrines were suppressed. In spite of this — as demonstrated in recent developments — a completely new way of thinking is opening up, one that no longer adheres to the mythologies of the Cold War but is a rather independent way of expressing real historical traditions.[4]

Only now do we become aware to what extent the Cold War was a conspiracy to dominate the Third World. As Noam Chomsky articulated: "To a significant extent, the Cold War has been a system of tacit cooperation, a massive propaganda system that has effectively disguised the actions taken by the super powers to maintain control over their domains. The Cold War has been in effect a war against much of the Third World, and for our tacit partners in global repression, was against their own subject population."[5]

A Shift of Tasks

The actual political changes and the new architectural realizations were in a structural correlation that developed out of its own momentum, and each articulated the new necessities on the level of authentic relevance. Part of this basic transformation has been an important shift in the purposes of buildings, which gave articulation to a new universal social responsibility, to services for sectors of the population that had never before been appropriately served. These new tasks have been geared toward a visionary state of architecture and society in terms of non-oppression and limitation of power.[6]

Among the spectacular solutions in this regard are housing for the masses, child care centers, homes for the aged, homes for the

4. Lützeler, (ed.), *Europa*, p. 52-53.

5. Noam Chomsky, *Towards a New Cold War*, New York, 1982.

6. Alexander Tzonis and Liane Lafaivre, *Architecture in Europe: Memory and Invention since 1968*, New York, 1992, p. 62. U. Kultermann, *Architecture in the Twentieth Century*, New York, 1993.

handicapped and homeless, and centers for single parents and battered women. Each of these special new tasks, surprisingly, benefits architectural design in general; for example, a library for the blind can apply to and improve other building tasks as well. A home for single parents not only offers design solutions of a new kind, but many of its features and details redefine housing in general. It is not by chance that even before the political changes began taking place in Europe, the most important architects dared to face these new and necessary building types, among them Aldo van Eyck and Herman Hertzberger in Holland, Reima Pietilae in Finland, Alvaro Siza in Portugal, and Giancarlo de Carlo in Italy.

In contrast, the buildings of High Tech architecture, continuing and exaggerating the potentials of technology of the past, are manifested in the 1976 Centre Pompidou in Paris by Piano and Rogers, the 1978-86 headquarters of Lloyds in London by Rogers, and in numerous other representational buildings such as Otto von Spreckelsen's "La Grande Arch de la Defense" 1982-89 in Paris.[7]

A European Identity?

It is not only in regard to the new tasks that the present situation of architecture in Europe is in line with international tendencies; there is also a transformation from the general to the specific, the large to the small, the international to the regional. There are numerous interrelated crossings of borders within the European countries — for example, architects from England and Italy working in Germany, Scandinavians in England and Switzerland, Portuguese and Spanish in France. This phenomenon is distinctly different from what is occurring in non-European countries.

European architects have consciously and creatively searched for their regional roots, and in many cases they have been able to establish new criteria for buildings in harmony with the history of the site and a continuation of place, as it was advocated so prominently by Aldo Rossi in Italy. In his basic theoretical statements and in his completed buildings Rossi established typological sys-

---

7. Colin Davis, *High Tech Architecture*, London, 1991.

tems that not only brought contemporary architecture in harmony with the memory of the site but also led to the new trend of building a city as it existed in the past. His housing of 1969-73 in Gallaratese near Milan was one of the pioneering monuments in which the new European identity was articulated, here with specific references to the old Lombardic tradition. Alexander Tzonis and Liane Lefaivre clearly understood its significance: "Gallaratese derives its long rectilinear form from the traditional Milanese tenement house which Rossi identified as a type. The building itself is 182 meters in length and 12 meters deep. The ground floor is an implacably rhythmical portico made up of pilaster elements, while the mostly 2-room housing units are located above, along a corridor".[8] But Rossi went beyond the tradition of the Milanese tenement house and incorporated older forms of Lombardic architecture, manifested in the complete urban integration of city and building in Brisighella, where a two-level transportation system, common in medieval cities, exists today.[9]

As pioneering as Rossi in Italy was the reintegration of historical regional elements in the work of James Stirling in England. His housing scheme of 1967-74 in Runcorn New Town near Liverpool redefined housing in the context of local traditions, such as the nearby still-existing Roman town of Chester with its two-level transportation system and the urban structuring of landscape squares and apartment blocks as it was historically prefigured in London and Bath.[10]

And, to give a third parallel to the tendencies in Italy and England, the German architect Gottfried Boehm similarly created buildings that continue the given physical presence of the past, such as in his Bensberg City Hall of 1962-64, or in his social housing of 1969-75 in Chorweiler near Cologne. In his City Hall Boehm respected and integrated the medieval structure as a constituting element for the work.[11] The Chorweiler housing

---

8. Diane Lefaivre, "'Dirty Realism' in der Architektur," *Archithese* 1, 1990.

9. Kultermann, "Mit Zitaten bauen."

10. Kultermann, "Diversity versus Uniformity." Runcom New Town housing has since been demolished.

11. Kultermann, "Mit Zitaten bauen."

integrated several building types and public spaces into a cohesive neighborhood.

Still another exemplary building in which tradition and new requirements are united is the Regional Library of 1992 in Karlsruhe by Oswald Mathias Ungers. The architect creatively related both the neighboring church by Weinbrenner and the earlier tradition of German architecture, such as the Festival Hall of 1910-1912 in Dresden-Hellerau by Heinrich Tessenow . Projects by Rob Krier, such as his design for squares in Karlsruhe and Berlin, take on the historical urban reality and use its shapes for contemporary purposes.

The new attention given to the site, the memory of place and of historic precedents in general, led to a basic reevaluation of architectural meaning in Europe. As a matter of fact, these transformations mirrored exactly the political transformations taking place during the same years. A completely new way of thinking was inaugurated, one that explored political, social, and economic concepts in an unprecedented manner, and one in which the architect reacted in his own professional language — the language of an autonomous architecture — rather than in the previous manner of delegating responsibilities to other disciplines such as economics and the social and political sciences.[12]

Southern Transformations

Other significant examples of regional differentiations in contemporary European architecture are works by architects in Southern Europe, who have established distinctly defined articulations based on the vernacular tradition of their country or on building typologies that strongly emphasize the culture of the region. One of the clearly recognizable architectural identities in the Italian part of Switzerland are buildings by Mario Botta, Reichlin and Reinhart and Luigi Snozzi, who have established a language that defines the climatic requirements and the cultural tradition of the region without folkloristic or illustrative use of picturesque elements. As in Rossi's buildings in Northern Italy,

---

12. Ernst Friedrich Schumacher, *Small is Beautiful: Economics as if People Mattered*, New York, 1973.

for the Swiss architects it is also the typology of elementary forms through which an autonomous but equally regional architecture has been created. Major examples are Botta's school of 1972-76 in Morbio Inferiore and his house of 1980 in Viganello in which his admiration for his master Louis I. Kahn and the specific requirements of his clients are harmonized.[13]

While French regional differentiations are not as strongly articulated and several of the major building programs of President Mitterand take refuge in monumental state representations — including the large-scale housing schemes by Ricardo Bofill in several new cities outside Paris — the situation in Spain and Portugal is quite differently manifested, especially in works by Rafael Moneo in Spain and Alvaro Siza in Portugal. Moneo's Museum of Roman Art of 1980-88 in Merida has a special place in this development, as it is the essence of regional identity. Housing more than 20,000 items of Roman excavations from the area, the museum incorporates parts of the old Roman buildings and continues their architectural language in the new building. Tzonis and Lefaivre commented in this regard: "The museum thus emerges as if mediating between 'time present and time past,' and the visitor moving through it becomes an unceasing explorer".[14] Spanish contemporary architecture here has achieved its full maturity and, at the same time, it continues and creates a unity with the regional past.

Alvaro Siza's work in Portugal is also based on local tradition but transcends it in a contemporary rearticulation. His Bouca Social Housing of 1973-77 in Porto provides a prototype for low-income housing and without any references to decorative elements, gives a new version of old architectural forms of the region. It is not by chance that on the basis of this still incomplete housing scheme, other architects have followed its principles and are in the process of developing a regional identity under the name "School of Porto." The work of Siza also had tremendous international reverberations.[15]

13. Francesco Dal Co., *Mario Botta. Architecture. 1960-1985*, London, 1987.

14. Tzonis and Leaivre, *Architecture in Europe*, p. 149.

15. V. Gregotti, La passion d'Alvaro Siza," *L'Architecture d'Aujourd'hui* 185, 1976.

Eastern European Transformation

In addition to the strong regional manifestations of architecture in
Central and Southern Europe, there are — similar to the political
transformations — even more spectacular developments to be
seen in Eastern Europe. While for many decades architects were
under the rule of Communism and subjected to the architectural
style dominated by the Soviet Union, recent developments have
shown a strong protest against the dictates of a political ideology
by reestablishing regional forms in architectural design.[16]

This development is clearly visible in buildings by Czech architects such as Alena Sramkova and the group SIAL in Liberec,
which continue the earlier Czech development of architecture.
Under the direction of Karel Hubacek, the SIAL group built a
department store in Prague and the TV Tower in Jested, and
participated in a competition in Berlin as well.[17] Architects in
Hungary, on the other hand, rediscovered the old Hungarian
rural tradition and established masterpieces — for example, Imre
Makovesz's House of Culture of 1974-77 in Sarospatak — in
which the material wood and the emotional energies of the old
rural Hungarian tradition are revitalized.[18]

Still other differentiations can be recognized in the various
parts of the former Yugoslavia, with distinct cultural features in
buildings by Croatian architects such as Boris Magas, Slovenian
architects such as Edvard Ravnikar, and Serbian architects such
as Stojan Maksimovic, who rearticulated the regional tradition of
their ethnic cultural identity. In the southern parts of the former
Yugoslavia the tendencies toward specific architectural language
are demonstrated in programmatically Moslem buildings like the
1980 White Mosque in Visiko by Zlatko Ugljen and the 1980

---

16. U. Kultermann, *Zeitgenössische Architektur in Osteuropa*, Düsseldorf, 1985.

17. U. Kultermann, " Das Werk der Architektengruppe SIAL. Zeigenössisches
    Bauen in der Tchechoslowakei," *AIT (Architektur, Innenarchitektur, Technis-
    cher Ausbau)* 1, 1985.

18. About Imre Makovesz: U. Kultermann, "Architecture as Folk Architecture:
    The Work of the Hungarian Architect Imre Makovesz," *Architecture and
    Urbanism*, March 1984.

National and University Library of Kosovo in Pristina by Andrija Mutnjakovic.In these buildings the revival of Islamic forms of architecture of the past is openly visible.[19]

The same phenomenon can be seen in the different regions of the former Soviet Union, where the architecture of the Russian and Ukrainian Republics is different from the architecture in the Republics of Armenia and Georgia. The Children's Library of 1980 in Kiev by Michael Budilovski transcends the doctrine of Socialist Realism forced upon architects for many years by adopting a regional Ukrainian solution. The Library is also innovatively a new building type.[20]

The fact that the movements for independence took place in architecture long before the advent of political independence in the various countries can best be demonstrated in selected examples of Lithuanian and Estonian architecture. The 1981 Recreation Center in Druskininkai Lithuania, by R. and A. Shilinskas is a free architectural manifestation that openly transcends the limits set by the previous Soviet cultural limitations.[21]

Furthermore, the Estonian architects in Tallinn created a movement in defiance of Soviet demands by erecting buildings for social purposes, apartment buildings, and one-family houses in which an Estonian identity was openly demonstrated. Toomas Rein's Public Sauna for Farm Workers of 1973-83 in Kobela and his Recreation Center of 1976-79 in Paatsalu are masterpieces of regional Estonian identity, built under the regime of the political power of the Soviet Union.[22]

19. Ivan Straus, *Arkitekture Jugoslavije*, Sarajevo, 1991.

20. Catherine Cooke, "Meaningful Messages of Post-Modernism," *Architectural Design*, News Supplement 1, 1982.

21. U. Kultermann, "Looking East," *Space and Society*, June, 1985.

22. U. Kultermann, Toomas Rein, "Towards an Estonian Identity," *Space and Society* 19, 1982; "Looking East." See also: U. Kultermann, Leonard Lapin – Visionary of a New Estonian Culture, Architektur, Fall/Winter 1993, 3-9.

Conclusion

European identity has emerged from a multiplicity of sources. There was a strong dividing line between the countries of Western Europe and Eastern Europe, resulting in opposite formal rules according to the ideology of the Cold War. There were nationalistic tendencies — such as expressions of power that were not in line with the natural ethnic and regional cultural traditions, that had to be overcome. There will continue to be obstacles to the diversity of regional manifestations in the various parts of Europe in years to come.

It would be a mistake to claim that architecture in Europe — like European politics — needs to be a homogeneous, uniform stylistic articulation. This would be a direct contradiction of what regional identity is meant to be. It is important to achieve a balanced and free diversity of regional manifestations which, nevertheless, remain united in their sharing of mutual values. The discovery of the specific inner characteristics of each small unit in the context of a family of nations may bring out new insights and innovative visions. Each country may have the opportunity to develop according to its own specific goals.

Architectural styles unfortunately will continue to be expressions of power, whether they are exaggerations of the new national consciousness of individual countries, or whether they are the oppressive economic power of large corporations, which to some extent has already interfered with the rediscovery of local values and regional traditions. A truly new architecture without style remains a vision for the future.

The European regeneration of the early 1990's in terms of political, economic, and cultural identity offers a potential for the realization of an architecture no longer based on power, as it was in the past — an architecture that does not articulate nations and empires or the dynastic aspirations of individual rulers or bureaucratic institutions. The recent developments of some of the major architects practicing in Europe and their clients have demonstrated that this direction is a realistic one.

18
Writers on European Identity

◆ ◆ ◆ ◆ ◆ ◆

Paul Michael Lützeler

"These poets!" Matthieu de Molé cried distractedly at the plenum of the French National Assembly. De Molé, a state representative, had quite obviously lost his composure. On this 17th day of July 1851, tempers were already flaring in the French Parliament, since the topic under discussion was the delicate matter of a constitutional change. This change was aimed at enabling the president Louis Napoleon to run for reelection, which was forbidden by existing law. At this point — of all times — the novelist and visionary Victor Hugo found it necessary to step into the realm of Utopia by presenting his unpatriotic vision of a United States of Europe. This was too much! In the eyes of those fighting for French *gloire*, Hugo was nothing but a renegade who had drifted out of the conservative faction to the left, where national matters were of no great concern. Charles de Montalembert was speaking to Hugo from the right wing, telling him that he must be out of his mind. The idea Hugo had dared to put forth was soon drowned out by the noise of jeering and by expressions of anger.

In contrast to Hugo's contemporaries, today most people do not question the realistic direction of thinking aimed at the integration of democratic states in a continental unity. To the contrary, many aspects of European cooperation have progressed so rapidly that the process is evoking opposition of a sort that Hugo could not possibly have envisioned. The French writer saw in European unification a practical means of countering the cultural chauvinism of individual countries, as well as a measure against the potential self-destruction of a continent predisposed to war because of its nationalistic structure. Present-day authors such as Hans Magnus Enzensberger argue that a pacified continent should maintain its sovereign nation states, since the political union of Europe could lead to an inner annihilation of the cultural diversity of its various countries, states, and regions. Because of its immense economic and military strength, such a union could outwardly threaten peace rather than ensure it.

The idea of a united Europe long preceded Hugo's speech to Parliament in 1851 and, for a variety of reasons, it met with opposition long before Enzensberger's comments in the 1980s. It is striking that in the European countries it has been especially the writers who have dealt with the idea of European unity so intensively for the past two hundred years. One of its prominent defenders, Heinrich Mann, went so far as to claim that European identity was an invention of the writers. Such a sweeping generalization is hardly convincing, since the pioneers of what Benedict Anderson called the "imagined community" of Europe included philosophers, educators, scientists and, of course, politicians. Nevertheless, it is a fact that the writers of the last two centuries have made a considerable contribution to the concept of a cultural and political European alliance. To ignore the impact of their works on the history of the unification process or to underestimate their influence would be tantamount to falsifying history. Like Hugo, they were often ridiculed by short-sighted intellectuals and politicians who professed to be "pragmatists" and who would have been content with what was "doable" in pursuing the course of least resistance and momentary success. As in Hugo's case, the authors of essays on Europe often recognized the signs of the times more clearly than those who were at the core of public opinion and political decisionmaking.

At the turn of the eighteenth century, the Holy Roman Empire of German Nations was in the final stages of disintegration. In Paris, Napoleon was putting into effect a foreign policy whose ultimate goal was France's domination of Europe. In his essay "Christianity or Europe" of 1799, Novalis reacted to both historical phenomena. It was at this point that German-speaking authors became intensely preoccupied with Europe. Yet Novalis's essay was made possible by the preparatory work of such European cosmopolitans of the seventeenth and eighteenth centuries as Herder, Wieland, Kant, Hume, Rousseau, Saint-Pierre, Fénelon, Leibniz, William Penn, the Duke of Sully, and Grotius.

The literary essays on Europe that have appeared since the time of Romanticism are not merely political blueprints for a future European federation. Of equal importance — and at times, of even greater impact — is the parallel discussion of European cultural identity, which is closely linked to the political debate. The political arguments for continental cooperation are supported by references to shared history, religion, and art. Like the political designs, ideas on cultural identity are not naturally derived phenomena but rather conscious constructs.

No other literary genre considered the pressing political and cultural questions of Europe so directly and from so many aspects as did the literary essays on Europe. Along with Novalis, the leading Europe essayists during the time of Romanticism were the Schlegel brothers, Arndt, Gentz, Coleridge, Wordsworth, and Madame de Staël. Their interests focused on a conceptualization of Europe that could serve as an alternative to Napoleon's idea of French dominance. In the course of the debate about Metternich's restoration strategy, essays on Europe were proffered by Saint-Simon, Görres, Franz von Baader, Schmidt-Phiseldek, Heine, Börne, Mazzini, Kühne, Mackay, Menzel, Ruge, and Fröbel. During the time of peace between 1871 and 1912, Nietzsche, Unamuno, Mithouard, Wildenbruch, and Paquet made important, though controversial, contributions on the topic of European identity. At the time of the First World War and in the early 1920s, Rolland, Hesse, Annette Kolb, Schickele, Heinrich Mann, Borchardt, Hofmannsthal, Pannwitz, and Theodor Lessing commented on European affinities. Coudenhove-Kalergi, Thomas Mann, Hiller, Olden, Tucholsky, Arnold Zweig, Flake, Klaus Mann, and Rychner supported the Europe politics of Briand and Stresemann in the period between the wars. After 1933, Lion, Thomas Mann, Unruh, Kahler, Heinrich Mann, and Döblin sounded a warning about Hitler as the destroyer of

Europe. Subsequent to the Second World War, after 1945, Ernst Jünger, T. S. Eliot, Stephen Spender, Andersch, Thiess, Bergengruen, Sartre, Klaus Mann, Reinhold Schneider, and George Saiko demanded — with varying sociopolitical goals in mind — a new beginning for Europe. The Europe discussion was revived in the 1980s by such Central European intellectuals as Kundera, Konrád, and Dalos, who demanded an end to the European order established at Yalta. They pushed for the reunification of Europe, ending the division of the continent by the Iron Curtain. In the Federal Republic of Germany, Enzensberger took the initiative, warning of a bureaucratic, stagnant, Common-Market Europe.

Writers on Europe have been greatly concerned with restriction of the European identity. Values such as unity, individualism, and idealism are at the center of the discussion; in this context, America and Asia are often used as a basis for demarcation and comparison. The roster of authors who have debated the unity and diversity of European culture ranges from Novalis's and Friedrich Schlegel's insistence on unity to those authors who believe that diversity is contained within unity (as asserted by Börne, Heine, Stadler, Schickele, Lion, Annette Kolb, and Stefan Zweig) as well as to the authors of the 1980s (i.e., Hans Magnus Enzensberger, Heiner Müller, and Peter Schneider) who rejected the concept of the unity of European civilization and instead insisted on an acknowledgment of total pluralism. It is generally assumed that in Europe idealism, individualism, and unity are embroiled in a constant struggle with materialism, collectivism, and diversity, whereas the image of an all-encompassing cultural unity is often projected onto Asia (ancient China and ancient India). However, as Edward Said has demonstrated, these images are generally Eurocentristic constructs.

What was it that drove the essayists to write about Europe, that moved them to their reflections, theses, postulations? In the last analysis they took up their pens for political reasons. Some of them were what might be termed "Euronationalists" or "Eurochauvinists." Their primary concern was the safeguarding of the spiritual and/or material European hegemony in the world, the maintenance of an ideological and/or real imperial European position. Such was the case with Schmidt-Phiseldek, Nietzsche, Alfons Paquet, the young Heinrich Mann, André Suares, Ortega y Gasset, the early Pannwitz, and Stefan Zweig. At times their studies express a fear of conquest or entrapment of Europe by the world powers: America and Russia (or the Soviet Union). Far more numerous, however, are the essayists who profess more humane and selfless motives for their attitudes and stances toward Europe. These authors are primarily concerned with preventing war in Europe, with eliminating national prejudices and hatreds, and with promoting friendship among European countries, especially between Germany and France. This is the basis for the arguments, rationalizations, and polemics of Novalis, Saint-Simon, Heine, Börne, Hugo, Heinrich Mann, Ernst Stadler, René Schickele, Hermann Hesse, Annette Kolb, Rudolf Borchardt, Hugo von Hofmansthal, Thomas Mann, André Gide, Jacques Rivières, Ivan Goll, Coudenhove-Kalergi, Emil Ludwig, Arnold Zweig, Rudolf Olden, Fritz von Unruh, and Klaus Mann. This goal is frequently combined with the fight for greater liberalization of the political condition and the demand for emancipation of underprivileged groups within the respective states. In this context Görres, Börne, Mazzini, Hugo, and Heinrich Mann are to be singled out.

Endless discussions have been devoted to the specific form of the alliance among the individual nation-states. Would a united Europe or a federation of states or a Europe of fatherlands be the best solution? Would a constitutional monarchy or a democratic republic be the most adequate form of government for the unified continent?

Another aspect of the literary essays on Europe is the idea of a "Sonderweg," or the particularized developmental pathway of each nation. Almost all the essays that deal with Europe respect each European nation's individuality and its distinctive historical development, while at the same time the cultural and historical affinity of the entire continent is stressed again and again. During the late nineteenth and early twentieth centuries, Tolstoy in Russia, Unamuno in Spain, Kipling in England, d'Annuncio in Italy, Barrès in France, and Thomas Mann in Germany took great pains to point out the uniqueness of the Russian, Spanish, English, Italian, French, and German *Sonderweg* in the course of European history. At times the descriptions of this uniqueness and the contrived delineations (by Unamuno and Thomas Mann, for example) resembled each other to the point that they became interchangeable. One must keep in mind that the above-named writers on the *Sonderweg* were simultaneously great Europeans who expressed their preference for either the idea of a common Europe or the concept of national uniqueness, depending on the historical situation. They never lost sight of the inevitable and insoluble intermeshing of European and national identity. One must not underestimate the ideological significance and the fatal consequences of the *Sonderweg* debate on the attempt to define national identities in the Germany of the nineteenth and early twentieth centuries. However, the *Sonderweg* discourse was but one among many in which the writers engaged. Following the Second World War, the shock and the enormity of the Holocaust and other crimes perpetrated by the National Socialists caused the blame for the catastrophe of the Third Reich to be laid upon the German *Sonderweg*. Historiographers have a tendency to isolate the old *Sonderweg* discourse as a cultural-historical debate. In parallel with the nationalistic *Sonderweg* debates going on in the individual European states, a discussion on Europe was taking place, which partially incorporated the *Sonderweg* arguments and partially neutralized or discredited them. Neither of these discourses should be relegated to a purely historical viewpoint, for they are being revived and continued in current discussions in Germany and elsewhere. In the Central European countries, which have escaped from the forcible embrace of the former Soviet Union, such an animated debate is currently taking place on a European level as well as on a national one. Indeed, in almost all of the European countries debates are being held and plans are being made on various levels: local, regional, national, European, and global. If the future is to be mastered in a European as well as an international context, it is essential that critical discussions be held not only about the old *Sonderwege* but also about the European concept as discussed in the literary essays on Europe. At the same time, there is no reason to glorify the

Europe debates in which the writers have engaged, since they reflect not just realistic appraisals of the present and the future. At times nationalistic ideas were simply expanded into Eurochauvinist concepts, as in the case of Nietzsche's idea of the "good European." By and large, however, the intent of the essays on Europe was to contribute to the elimination of national prejudice, hatred, and warmongery.

A glance at the history of European identity formation shows that it was constantly subject to change. What direction this change will take in light of the intensified confrontation with other cultures cannot be predicted at this point in time. It is clear, however, that the old polarities of anarchy and order, individualism and communality, rationality and faith, idealism and materialism, reason and critique of reason, science and ideology, logos and myth, history and utopia, tradition and progress, unity and plurality are at odds with each other in new ways and with new results. They are the same polarities that Karl Jaspers saw as the signs of European freedom. In his book *Imagining Europe*, the French philosopher Edgar Morin also views this *unitas multiplex* as the essence of European identity. In order to explain this multilayered and contradictory identity he employs the term "dialogic," which he borrows from Bakhtin. He writes:

> The principle of "dialogic" means that two or more different kinds of "logic" are joined together in a complex manner (complementary, concurring, antagonistic) without losing their duality in this unity. Thus, what creates the unity in European culture is not the Jewish-Christian-Greek-Roman synthesis, not just the complementary quality of these elements, but also the concurrence and the antagonism which exist between all these instances, all of which have their own logic: their "dialogic." (29)

In every country, in every region of Europe the adaptations of cultural identity will differ, and thus there is no reason to fear that in the future the continent will present a picture of colorless uniformity. The cultural European scene will always continue to resemble a laboratory. The fact that the uniqueness of the current European identity is paralleled by sociohistorical manifestations has been shown by Hartmut Kaelble. He has defined the special aspects of Europe's societal composition in comparison to that of Japan, the Soviet Union, and North America.

I would like to add a postscript on solidarity and subsidiarity in Europe in order to put into perspective the present discussion on Europe. During the First World War, Heinrich Mann and Hugo von Hofmannsthal introduced the term "European solidarity" into the discussion. European solidarity is necessary to overcome the conflicts and dangers that originated in the restructuring of Central and Eastern Europe subsequent to the generally peaceful revolutions of 1989 and 1991. Because of the dynastic and national traditions of the European continent, there exists the ever-present danger in Europe that solidarity will be lost, and it takes a great effort to steer clear of this threat. Writers have attained a growing awareness that the events in Central and Eastern Europe demand an encompassing European solidarity. In the past most authors did not become Europeans until after their fatherlands had suffered catastrophic defeats; European solidarity then appeared to provide salvation. The most avid Europeans were likewise the greatest national losers. Whenever the national identity became blemished, the European angle was rediscovered. This was the case in the German countries during the Napoleonic era when the French emperor stripped them of their power, a process that caused Arndt, Görres, and Gentz to search for a European solution. So it was also in 1814, after the defeat of France, when Saint-Simon and Thierry devised their design for a united Europe in which their fatherland would once again play an honorary role. The same was true in 1870, when the realm of Napoleon III was destroyed by the Germans. At that time Victor Hugo called for the unification of the continent. It was the situation in 1917 as well, when authors like H. Mann, Borchardt and Hofmannsthal, surveying the misery of their fatherlands, looked to European solidarity. It was thus in 1945, when Ernst Jünger demanded the unification of Europe, which would have ensured the survival of Germany. And once again in the mid-1980s, when Milan Kundera and György Konrad made an appeal in the name of their oppressed Central European countries for the solidarity of Western Europeans. On Christmas eve of 1989, a group of

Rumanian students marched toward the guns of the security police in Bucharest, shouting the slogan: "Europe is with us! Europe is with us!" This was probably the most desperate plea for help from Europe that year.

In the course of the centuries the hope for a European association continuously expressed by the national losers has evolved into something akin to a limited liability corporation, namely, the current European (economic) Community. One may assume with some degree of certainty that the Western and Eastern European nations will see eye to eye when it comes to the expansion and strengthening of the economic community. Although this expansion will exceed the bounds of the Commission as the central planning committee in Brussels, it is underway. As was foreseen in the nineteenth century, economic conditions demand the abolition of national boundaries, and it could be a matter of time before trade, labor, and possibly currency will function freely within Europe. None of the continent's nations seems to be in a hurry to achieve European political unity, although the vision of political unity is part of the Maastricht Treaty. The elected parliaments, leaders, and heads of state of the various countries are reluctant to yield political sovereignty, since such an act entails the actual relinquishing of power. Nevertheless, more and more sectors will work together on a European level, and this increased cooperation goes hand in hand with the gradual takeover of national governmental functions by a European consortium. Whether the old idea of a United States of Europe can be realized — or whether such a realization is indeed desirable — is one of the questions that the authors, along with others, will be debating for a long time to come.

Whatever forms of European representation or government eventually come to be established, it would be worthwhile to support the principle of subsidiarity. This principle — endorsed by the Maastricht Treaty — suggests that only those elements should be delegated to the next-higher level that cannot be dealt with on a lower level. Anything that can be resolved on the local, regional, or national level should not be passed on to the highest agency. It is thus the reverse of the concept of a central government in which all actions must be sanctioned by a government agency in the state capital; the inefficiency of such a system was evidenced in the countries of the former Socialist Bloc. One must beware of a superbureaucracy in Brussels attempting to make detailed decisions for the whole European continent. It is likely that in the Europe of the future the discrete nations as well as (increasingly) the regions will continue or will resume playing an important role in the decisionmaking process. The old European regions were often restricted in their development because of national borders and artificial district boundaries. In the pursuit of certain demands, it is the regions especially that would benefit from a legally ensured subsidiarity principle. If one visualizes the government of a united Europe as a building, it would be made up of a local, a regional, a national, and a European floor. On the European floor only those problems would be dealt with that could not be handled on the national floor; this floor, in turn, would be faced only with problems too difficult for the regional floor, which would occupy itself only with matters beyond the scope of the local level. Perhaps a Europe organized along these lines would pacify those critics of Brussels — Hans Magnus Enzensberger among them — who are concerned with the preservation of local color and regional/national variety in Europe and who despise nothing more than central bureaucracy.

The parallel to a subsidiary structure is found in human identity per se, where gender, family, professional, social, religious, local, regional, national, continental, and global identities are — in the sense of Edgar Morin's and Bakhtin's dialogic — intertwined in conflict. It is to the lasting credit of the European writers that they committed themselves to the European dimension of their identities during the nineteenth and twentieth centuries, i.e., at a time when nationalistic movements insisted on the unity and totality of a specific nation's identity and proceeded to enforce these demands with catastrophic consequences. On the other hand, it is also to the credit of contemporary authors that they insist on the importance of regional and national identities when these identities seem to be threatened by the Brussels project. Europe would indeed no longer be Europe if its regional and national identities were to be standardized; a European identity needs to encompass national and regional — and for that matter, global — identities in the spirit of multiculturalism.

Bibliography

Anderson, Benedict R., *Imagined Communities: Reflections on the Origin and Spread of Nationalism* (London, 1983).

Foerster, Rolf Hellmut, Europa. Geschichte einer politischen Idee (Munich, 1967).

Gollwitzer, Heinz, *Europabild und Europagedanke. Beiträge zur deutschen Geistesgeschichte des 18. und 19. Jahrhunderts* (Munich, 2nd ed., 1964).

Heer, Friedrich, *Europa, Mutter der Revolutionen* (Stuttgart, 1964).

Jaspers, Karl, *Vom europäischen Geist* (Munich, 1947).

Kaelble, Hartmut, *Auf dem Weg zu einer europäischen Gesellschaft. Eine Sozialgeschichte Westeuropas 1880-1980* (Munich, 1987).

Lepenies, Wolf, *Die drei Kulturen. Soziologie zwischen Literatur und Wissenschaft* (Munich, 1985).

Lützeler, Paul Michael, *Die Schriftsteller und Europa. Von der Romantik bis zur Gegenwart* (Munich, 1992).

Meulen, Jacob ter, *Der Gedanke der internationalen Organisation in seiner Entwicklung* (The Hague, 1968).

Morin, Edgar, *Europa denken* (Frankfurt/Main, 1988).

Weidenfeld, Werner, ed., *Die Identität Europas* (Munich, 1985).

Notes on the Contributors

◆ ◆ ◆ ◆ ◆ ◆

George A. Bermann
Charles Keller Beekman Professor of Law at Columbia University School of Law and editor of the *Columbia Journal of European and Community Law*. He received his JD from Yale Law School, where he served as editor of the *Yale Law Journal*. He has been Visiting Professor at Tulane Law School and at the University of Paris I — Sorbonne. His publications include *Cases and Materials on Transnational Litigation* (1993), *French Law: Constitution and Selective Legislation* (1988, co-author) and *Cases and Materials on European Community Law* (1994), as well as numerous book chapters, articles, and presentations on European law.

Dieter Dettke
Executive Director of the Washington Office of the Friedrich Ebert Foundation since 1985. He received his PhD in political science from the Free University of Berlin. Until 1972 he was a research associate at the German Society for Foreign Affairs in Bonn, then served as political counselor of the SPD Parliamentary Group of the German Bundestag. Between May and October 1982, he was Staff Director at the Office of the State Minister of the German Foreign Ministry. He has published widely on security issues, East-West relations, and U.S. foreign and domestic policy, including *Allianz im Wandel*, Frankfurt, 1984.

Yuri V. Fedotov
Associate Professor and Head of the Department of Economics of the Firm in the School of Management at St. Petersturg State University, he graduated from Leningrad State University. He has spent two years as a guest researcher in the Department of Economics at Stockholm University. He is the director of the Center of Public Administration Studies at St. Petersburg University. The author of numerous articles on economic efficiency measurement,

production, and growth theory, he has also written textbooks and teaching materials for courses in microeconomic theory and modeling of technical change, as well as translating books and articles by Western economists.

Caroline Jackson

Conservative Member of the European Parliament for Wiltshire (England) since 1984. She was formerly a research student at Nuffield College, Oxford, where she obtained a PhD with a thesis on nineteenth-century politics, and then a research fellow at St. Hugh's College, Oxford. In the European Parliament she specializes in environmental protection and consumer issues. She is the author of numerous articles and pamphlets on contemporary European issues, including "The First British MEPs, 1974-1979," published in the *Journal of Contemporary European History* (1993).

Hartmut Kaelble

Professor of Social History at Humboldt University in Berlin, he received his PhD and his *venia legendi* at the Free University of Berlin. He was previously professor at the Free University of Berlin and research fellow at Harvard University, at St. Antony's College in Oxford, and at the Maison des Sciences de l'Homme in Paris. He is the author of numerous books, including *Social Mobility in the 19th and 20th Centuries: Europe and America in Comparative Perspective*, 1985; *Industrialization and Social Inequality in 19th Century Europe*, 1986; *A Social History of Western Europe, 1880-1980*, 1990; *Nachbarn am Rhein: Entfremdungen und Annäherungen der französischen und deutschen Gesellschaft, 1880-1980*, 1991.

Udo Kultermann

Ruth and Norman Moore Professor of Architecture at Washington University in St. Louis, he graduated from Münster University. He has lectured at major universities on all continents and has acted as consultant to government agencies. Among his book publications, which have been translated into ten languages, are *Kenzo Tange — Architecture and Urban Design* (1970), *Art and Life — The Function of Intermedia* (1970), *Architecture in the 20th Century* (1977), *Architecture in the Seventies* (1980), *History of Art Theories* (1987), *Art and Reality: From Fiedler to Derrida. Ten Approaches* (1991).

James T. Little

Professor of Economics and Finance at the John M. Olin School of Business at Washington University in St. Louis, he graduated from the University of British Columbia and received his PhD from the University of Minnesota. He is the author of *Neighborhood Change: Lessons in the Dynamic of Urban Decay,* 1976, as well as articles on consumer theory, urban policy, corporate financial policies, and joint ventures.

Paul Michael Lützeler

Rosa May Distinguished University Professor in the Humanities, he teaches in the German Department, the Comparative Literature Committee, and the European Studies Program, of which he is the director, at Washington University in St. Louis. He has been a Visiting Professor at Indiana, Tübingen, Princeton, Monash, and McMaster Universities. His awards include the Austrian Cross of Honor for Arts and Sciences, the German *Bundesverdienstkreuz,* and the Outstanding Educator Award of the American Association of Teachers of German. The author of *Hermann Broch. Eine Biographie* (1985), *Zeitgeschichte in Geschichten der Zeit* (1986), *Geschichte in der Literatur* (1987), *Die Schriftsteller und Europa* (1992), he has also written many articles and edited numerous editions on German and European literature, culture, and politics.

Joyce Marie Mushaben

Associate Professor of Comparative Politics, Women's Studies, and a Research Fellow in the Center for International Studies at the University of Missouri-St. Louis. She received her PhD from Indiana University. A former DAAD-Fulbright Scholar, Alexander von Humboldt Fellow, and Ford Foundation Fellow in GDR Studies, her publications focus on peace, feminist and ecology movements, German national identity, and right-wing radicalism. Her recently completed book, *The Post-Postwar Generations: Changing Attitudes towards the National Question and NATO in the Federal Republic of Germany, 1949-1989* will appear in late 1994.

Robert Picht

Director of the Deutsch-Französisches Institut (Franco-German Institute) in Ludwigsburg, he has also served as Professor of Sociology at the College of Europe at Bruges and at the Fernuniversität Hagen. He was vice-president and director of the Executive Committee of the European Cultural Foundation in Amsterdam. His publications include *Deutschlandstudien* I and II, Bonn, 1975/8; *Das Bündnis im Bündnis. Deutsch-französische Beziehungen im internationalen Spannungsfeld*, Berlin, 1982; *Esprit-Geist. Hundert Schlüsselbegriffe für Deutsche und Franzosen*, Munich, 1989; and *L'identité européenne*, Brussels, 1994.

Peter G. Rogge
Economic adviser to a number of European governments, public institutions and leading companies, he studied in the U.S. (California State University), Germany, and Switzerland. He obtained his PhD in economics from Basle University with a thesis on "The US Credit Programs for West Berlin." He was CEO of PROGNOS AG, a leading economic research and consulting organization in Basle, before joining Swiss Bank Corporation, where he served as Senior Vice President in charge of Economics and Corporate Systems prior to his retirement in March 1994.

Alberta Sbragia
Professor of Political Science and Director of the West European Studies Program at the University of Pittsburgh, she received her PhD from the University of Wisconsin-Madison. She carried out her dissertation research as a Fulbright scholar in Milan. She taught "Government, Business, and the International Economy" at the Harvard Business School (1983-4) and directed a project for the Brookings Institution on "Politics and Policymaking in the European Community." She recently published *Euro-Politics: Institutions and Policymaking in the "New" European Community* (1992). Her current research focuses on environmental policy within the European Community/Union.

Theo Sommer
Formerly editor-in-chief and now publisher of *DIE ZEIT* (Hamburg), he received his education in Sweden, Tübingen, and Chicago. He was a participant in Henry Kissinger's International Summer Seminar at Harvard University in 1960. He is a TV commentator and the moderator of a monthly program. The recipient of several prestigious awards, including an honorary Doctor of Laws degree from the University of Maryland, he writes mainly on international affairs, strategic questions, and German and European problems. In addition to being a contributing editor to

Newsweek International and *Yomiuri Shimbun,* he has written or edited several books: *The Chinese Card* (1979), *Changing Alliance?* (1982), *Look Back Into the Future* (1984), *Journey to the Other Germany* (1986).

Andrzej Stępniak
Professor of Economics and the Didactics of International Economics and European Integration as well as director of the Research Centre on European Integration at the University of Gdańsk, where he received his PhD. He has been a Visiting Professor at Zürich University and a Jean Monnet Fellow at the European University Insititute in Florence. Co-founder of the Polish European Community Studies Association, he has written and edited books on international affairs, European integration, and Polish-EC cooperation: *Joint Ventures between the Member States of the EEC and CMEA,* Saarbrücken, 1985; *Poland-EC: Selected Aspects of Adjustment in the Light of 1992 Single Market and the Agreement on Association,* Gdańsk, 1993; *Poland-EC. Investment Opportunities in the European Community,* Gdańsk, 1993.

Michael Strübel
Professor of Political Science at the University of Erfurt, he received his PhD and his *Habilitation* at the University of Heidelberg. He was a Jean Monnet Fellow at the European University Institute in Florence and Visiting Professor at Stuttgart and Humboldt Universities, Berlin, and Washington University in St. Louis. He is author of *Die Internationale Politik der Italienischen Kommunisten,* 1982 and *Internationale Umweltpolitik,* 1992, as well as author of numerous articles on international relations, European integration, security politics, and environmental policies.

Sergei F. Sutyrin
Professor and Head of the Department of International Economics at St. Petersburg State University, he graduated from Leningrad State University, spent a year as research fellow at the London School of Economics, and received his PhD degree from Leningrad State University. He is the author of *Sovietological Economic Theory in Critical Retrospective,* Leningrad, 1989, as well as articles on the history of economic thought, economic history, and international economics. He has also written textbooks and teaching materials for courses on the economics of taxation and international economics.

Elke Thiel
Senior Research Associate at the Stiftung Wissenschaft und Politik (German Research Institute for International Affairs) in Ebenhausen (near Munich) and *Honorarprofessor* for European Politics at the University of Bamberg. She is the author of *Dollar-Dominanz, Lastenteilung und amerikanische Truppenpräsenz in Europa*, Baden-Baden, 1979; *Die Europäische Gemeinschaft*, Munich, 1992; and several articles on international and European economics, in particular U.S.-EC and trilateral relations as well as the economics and politics of European integration.

Murray Weidenbaum
Mallinckrodt Distinguished University Professor at Washington University in St. Louis and Director of the University's Center for the Study of American Business, he also has held senior positions in government and business. He served as chairman of President Reagan's Council of Economic Advisers in 1981-2 and earlier was the Assistant Secretary of the Treasury for Economic Policy and Corporate Economist for the Boeing Company. He is the author of *Economics of Peacetime Defense*, 1974; *Rendezvous With Reality: The American Economy After Reagan*, 1988; *Business, Government, and the Public* (fourth edition), 1990; *Small Wars, Big Defense*, 1992. He is also co-chair of the International Research Council of the Center for Strategic and International Studies.

Leila Sadat Wexler
Associate Professor of Law at Washington University in St. Louis, she received her JD, *summa cum laude*, from Tulane Law School and clerked for the Honorable Albert Tate, Jr., United States Fifth Circuit Court of Appeals, before attending Columbia Law School (LLM 1987) and the University of Paris I — Sorbonne (DEA 1998) as a Jervey Fellow of the Parker School of Comparative Law. Prior to joining Washington University, she practiced international law in Paris and is a French *Avocat*. She is on the Board of Editors of the *American Journal of Comparative Law* and is a member of the French *Société de Législation Comparée*. In addition to her work on the European Community, she has two articles forthcoming.